WORLDWIDE
WARD
COOKBOOK
MOM'S BEST RECIPES

More Than 250 Recipes from LDS Moms Around the Globe

WORLDWIDE WARD COOKBOOK

MOM'S BEST RECIPES

More Than 250 Recipes from LDS Moms Around the Globe

Adjustments for Altitude

Because the recipes in this cookbook have been submitted by people from throughout the world, it's important to compare the altitude where you live to the altitude where the recipe originated. Keep in mind that many recipes originated in Utah, which has an elevation of 3,500 feet and higher.

If the recipe comes from an area similar in altitude to yours, no changes are necessary.

If you are at a higher altitude than where the recipe originated, keep the following in mind:

• Water boils at a lower temperature at high altitudes, so foods take longer to cook. If you're making stews or braised meats, add 1 hour for every 1,000 feet above sea level. Beans may take twice as long to cook. Pasta needs to cook at a hard boil for a longer period. When making baked goods, increase your oven temperature by 15–25 percent at elevations of 3,500 to 6,500 feet; you may also need to increase baking time.

• Air pressure is lower at higher elevations, so baked foods rise faster. Don't use self-rising flour at high elevations; it will over-expand. Watch yeast breads; don't let them rise to more than double in size.

• Too much leavening in baked goods will cause them to rise too fast and then fall, resulting in dry or tough foods. At higher altitudes, reduce the amount of baking powder or baking soda in a recipe by 25 percent.

• Liquids evaporate more rapidly at higher elevations, so candies and cooked frostings will get harder faster. Decrease cooking time.

• Flour gets drier at higher altitudes and will absorb more of the liquid in a recipe; increase liquid by 2–4 tablespoons for every cup of flour used in the recipe.

• At higher altitudes, use eggs at room temperature. Beat them less; beat egg whites only to soft-peak consistency.

• Fill pans for cakes, cupcakes, muffins, and other baked goods only half full, not two-thirds full.

• Cakes and other baked goods stick more at higher altitudes, so grease pans more heavily and dust the greased pans with flour.

If you're at a significantly lower altitude from where the recipe originated, simply reverse the directions above!

Table of Contents

I grew up on a farm in Illinois. We lived in a farmhouse and had a big barn for the pigs and the cows and an old horse named Jim. The barn had a hay mow where my two brothers and I built forts with the straw bales, swung from a huge rope, and searched for nests of mice so we could marvel at their brand new naked pinkness.

There was an enormous machine shed where the combines and tractors and plows were kept. There were acres and acres of soybeans and sweet corn. The fields seemed endless and the rows of corn stood taller than a man. How we loved to race through the fields, always with a sniggling of fear that we would get lost and never be found.

My favorite winter was the one when the blizzard left snow drifts as high as the roof, swallowing the entire house on one side. The trees were covered with ice and every tiny twig was outlined with glass, making the limbs so heavy that branches broke, blocking the dirt road that was our only access to town—Allerton, a mile away. Power lines were down and we had no electricity, but we had a wood stove on which my mother made wonderful food and we played Sorry for hours by the light of a lantern.

Summertime meant running barefoot across the great expanse of lawn, dancing through the sprinkler, climbing trees, and catching lightning bugs in canning jars at twilight. And we had a garden—a huge garden. We grew nearly every vegetable you can name, and my mother put them all in the freezer or in canning jars, arranged in beautiful rows on shelves. My mother cooked splendid meals. I remember steaming piles of corn on the cob, picked from our garden only minutes earlier,

which she put on the table last. She insisted we eat the rest of our dinner first; otherwise, we would eat nothing other than sweet corn.

She made breakfast every morning just before dawn so that my father had a hot meal before heading off to the fields. We all ate breakfast together, no matter how early the hour. At the height of the season, my mother made a hot lunch every day, loaded it and us three kids into the station wagon, and drove out to wherever my father was toiling. We sat on the back door of the car and ate lunch together. But it wasn't called *lunch;* it was called *dinner,* because it was the main meal of the day. In the evening we had *supper,* which was always lighter fare.

I helped my mother with whatever chore needed to be done—and in the process, I learned to cook and to bake and to garden and to can the bounty. I'm sometimes asked why I do something the way I do; the answer will always be, "Because my mother did."

Life seemed simpler then . . . and maybe it was, or maybe I was too young to notice the complications of life. Just the same, all the stuff that is now meant to make life easier somehow complicates it, filling up all the little crannies that used to be filled with running barefoot and catching lightning bugs. But, simple or complicated, life marches on. Now I am the mother, and my mother has become the grandmother. The miracle of birth has happened four times for me, and now there are four splendid people who call me "Mom." And if that is not enough happiness, I just learned that my sweet little firstborn daughter—who seems to have been a baby only a minute or two ago—is going to be a mommy herself in a few months. Soon there will be a new and beautiful little person who will be the first to call me "Grandma." How marvelous! . . .

—Deanna Buxton

Pictured above, four generations of Deanna's family: Deanna Buxton, right, with her infant daughter (now Erin Buxton Miner); her mother, Shirley Drudge, left; and her grandmother, Ilene Jenkins, top center.

If you would like to be included in the next Worldwide Ward Cookbook, go to www.worldwidewardcookbook.blogspot.com and submit your recipe!

{ APPETIZERS }

A mother is she who can take the place of all others but whose place no one else can take.

{ Cardinal Mermillod }

Guacamole

5 large ripe black Hass avocados

Juice of 2 large limes

1 medium onion, chopped

⅔ C. cilantro, chopped

1 large tomato, chopped

Salt to taste

Fresh jalapeño peppers, chopped (optional)

Slice avocados in half; remove the pits and scoop the flesh out of the shells. Place in bowl. Add juice of one fresh lime to prevent browning. Mash with a fork; it's okay if it is still lumpy. Add onion, cilantro, and tomato; stir gently to mix. Add the juice of second lime and salt to taste. Stir just enough to blend. Add jalapeño until it's as hot as you like (we like it really hot!). If you accidentally make it too hot, add another avocado.

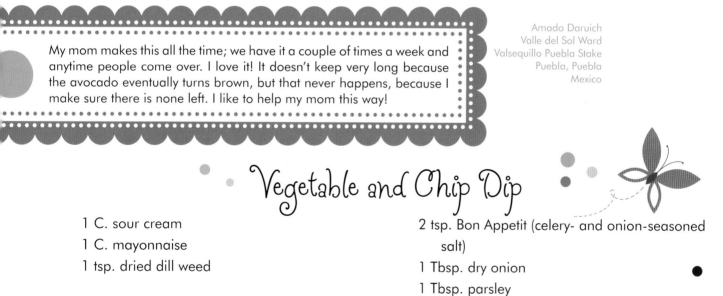

My mom makes this all the time; we have it a couple of times a week and anytime people come over. I love it! It doesn't keep very long because the avocado eventually turns brown, but that never happens, because I make sure there is none left. I like to help my mom this way!

Amado Daruich
Valle del Sol Ward
Valsequillo Puebla Stake
Puebla, Puebla
Mexico

Vegetable and Chip Dip

1 C. sour cream

1 C. mayonnaise

1 tsp. dried dill weed

2 tsp. Bon Appetit (celery- and onion-seasoned salt)

1 Tbsp. dry onion

1 Tbsp. parsley

Mix all ingredients and refrigerate a few hours before serving. Terrific with celery, carrots, and potato chips! Makes about 2 cups.

Chad Carpenter
Pleasant View 9th Ward
Pleasant View Utah South Stake
Pleasant View, Utah

This dip is a favorite of our family for get-togethers. With the great combination of spices, this dip is worlds above the ordinary sour cream and Ranch mix. We all like it when Mom gets assigned the relish tray for a party, because we know we will get the good dip!

Chicken Enchilada Dip

1 8-oz. pkg. cream cheese, softened

1⅓ C. cheddar cheese, shredded

1 tsp. garlic, minced

1½ Tbsp. chili powder

1 tsp. oregano

1 tsp. cumin

1 tsp. paprika

Cayenne pepper to taste

Hot pepper sauce to taste

3 chicken breasts, cooked and finely chopped

1 bunch cilantro leaves, chopped

4 green onions, chopped

1 10-oz. can diced tomatoes with green chiles

In a large mixing bowl, mix cheeses until creamy and blended. Add garlic, spices, and pepper sauces; mix well. Gently fold in chicken, cilantro, green onions, and tomatoes. Refrigerate overnight to fully blend flavors. Serve with tortilla chips. Makes about 6 cups.

Heidi Miller
Texarkana Ward
Shreveport Louisiana Stake
Ashdown, Arkansas

Deep-Fried Tofu

3 Tbsp. soy sauce

1 tsp. white rice wine vinegar

1 tsp. white sugar

½ tsp. red chile flakes

1 spring (green) onion, chopped

1 clove garlic, minced

Pinch pepper

1–2 cakes firm tofu (quantity is not important), cut into 1-inch cubes

5 C. oil

To make dipping sauce: In a small bowl, mix soy sauce, vinegar, and sugar well. Add chile flakes, onion, garlic, and pepper; stir to combine. Set aside. Rinse tofu and drain well. Heat oil in a wok or pot to about 350. Optional: For a crisper tofu, dust tofu lightly with cornstarch or flour before frying. In manageable portions, fry tofu quickly until golden brown. Drain well. Serve at once, dipping tofu into sauce.

Yue Cai-Han
Xuang-He 1st Ward
West Taipei Stake
Taipei, Taiwan

Shanghai Lumpia (Egg Roll)

1 lb. ground pork
1 lb. ground beef
1 lb. shrimp, chopped
3 cloves garlic, chopped
1 medium jicama, chopped
⅓ C. parsley, chopped
2 carrots, chopped
3 eggs, beaten

½ C. soy sauce
½ Tbsp. salt
2 tsp. pepper
Egg roll wrappers
Oil for deep frying
1 egg, beaten
1 Tbsp. water

In a large bowl, combine ground pork, ground beef, shrimp, garlic, jicama, parsley, carrots, 3 beaten eggs, soy sauce, salt, and pepper. For each lumpia, scoop about 3 Tbsp. filling mixture onto one side (about ½ inch from edge) of an egg roll wrapper; filling should be about ½ inch from the edge, aligned in a straight line with the edge. (If you put too little filling on the wrapper, there won't be enough meat; if you use too much filling, you'll have to fry them longer to cook the meat.) Roll the wrapper around the mixture to completely wrap the filling. To seal the lumpia roll, make an egg wash by combining 1 beaten egg and water. Spread the egg wash along the edge of the roll, and press the edge closed. Repeat for each lumpia. Cut each lumpia roll into thirds. Deep-fry the lumpia rolls until golden brown; if the rolls are thick, fry until the meat is cooked. Makes about 45.

Grace Buxton
Cheyenne Ridge Ward
Lone Mountain Nevada Stake
Las Vegas, Nevada

My mom has been making Shanghai Lumpia for years and serves it at every family party. It's so delicious, her friends also ask her to make it for their parties. In fact, a family friend used to purchase them from my mom to serve at his restaurant. When I told my mom that the teachers who mentored me while I was student teaching loved egg rolls, she made a batch just for them for lunch one day. They were a hit. They don't taste like regular egg rolls—they are amazing. The last time my mom made these was for my twins' first birthday party. Good food equals good times and good memories!

Tom Ka Kai (Thai Chicken Coconut Soup)

1 lemongrass stalk OR 3 Tbsp. frozen prepared lemongrass

6 C. chicken broth

2 C. roasted chicken

Handful of fresh or dried shiitake mushrooms, sliced (if dried, be sure to soak them in hot water for several hours)

1–3 fresh red chiles, according to taste (1=mild, 2=medium, 3=spicy hot)

1 thumb-size piece ginger, grated

1 can coconut milk

2 Tbsp. fish sauce

1 tsp. brown sugar

Vegetables, chopped (optional)

2 Tbsp. lime juice

Handful fresh coriander leaves (garnish)

Handful fresh basil leaves (garnish)

3 spring (green) onions, sliced (garnish)

Slice and mince the lower portion of the lemongrass stalk. Retain the upper stalk for the soup pot. Place chicken broth in a large soup pot over medium-high heat. Bring to a boil. Add chicken (if you have leftover chicken bones, add those too) and mushrooms. Also add the lemongrass (including upper stalk pieces) and fresh chiles. Boil 5–8 minutes. Turn heat down to medium. Add the ginger, coconut milk, fish sauce, brown sugar, and extra vegetables (if using). Stir well. Simmer gently 1–2 minutes. Reduce heat to simmer. Add lime juice and stir. Taste; there should be a good balance between spicy, sour, salty, and sweet flavors. Start with salty; add more fish sauce if not salty enough (1 Tbsp. at a time). If too sour, add a little more brown sugar. If too spicy (hot), add a little more coconut milk. If not spicy enough, add more fresh chiles. Ladle soup into serving bowls. Sprinkle a little fresh coriander, basil, and spring onion over each bowl. Makes 4 appetizer bowls.

Summer XiaChen
Bangkok International Ward
Bangkok Thailand Stake
Bangkok, Thailand

My mother lives in China; I live in Bangkok, where I am working on my master's degree and writing my thesis. I am also doing a six-month internship here. I love this soup. It is meant to be an appetizer, but my mother sometimes adds cooked noodles to the soup and it becomes our dinner. My mother taught me that this soup brings warmth in the winter and helps prevent colds and flu. Enjoy!

Curry Dip

1 8-oz. pkg. cream cheese

1 Tbsp. Worcestershire sauce

3 Tbsp. light cream

½ tsp. seasoned salt

½ tsp. curry powder

In the bowl of an electric mixer, beat cream cheese with remaining ingredients until light and fluffy. Chill. Serve with crackers or crisp vegetables. Makes 8 servings.

Val McTee
Ewa Beach 1st Ward
Waiphau Hawaii Stake
Ewa Beach, Hawaii

Camarones al Ajillo (Garlic Shrimp)

3 Tbsp. garlic a pilonázos (minced)

3 Tbsp. olive oil

1 lb. medium shrimp, cooked, peeled, and deveined

¼ C. lime juice

Salt and pepper to taste

Parsley or cilantro, chopped

In a deep frying pan, sauté the garlic in olive oil. Once the garlic is a little brown, add the shrimp, lime juice, salt, and pepper. Cook for 8–10 minutes to blend the garlic and shrimp flavors. Sprinkle with parsley or chopped cilantro.

Alex Torres
Guaynabo Ward
San Juan Puerto Rico Stake
Rio Piedras, Puerto Rico

My mom makes very delicious food. Often when we have this, she makes *tostones*, deep-fried plantains. She cooks pieces of plantain in hot oil for 3 minutes on each side. Then she removes them from the hot oil, flattens them with a plate, dips them in water, and then puts them back in the hot oil for a minute on each side. When they are done, she sprinkles them with salt. We eat the *tostones* with this delicious shrimp. We also have white rice and bread that we dip in the sauce from the shrimp. It is so delicious!

Cheese Dip

1 lb. sausage
2 10-oz. cans tomatoes with green chiles (Rotel)
5 8-oz. pkgs. cream cheese

Fry the sausage until cooked through, but do not add any spices. Add the tomatoes and cream cheese. Put mixture in a slow cooker. Stir after 10 minutes. This is great as an appetizer for parties, and is also good to eat with rice, tortillas, and bread. Makes 15–20 servings.

Tatiana Pryor
Aldeota Ward
Fortaleza Ceará Stake
Fortaleza, Ceará
Brazil

When I was seventeen, I came to the United States as an exchange student. I was blessed to be able to live with an adorable woman, Donna Lexa, who helped me so much and was always there for me. My own family was very close, and without my host parents—who were very family-oriented—I would have been very sad. Donna created this recipe; I modified it a little so it was not so spicy. Much of what I learned—and many wonderful memories—came from this wonderful family.

Cheese Ball

1 jar English Sharp Cheese (Kraft)

1 jar Roka Blue Cheese (Kraft)

2 8-oz. pkgs. cream cheese, softened to room temperature

1 Tbsp. Worcestershire sauce

2 small green onions, chopped

1 C. pecans or walnuts, chopped

1 C. parsley, chopped

In a large bowl, combine cheeses, Worcestershire sauce, and green onions; mix with beater until just combined. Refrigerate for several hours until mixture is firm. Divide mixture into thirds, and form into three balls. Roll each cheese ball in nuts and garnish with parsley. Makes 8–10 servings.

Kelli Allen
Sharjah Ward
Manama Bahrain Stake
Dubai, United Arab Emirates

For as long as I can remember, my mother made these cheese balls during the holidays for our family and to share with the neighbors. When she passed away almost twenty years ago, I treasured her copy of this favorite family recipe. My sisters and I have continued this tradition, and we each make cheese balls for our families and neighbors every year. Each year when I pull out this favorite recipe in my mother's handwriting, I think of her and all the wonderful memories associated with her—especially since I am now living so far away from where I grew up. She was a wonderful mother, a great cook, and a person who gave service to all.

Make Mom Proud
Savory Sun-Dried Tomato and Artichoke Cheesecake

1 medium onion, thinly sliced

1 tsp. sugar

½ C. dry bread crumbs

1½ Tbsp. butter, melted

3 8-oz. pkgs. cream cheese, room temperature

4 oz. feta cheese, crumbled

3 eggs, lightly beaten

1 tsp. dried basil

1 tsp. salt

1 tsp. pepper

1 clove garlic, minced

1 14-oz. can artichoke hearts, coarsely chopped; reserve 2 Tbsp. liquid

½ C. sun-dried tomatoes in oil, chopped

¼ C. Parmesan cheese, shredded

1 tsp. sugar

In a frying pan, caramelize the sliced onion by cooking with the sugar over medium-low heat for about 30 minutes. Set aside. Mix the bread crumbs and melted butter and press into the bottom of a 9-inch spring-form pan. In a large bowl, beat the cream cheese with a hand mixer until smooth. Add the feta cheese and beat until well mixed. Add the eggs, basil, salt, pepper, garlic, and 2 Tbsp. reserved artichoke liquid; mix until just incorporated. Fold in the caramelized onions, artichoke hearts, sun-dried tomatoes, and Parmesan cheese. Pour filling into the prepared 9-inch spring-form pan; bake at 325 for 35 minutes. Allow cheesecake to sit at room temperature for 30 minutes on a wire rack, then chill for at least 4 hours before serving. To serve, slice cheesecake into wedges and spread on crackers, toast, or crusty bread. Enjoy! Makes 12 servings.

Emily Liechty
Cedar City 16th Ward
Cedar City Utah Stake
Cedar City, Utah

This Savory Sun-Dried Tomato and Artichoke Cheesecake is one of my very favorite recipes from my mom that I have ever made! For me it has always been such a thrill when I can wow my mom with my cooking. This appetizer cheesecake is one of the recipes that my mom absolutely loves and had to tell everyone about! My mom is the one who taught me how to cook and who encouraged my excitement for cooking. Now that I am married it is an even greater thrill to still see her get excited about what comes out of my kitchen—and it reminds me how I want to be with my own children one day! Thanks, Mom, for sharing a love of cooking and being such a great taster and inspiration!

Mustard Pickles

Pickles:

9–10 large cucumbers, peeled, seeded, and cut in half

1½ lb. onions, diced

1 small cauliflower, cut up

1 red pepper, chopped

1 green pepper, chopped

Sauce:

3½ C. sugar

3 Tbsp. pickling salt

1 Tbsp. turmeric

1 tsp. black pepper

¾ C. flour

1 Tbsp. mustard seed

1 Tbsp. dry mustard

2 C. vinegar

Put vegetables in a large saucepan. Mix sauce ingredients until smooth and pour over vegetables in saucepan. Cook until sauce comes close to a boil. Be careful not to burn. Remove from heat and bottle in hot, sterilized jars. Makes about 6 pints.

Anne Donovan
North Sydney Branch
New Glasgow Nova Scotia District
North Sydney, Cape Breton Island
Nova Scotia, Canada

This mustard pickle recipe is one I make every year and it is so delicious. It has become a tradition to make Mustard Pickles and give them as gifts at Christmas to the sisters I visit teach or to my beloved children when they come home to Cape Breton Island to visit.

{ BEVERAGES }

An ounce of mother is worth a pound of clergy.

{ Spanish proverb }

Strawberry Limeade

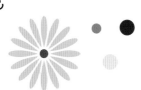

2 liters lemon-lime soda

1 qt. frozen strawberries with syrup

6 limes

Pour lemon-lime soda into punch bowl. Stir in strawberries. Squeeze the juice of 4 limes into punch. Slice the 2 remaining limes and add to the bowl. Makes 24 servings.

Starr Thomsen
Star 3rd Ward
Eagle Idaho Stake
Star, Idaho

> I have such a deep love for my family. I was not raised in the Church and did not have the chance to learn the gospel in my youth as part of a family. I joined the Church in 1997, and am the only member in my family. I have had many struggles, but I know I made the best decision; I would hate to see what my life would be like without the gospel. I am so excited as a mother to be able to raise my children in The Church of Jesus Christ of Latter-day Saints—to be able to teach them how to can produce, bake bread, learn right from wrong, and simply love each other. I did not have this chance as a child, but I am glad to be able to have this experience with my children. I love being a mom.

Coquito (Coconut Eggnog)

2 eggs, separated (use only yolks)

1 12-oz. can evaporated milk

1 14-oz. can cream of coconut

1 14-oz. can sweetened condensed milk

1 C. milk

1 C. water

¼ tsp. ground cloves

½ tsp. ground cinnamon

1 tsp. vanilla

In the top of a double boiler, combine egg yolks and evaporated milk. Stirring constantly, cook over lightly simmering water until mixture reaches a temperature of 160. The mixture should be thick enough to coat the back of a spoon. Transfer mixture to a blender, and add cream of coconut, sweetened condensed milk, milk, water, cloves, cinnamon, and vanilla. Blend for about 30 seconds. Pour into glass bottles; chill overnight. Makes 10 servings.

Starr Thomsen
Star 3rd Ward
Eagle Idaho Stake
Star, Idaho

Lush Slush Punch

1 ¼ C. white sugar

6 C. water

2 3-oz. pkgs. strawberry-flavored gelatin mix

1 46-oz. can pineapple juice

⅔ C. lemon juice

1 qt. orange juice

2 2-liter bottles ginger ale

In a large saucepan, combine sugar, water, and strawberry-flavored gelatin. Boil for 3 minutes, then stir in pineapple juice, lemon juice, and orange juice. Divide mixture in half and freeze in two separate gallon freezer bags. When ready to serve, place the frozen contents of one container in a punch bowl and stir in 1 bottle of ginger ale until slushy. Makes 30 servings.

Alexandria Simpson
Bedford Ward
Concord New Hampshire Stake
Bedford, New Hampshire

This is the punch my mom made for my wedding and those of my sisters. She later made it for our baby showers. We all continue to make this for birthday parties, church events, and other activities. I don't know where Mom discovered this, but we all LOVE this punch! It's addicting!

Wedding Punch

½ C. lemon juice

1 full hand of bananas, sliced (about a mixing bowl full)

2 3-lb. bags frozen strawberries

3–4 46-oz. cans pineapple juice

3 12-oz. cans frozen lemonade concentrate

About 14 2-liter bottles lemon-lime soda (to be opened at serving time)

Pour lemon juice over bananas to prevent browning. Blend all ingredients except soda using a blender. Freeze in 1-gallon freezer bags. At serving time, mix 1 gallon frozen punch mix with 2 2-liter bottles of lemon-lime soda. Makes 7 gallons of punch mix.

Darleen Frank
Battle Creek 10th Ward
Pleasant Grove Utah East Stake
Lindon, Utah

My mom, Eula Lunt Romney, didn't love to cook, and often chose not to. But she did love to sew. She converted her walk-in closet into a sewing room, and I spent countless hours talking with her as her sewing machine hummed along—making dresses for me, dresses for her, Halloween costumes, high school performance group costumes, Scout patches, Christmas decorations, missionary suits, drapes, prom dresses, wedding gowns, aprons, and teddy bears. She helped me gain my testimony as we sat together in her sewing closet. Her final sewing project was thirteen quilts for her grandchildren. She was only fifty-nine, but she knew her time was short. To each quilt she attached a handwritten personal note with her testimony of the joy she felt knowing that she would be their grandma for eternity. She finished the last one a few days before she died in November 1990. She had arranged to have them wrapped for Christmas—precious Christmas gifts from an angel grandmother! Her love for sewing lives on. My dad gave me her sewing machine, with the familiar hum that had accompanied mom for so many miles of sewing. I have sewn many more miles over the years with my daughters by my side. One of those daughters is now sewing her way through college, working as a seamstress. Mom is smiling from above and testimonies are still growing here on earth as her sewing machine continues to hum along.

Blue Baby Shower Punch

1 0.13-oz. envelope blue berry-flavored
   Kool-Aid
1 2-liter bottle lemon-lime soda
1 64-oz. bottle white cranberry juice

1 C. sugar, to taste
8 scoops vanilla ice cream

In a large punch bowl, stir together the Kool-Aid, lemon-lime soda, and white cranberry juice (can use white grape juice if desired). Taste, and stir in sugar to your liking. (I like to add the whole cup of sugar.) Float scoops of ice cream on the top. The ice cream melts a little and turns the punch a beautiful baby blue color with frothy white clouds floating on the top. Makes 20 servings.

Alexandria Simpson
Bedford Ward
Concord New Hampshire Stake
Bedford, New Hampshire

When we found out my sister was having a little boy (the first boy after nine granddaughters), we were ecstatic. When it was time to plan her baby shower, we wanted a blue punch. I couldn't find any punch concoctions that were blue, so we made our own. It was awesome, and I have given this recipe out countless times to others who ran across the same problem when planning a baby shower for a boy. We floated rubber ducks in our punch, and it was adorable.

Tía Chuy's Jamaica (pronounced "ha-my-ka")

6 C. water
2 C. hibiscus flowers
¾ C. sugar

Bring 4 C. water to a boil and pour over hibiscus flowers. Let the flowers soak in the water for about an hour. Pour the liquid and flowers through a strainer into a large pitcher. Add sugar; stir for 1–2 minutes or until sugar is dissolved. Add remaining 2 C. water; taste for sweetness, and adjust if needed by adding more sugar or water. Add ice when you serve the drink. Makes 5–6 servings.

Margaret Zarate-Goebel
Sierra Ranch Ward
North Las Vegas Nevada Stake
North Las Vegas, Nevada

My aunt is María de Jesus Aldaz Zárate. We call her Tía Chuy—*Tía* means "aunt" in Spanish, and *Chuy* is the Spanish nickname for María. When I was nineteen, I went to live with her, her husband, and their three sons while I attended the University of Guadalara in Jalisco, Mexico, and she often made this refreshing drink for me when I came home from a day of classes at the university. Tía Chuy did not have a daughter, and she treated me with the kind of love that I imagine she would have shown to a daughter of her own. While living with her and her family, I had some experiences that changed my life. The most memorable and special moment was watching her entire family join the Church and seeing the complete change in their lives as they accepted the gospel. That was definitely one of the best days of my life! We enjoyed this delicious Jamaica at the after-baptism fiesta at their home that night.

Snowflake Cocoa

2 C. cream
6 C. milk
1 tsp. vanilla
1 12-oz. pkg. white chocolate chips

Whipped cream (for garnish)
Candy canes (for garnish)

In a slow cooker, stir together the cream, milk, vanilla and white chocolate chips. Cover and cook on low for 2 to 2 ½ hours, stirring occasionally, until mixture is hot and chocolate chips are melted. Stir again before serving. Garnish with whipped cream and candy canes, as desired. Makes 10 servings.

Anna Henwood
Kerrville Ward
San Antonio Texas Hill Country Stake
Kerrville, Texas

Agua Fresca

3 C. fresh fruit, coarsely chopped
6–8 C. water

½–¾ C. sugar
¼ C. lime juice (optional)

Pour the fruit and 2–3 C. water into a blender; puree until smooth. Strain through a sieve into a large pitcher. Add the remaining water, ½ C. sugar, and lime juice if desired. Stir well; taste, and add more water or sugar as needed to adjust the sweetness. Chill well to serve. Makes 2½ quarts.

Use the following fruits for these variations: Agua de Fresa—strawberries; Agua de Melón—cantaloupe or any other melon; Agua de Papaya—papaya (lime juice makes it delicious); Agua de Sandía—watermelon; Agua Fresca de Pepino—peeled, seeded cucumbers and lime juice (use a little less sugar).

Lupe Plascencia
Chula Vista Branch
Puerto Vallarta Mexico Stake
Chula Vista, Nayarit
Mexico

Water is good, but water with fruit is better! My mother taught me to make this when I was very young and I have enjoyed it my whole life and make it often for my family and friends. My favorite is made with watermelon.

Pumpkin Spice Hot Chocolate

½ C. dark chocolate hot cocoa

Water or milk

2 C. milk

2 Tbsp. canned pumpkin

2 Tbsp. sugar

2 Tbsp. vanilla extract

½ tsp. pumpkin pie spice

Whipped cream (optional)

Make ½ C. dark chocolate hot cocoa as directed on package with water or milk and set aside. In a saucepan, combine milk, pumpkin, and sugar; cook on medium heat, stirring, until steaming. Remove from heat, stir in vanilla and spice, transfer to a blender, and process for 15 seconds until foamy. Pour into two mugs and pour half of the dark chocolate hot cocoa into each mug. Top with whipped cream and a sprinkle of pumpkin pie spice. Makes 2 servings.

Christina Marcano
Dry Creek Ward
Lehi Utah South Stake
Lehi, Utah

Orange Cream Punch

1 qt. vanilla ice cream

1 qt. orange sherbet

1 qt. cold milk

1 12-oz. can lemon-lime-flavored carbonated beverage

Place the ice cream and sherbet in a punch bowl. Pour in the milk and lemon-lime soda. Stir gently and serve immediately. Makes 24 servings.

Tylie Vick
Hanalei Branch
Kauai Hawaii Stake
Princeville, Hawaii

This is special because it reminds me of all my wonderful friends who gave me a bridal shower and served this wonderful punch. Delicious punch, good friends, good memories. . . .

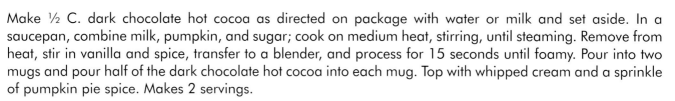

{ BREAKFASTS }

All that I am or hope to be, I owe to my angel mother.

{ Abraham Lincoln }

Bilini (a crepe-like pancake)

½ C. milk

4 Tbsp. sugar

1½ C. sifted flour

Dash of salt

3 eggs

1 Tbsp. butter, melted

1½ C. milk

½ C. flour

Powdered sugar (for garnish)

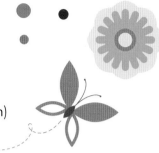

Combine milk, sugar, flour, salt, and eggs. Add melted butter, milk, and remaining flour. Mix well and fry in butter. Sprinkle with powdered sugar and serve with jelly or fruit. Makes 6 servings.

Sandi Henderson
Nakhodka Branch
Russia Vladivostok Mission
Nakhodka, Russia

Budin de Pan

8 slices white bread, torn into small pieces

3 eggs, lightly beaten

1½ C. milk

1 C. sugar

½ C. raisins

½ C. flour

3 Tbsp. butter, melted

1 tsp. vanilla

¼ tsp. baking powder

¼ tsp. cinnamon

Preheat oven to 350. Combine all ingredients and pour into a greased 1½-quart baking dish. Bake at 350 for 45–55 minutes. Allow to cool, cut in squares, and serve warm or at room temperature. Makes 4 servings.

Walter Rivas
Palermo Ward
Buenos Aires Belgrano Stake
Buenos Aires, Argentina

I love it when my mom makes this for breakfast. It is my favorite! My brother and I fight over the last bit in the pan, because my mom is such a good cook and she makes Budin de Pan better than anyone else!

Best Ever Cinnamon Rolls

Cinnamon Rolls:

1 C. milk

¼ C. butter

1 Tbsp. (1 pkg.) dry yeast

¼ C. warm water

1 Tbsp. sugar

1 small package instant
   vanilla pudding mix

1 egg, room temperature

½ tsp. salt

4 C. flour

Filling:

½ C. butter, softened

1 C. packed brown sugar

Cinnamon to taste

Frosting:

1 8-oz. pkg. cream cheese,
   softened

¼ C. butter, softened

1 C. powdered sugar

½ tsp. vanilla extract

1½ tsp. milk

In saucepan, warm 1 C. milk and ¼ C. butter until butter is melted. Set aside. In large bowl, combine yeast, warm water, and 1 Tbsp. sugar. Let yeast mixture rise while milk mixture cools. Stir in cooled milk mixture, vanilla pudding mix, egg, and salt. Beat with electric mixer. Stir in flour. Knead on floured board until elastic. Return to greased bowl. Cover and put in warm spot until double in size. Punch dough down. Roll into rectangular shape (about 17 x 10 inches). Spread with ½ C. softened butter, then sprinkle with brown sugar and cinnamon. Starting at long side, roll up dough. Pinch off ends. Slice into 1-inch slices and place in buttered 9 x 13-inch pan. Let rise in a warm place until doubled (about 45 minutes). Bake at 350 for 15–20 minutes. While rolls bake, make frosting by combining all frosting ingredients (for us, one frosting recipe is enough for a double roll batch). This can also be made in a bread machine. Makes 16 servings.

Jenni McCall
BYU 156th Ward
BYU 13th Stake
Provo, Utah

These rolls are a must-have for all our holidays. Mom loves to bake and has tried many cinnamon roll recipes, but this is our favorite.

Hills and Valleys

6 eggs

1 C. milk

1 C. flour

¼ tsp. salt

5 Tbsp. butter

Preheat oven to 450. Whip eggs until thick and lemon colored. Add milk, flour, and salt. Place the butter in a 9 x 13-inch pan and heat it in the oven until melted. Pour batter into the melted butter. Bake at 450 for 15–20 minutes. As the pancake puffs it makes "hills and valleys." Serve with syrup. Makes 6 servings.

It was always a treat for my mom to make Hills and Valleys. After my mom put the pan in the oven, we anxiously waited for the timer to announce the pancake's arrival. After hearing the timer's beeping, we rushed into the kitchen to see hills bursting out of the pan accompanied by low valleys. I can't wait for my girls to get to the age where we can carry on this tradition of a delicious and fun breakfast.

Laura Lee Musson
Westland Ward
Columbus Ohio Stake
Galloway, Ohio

Dutch Honey

1 C. packed brown sugar

1 C. light corn syrup

1 C. cream

½ tsp. vanilla

¼ tsp. maple flavoring

Mix the brown sugar, corn syrup, and cream in a 2-quart saucepan. Cook over medium heat until mixture starts to boil; cook for an additional 15–20 minutes, stirring the mixture occasionally. This is great either hot or cold on hot bread, toast, and pancakes. Makes 20 servings.

Marla Newkirk
Raton New Mexico Ward
Pueblo Colorado Stake
Folsom, New Mexico

Dutch Honey is a tradition in the Newkirk family. Every Christmas my mother-in-law made Dutch Honey for her four sons. Christmas breakfast consisted of bacon, sausage, fried eggs, and biscuits with milk gravy. The boys liked to break several biscuits in half, smother them in gravy, then drizzle Dutch Honey over the top. This tradition was unique to my husband's family, and he has carried it on to our family. Each Christmas his mother gives us Dutch Honey, and it continues to be a favorite for our children.

Sweet Puffs

1 sheet puff pastry (Pepperidge Farm Puff Pastry Sheets), thawed

1 8-oz. pkg. cream cheese, softened

½ C. sugar

1 tsp. lemon juice

1 egg

1 tsp. vanilla

Powdered sugar (for garnish)

Unfold puff pastry sheet and cut into 9 squares. Put one square into each cup of a muffin tin, pressing gently into cup. To make the filling, combine all remaining ingredients and mix with an electric mixer until smooth and fluffy. Divide the filling between the 9 cups. Bring corners of puff pastry together in the middle and bake at 375 for 20–25 minutes. Remove from pan and sprinkle with powdered sugar. Makes 9 servings.

Beth Pearson
Spanish Fork 14th Ward
Spanish Fork Utah Canyon Ridge Stake
Spanish Fork, Utah

After I married and moved away from home, my parents opened a bed-and-breakfast. When I was visiting and they also had guests, I enjoyed coming into the dining room and eating breakfast with the guests so I could sample my mom's great cooking and the beautiful table she set. I fell in love with these Sweet Puffs and couldn't believe how easy they were to make. I like to make them for friends or family on special occasions. A few years ago, my parents sold their bed-and-breakfast so they could go on a mission. After living across country from me longer than I had ever lived with them, they bought a much smaller home in the town where I lived and began preparations for a mission. It was wonderful having them close but it took me quite awhile to get used to the idea that they were living close by instead of just here for a visit. Due to my father's health problems, they lived by me for a little more than a year before they were able to go on a mission. They were called to serve in Kirtland, Ohio, and spent their time at the John Johnson Farm in Hyrum, Ohio, which is where the Prophet Joseph Smith was tarred and feathered. I was proud of them for their willingness to sacrifice and serve, but I had been very content with my parents being a daily part of my life. Thankfully, we were able to email and talk regularly by phone, and my husband and I took our three children to visit for our summer vacation. Three years later, we still refer to things we were taught by my parents on their mission. Church history and events from the Doctrine and Covenants now play out in our minds in living color; it was a positive experience for all of us.

Fluffy Thick Homestyle Pancakes

1½ C. flour

3½ tsp. baking powder

1 tsp. salt

1 Tbsp. sugar

1¼ C. milk

1 egg

3 Tbsp. butter, melted

In a large bowl, sift together flour, baking powder, salt, and sugar. Make a well in the center and pour in the milk, egg, and melted butter; mix until smooth. Heat a lightly oiled griddle or frying pan over medium-high heat. Pour or scoop the batter onto the griddle, using approximately ¼ C. for each pancake. Brown on both sides and serve hot. Makes 8 servings.

Anna Wixom
Champions Ward
Klein Texas Stake
Houston, Texas

This is a recipe my mom always used while I was growing up, and it has been in our family for a long time. I have never even made pancakes from a box, because this recipe is just that easy, and the ingredients are simple items that are always in the pantry. We make these at least once a week. My mom's pancakes are always a hit, and I still can't believe how fluffy and pretty these always turn out. I promise once you see how easy and delicious these are you will never go back. It's a no-fail recipe for sure, and it always makes me think of my mom.

Rice Pudding

1 C. cooked rice
3 eggs
¾ C. sugar
¼ tsp. salt

3 C. milk
1 tsp. vanilla
Cinnamon (for garnish)

Spread rice out in an 8 x 8-inch pan. In a separate bowl, beat eggs, sugar, and salt. Stir in milk and vanilla. Pour over rice. Lightly sprinkle the cinnamon over the top. Place the baking dish in a larger pan, and fill the larger pan with water to at least halfway up the sides of the smaller pan. Bake at 325 for 1½ hours. You can tell the pudding is done when the custard jiggles equally—in other words, the middle does not jiggle more than the rest. Technically, this pudding makes 12 servings, but it really depends on who gets to it first. One person has been known to eat it all by herself. Note: This recipe creates a custard-style rice pudding with a layer of custard on top. If you like less custard on top, just add more rice.

Katey Clark
Turlock 1st Ward
Turlock California Stake
Denair, California

Mother was a "pull yourself up by the bootstraps" kind of gal. Her mother before her taught her to find something positive in each day, so when life got hard, she tackled it head-on. Rhoda Riggs Turley believed in two things: one was caring for and feeding others, and the other was preaching the gospel. She is no longer with us, but even while her body was giving out, she was still feeding others and spreading the word of God. There is no building with her name on it, but her name is stamped on the hearts of hundreds of people.

Dan Bing

6 eggs

Salt

Oil for cooking

Sesame oil

Dan Bing skins (you can substitute flour tortillas)

3 Tbsp. scallions, chopped and divided

Dark soy sauce (for dipping)

Beat the eggs with salt to taste. Heat a little oil plus a drop of sesame oil in a small pan. Pour about 1/3 of eggs into the pan and immediately add 1 Tbsp. chopped scallions. Immediately put a Dan Bing skin or tortilla on top of the eggs. Press the skin or tortilla down with your hands until the egg sticks to it. When the egg is cooked and beginning to brown, flip it over! Brown the skin/tortilla a bit. Lift up the edge of the skin/tortilla and add a little bit of water to steam the skin a bit, then finish browning. Roll up, cut into pieces, and dip in thick dark soy sauce. Makes 3 servings.

Yue Cai-Han
Xuang-He 1st Ward
West Taipei Stake
Taipei, Taiwan

I like to cook very much, but I don't like to do the dishes. My mother didn't teach me how to cook, but my father did a little. My eight-year-old son and seven-year-old daughter can both cook rice, noodles, sandwiches, and dumplings. If you visit Taiwan, we will cook lots for you!

Chorizo Con Huevos

1 Tbsp. canola oil

1 lb. chorizo sausage

1 medium onion, diced

2 serrano chiles, finely chopped

8 large eggs

½ bunch cilantro leaves, chopped

4 flour tortillas

1 large avocado, mashed

Salsa

Heat the oil in a large skillet over medium heat. Fry the chorizo in the oil until browned, breaking up the sausage with a fork as it cooks. The sausage will look almost burned, but that's just because this sausage is darker than other sausage. Drain off any excess oil. Add the onion and chiles and cook about 2 minutes until the onion is soft. Beat the eggs and add to the chorizo. Stir with a fork or spatula. Add cilantro just before eggs are completely set. Serve with flour tortillas, mashed avocado, and fresh salsa. Makes 4 servings.

In Mexico, we love breakfast with tortillas. We have tortillas the way other people have toast with breakfast. I make this for breakfast because my family and I love it—and also because my mother always made this for breakfast.

Maria Plascencia
Chula Vista Branch
Puerto Vallarta Mexico Stake
Chula Vista, Nayarit
Mexico

Arepas de Queso

1 C. cornmeal

1 C. warm water

⅓ C. white or mozzarella cheese, shredded

2 Tbsp. butter, divided

Salt

Combine the cornmeal, warm water, cheese, 1 Tbsp. butter, and a little salt. Set aside for 5 minutes. Knead with wet hands for about 3 minutes. Wet your hands as you work. Form 4 small balls with the dough. Place each ball in a plastic bag or between sheets of plastic. Flatten to ¼ inch. Melt butter in a skillet over medium heat; don't let the pan get too hot. Place the arepas in the pan, and cook about 3 minutes on each side, until a crust forms or they are golden brown. Spread with butter and cheese on top and serve with a delicious cup of hot chocolate. These arepas are an essential part of the Colombian daily diet. Makes 4 servings.

Julieta Arturo Sandoval
Las Villas Ward
Soacha Stake
Bogota, Colombia

Torta de Huevo

2 corn tortillas, cut into triangles
½ C. oil
4–5 eggs
1 lb. Roma tomatoes

2 garlic cloves
1 tsp. salt
2 Tbsp. oil
1 yellow onion, sliced

In a skillet, fry tortillas in ½ C. oil until they are very crispy. Drain oil from pan, leaving a few tablespoons of oil in pan. Pour eggs over the tortilla pieces and scramble. Do not overstir; the eggs need to be flipped over in large pieces. Place cooked eggs onto a platter. Put tomatoes into a saucepan and cover with water. Boil until skin begins to peel; remove most of the skin. Put tomatoes, garlic, and salt into a blender and puree. In a large frying pan, heat 2 Tbsp. oil. When the oil begins to sizzle, add the onions and sauté until almost transparent. Add tomato mixture to the onion and simmer about 8 minutes. As it is simmering, put egg into the tomato puree and reheat egg. Serve with rice, beans, and corn tortillas. Makes 4 servings.

María de Jesus Aldaz Zárate
Libertad Ward
Guadalajara Mexico Reforma Stake
Jalisco, Guadalajara
Mexico

Torta de Huevo is a favorite breakfast of mine. It is especially good served with a side of refried beans, white rice boiled with an onion, and some warm homemade corn tortillas. All of my relatives eat this entire dish with no utensils. With practice you can also eat this entire dish (tomato puree and all) using a few warm tortillas.

{ BREADS }

Mother is the name of God on the lips and hearts of children.

{ William Makepeace Thackeray }

Refrigerator Bran Muffins

1 C. shortening

2 C. sugar

4 eggs

1 qt. buttermilk

2 C. 40% bran flakes

4 C. All Bran

5 C. flour

1 Tbsp. salt

5 tsp. baking soda dissolved in 2 C. water

Cream shortening, sugar, and eggs. Add remaining ingredients, alternating dry and liquid ingredients and adding a little at a time. Put batter in covered containers and refrigerate up to 6 weeks. For muffins, bake at 350 for 10–15 minutes. Makes about 4 dozen.

Darleen Romney Frank
Battle Creek 10th Ward
Pleasant Grove East Stake
Lindon, Utah

My first day alone with my brand-new baby girl the telephone rang, and it was my sweet mother. We had spent some joyous time during the previous few days after the birth of my first baby, but now there was sadness in her voice. She had just returned from a doctor's appointment, where she learned that her cancer had returned. She was facing chemotherapy that would slow the cancer, but would not cure it. We cried together, and she expressed regret that this news came at a time when she wanted me to experience only happiness. We then both found great peace and comfort as we discussed the beauty of life. Even as my heart was breaking at the thought of losing my mother so soon, my heart was filled with joy as I looked into the eyes of my precious baby. My little baby needed me to be happy, and I knew I wouldn't mourn for long because I had a firm understanding that we would all be together in the eternities and that birth and death are both an important part of our beautiful lives. In my scriptures, I have the word *Mom* written next to Alma 7:11–12; it was her favorite scripture. For three years Mom fought cancer with courage, faith, and good cheer. To the very end she went about serving and uplifting others. When others asked about her joy amidst such pain, she quoted that favorite scripture. Because of our Savior, she did not fear death, and He helped her through the sickness and pain. She said that she felt His love so strongly that it was tangible to her. I will ever be thankful for the strength of my faithful mother and find such joy in knowing I will be with her again.

Grandma West's Soft Rolls

2 pkgs. yeast

3 C. warm water

1 tsp. salt

½ C. sugar

⅔ C. oil

2 eggs, slightly beaten

8 C. flour

1 C. powdered milk

Dissolve yeast in the warm water. Add salt, sugar, oil, and slightly beaten eggs to yeast mixture. Add half of the flour and all the powdered milk solids. Beat with a mixer until smooth. Gradually add the remaining flour until it can be worked with the hands. Knead until smooth (about 5 minutes). Place in greased bowl and cover with a cloth. Let rise in warm place until doubled (about 1 ½ hours). The dough is sticky, and hard to work with; you will need a lot of flour on your rolling pin and surface to roll them out, but the stickier the dough, the better the rolls. Shape into desired rolls and place on greased cookie sheets. Let rise 1½ hours, then bake at 375 for 10–12 minutes. Makes 4 dozen rolls.

Susan West
Meridian 8th Ward
Meridian Idaho East Stake
Boise, Idaho

Grandma West taught me how to make these rolls when I was engaged to my husband, Kevin, because he loved them so much. I taught my girls how to make them before they got married. After we were first married, I didn't make rolls very much, but one year on Christmas Eve I went to the grocery store to buy some soft rolls for Christmas dinner. The grocery store was completely out of rolls and the checkout lines went clear to the back of the store, so I decided I would just go home and make Grandma West's roll recipe. They tasted so good and were so easy to make that I rarely ever bought rolls after that.

The Best 100% Whole Wheat Bread

4½ tsp. yeast (2 packets)

¾ C. warm water

7–9 C. whole wheat flour from hard white
    wheat, divided

2½ C. warm water

½ C. wheat gluten

⅓ C. honey

1½ Tbsp. salt

2½ Tbsp. vegetable oil

(recipe continued on next page)

(The Best 100% Whole Wheat Bread, continued)

Combine yeast with ¾ C. warm water; add 1 C. flour. Mix vigorously. Let sit for 45 minutes or until it starts to settle back down. Add 2½ C. warm water and 2 C. whole wheat flour. Stir very well. Add wheat gluten, honey, salt, and oil. Mix well. Slowly add 4–6 C. whole wheat flour until good bread consistency. Knead 10–15 minutes. Place in greased pans and let rise 45 minutes to 1 hour. Bake at 325 for 30 minutes. It should be very light brown and super yummy! Makes 2 loaves.

My mom is the best mom in the world. I've never met a person more unselfish than her. All of my memories of her include her serving either our family or someone else in need. Whenever I compare my mothering to hers, I fear my children will take a hit, because I could never give and share as much as she has.

Laura Bernard
Story City Branch
Ames Iowa Stake
Iowa Falls, Iowa

Zucchini Bread

2 C. zucchini
3 eggs
2 C. sugar
1 C. oil
3 tsp. vanilla
3 C. flour

1 tsp. salt
1 tsp. baking soda
3 tsp. cinnamon
1¼ tsp. baking powder
½ C. nuts, chopped (optional)

You don't have to peel the zucchini or remove the seeds; simply wash, cut into chunks, and blend in a blender until pureed. In a large bowl, beat zucchini, eggs, sugar, oil, and vanilla. Stir in all dry ingredients and beat well. (I use a 3-cup sifter to sift the dry ingredients into the zucchini mixture; it mixes everything very well.) Stir in the nuts if desired. Grease and flour two bread pans; pour batter into pans. Bake at 325 for 50 minutes or until a cake tester comes out clean. You may add raisins, dates, coconut, or anything else you would like to the batter. *Note:* If you use smaller bread pans, adjust your baking time accordingly. This bread is very moist and freezes very well for some time. Enjoy. Makes 2 regular loaves or several small ones.

Heather Whipple
Piedmont Ward
Fredericksberg Virginia Stake
Culpeper, Virginia

I just recently learned how to make this recipe of my mom's; she is sixty-seven years old and still going strong. She has a lot of really good recipes, but this is one of her best. Recently she made it and put chocolate chips in the batter just to try something new, and it was delicious. I love my mom and her cooking!

Favorite Rolls or Ham Rolls

2 Tbsp. dry yeast or 2 yeast cakes	½ C. sugar
1 C. lukewarm water	½ C. shortening, melted
2 C. milk	4 eggs
2 Tbsp. salt	7 C. flour

In a large bowl, dissolve yeast in water. In a medium pan, scald milk; add salt, sugar, and shortening. Cool and stir into yeast mixture. Add beaten eggs and flour. Stir until well-blended. DO NOT add more flour. Let rise for 3 hours, stirring down occasionally, or refrigerate overnight (I prefer this method). Turn out onto floured board, roll out, and cut. (Depending on your flour, you may need to add a little more to the dough.) Place rolls on greased pan and let rise. If you refrigerate dough overnight, let rolls rise 2 hours. Bake at 350 for 15–20 minutes.

Ham Rolls:

When rolling out the dough, roll into large rectangle and cut into 4-inch squares. Combine cooked ground ham with enough salad dressing (such as Miracle Whip) to moisten. Stir in a little sweet pickle relish (we love the home-canned variety of sweet relish). Place about 1 tablespoon of ham filling the in center of each square, bring edges together, and seal. Place seam side down on pan. Bake as directed above. Makes about 40 rolls.

Sheri Willoughby
Sage Creek Ward
Idaho Falls Idaho North Stake
Idaho Falls, Idaho

As children, when we would smell the delectable aroma of Ham Rolls wafting through the house, we knew it was Christmas morning! When we were small, our mom—Beverly Tanner of Blackfoot, Idaho—wanted to come up with a healthy Christmas morning breakfast. She tried fruit pizza, decorated brown bag breakfasts, and other things. One day she was reading a novel that mentioned ham rolls. When she couldn't find a recipe for them in any cookbook, she made up her own recipe. She has made these rolls every Christmas morning for forty years. My sisters and I now make them on Christmas morning. Mom still makes them for her and Dad and whoever drops in. They are delicious served with homemade eggnog.

Southern Corn Bread

1 ½ C. rice milk

1 ½ C. white cornmeal

1 tsp. salt

2 Tbsp. shortening, melted

½ tsp. baking powder

1 egg, separated

In a large bowl, combine milk and cornmeal; stir in salt and melted shortening. Cool. Add baking powder and egg yolk and mix well. Fold in stiffly beaten egg white. Pour into greased 8 x 8-inch pan and bake at 400 for 20 minutes. *Note:* Sprinkle with cooked crumbled bacon before baking to make Bacon Corn Bread. Makes 9 servings.

This is a recipe I improvised for those who are allergic to milk and wheat. You can also add the beaten egg whole, but separating the egg as above gives a nicer texture.

Carol Clarke Kennedy
Eustis Ward
Leesburg Florida Stake
Tangerine, Florida

Coconut Bread

4 eggs, beaten

2 C. sugar

1 C. oil

2 tsp. coconut extract

3 C. flour

½ tsp. baking powder

½ tsp. baking soda

1 C. buttermilk

1 C. coconut

Combine all ingredients and pour batter into 2 regular greased loaf pans. Bake at 350 for 45 minutes. Makes 2 loaves.

Melissa Horner
LaBelle 1st Ward
Rigby Idaho East Stake
Rigby, Idaho

Best Flour Tortillas Ever

8 C. flour
4 tsp. salt
1 tsp. baking powder

1 C. oil
3 C. boiling water

Stir together flour, salt, and baking powder. Mix in oil; there will be small lumps of oil in the dough. Stir in boiling water (boiling water makes the dough a lot easier to roll out when it is finished). The dough should be soft and pliable, but not sticky or stiff; you may have to add a little more flour or water to get the right consistency. When the dough cools down, finish mixing it with your hands. Some oil lumps will remain; don't overmix the dough trying to get rid of them. Using a piece of dough about the size of a small apple, roll the dough out on a floured surface with a floured rolling pin. Roll in one direction first, then pick up the dough, flip it over and around, and roll in the other direction. Do that a couple of times. Don't worry if the tortilla is not perfectly round. Bake the tortilla over medium-low heat on a DRY pan—do not use oil! When the tortilla bubbles up, flip it over and bake the other side for a few seconds. Use for fajitas, burritos, wraps, soft tacos—or even eat them plain or with cheese melted on top. Makes 15 tortillas.

Ryan Lee
Fort Smith Ward
Fort Smith Arkansas Stake
Fort Smith, Arkansas

When my mom was gathering recipes just before she got married, she came across this flour tortilla recipe, lost and forgotten, in one of her mother's old recipe boxes. When she tried it out she discovered that it was fairly easy and super delicious. It became a staple in our home. For the last thirty years she has served these flour tortillas to many missionaries and other visitors, and they were always a favorite for family meals. She has even served them at a zone conference, where they made a big hit. When I went on my mission to Montana, I took the recipe with me. One day I decided that I just had to have some of my mom's flour tortillas. I got busy and mixed up the dough. But I was surprised when I realized that there wasn't a rolling pin anywhere in the apartment. So I found an empty 2-liter soda bottle, filled it with water, and went to work. Finally I had my tortillas—just like Mom's!

Italian Rosemary Bread

1 C. water

3 Tbsp. olive oil

1½ tsp. sugar

1½ tsp. salt

¼ tsp. Italian seasoning

¼ tsp. pepper

1 Tbsp. dried rosemary

2½ C. bread flour

1½ tsp. active dry yeast

This delicious recipe is designed for a bread machine, but could also be made like regular bread. Place all ingredients in the pan of bread machine in the order suggested by the manufacturer. Select white bread cycle; press start. Makes 10 servings.

My mom makes the most wonderful bread for dipping in olive oil and spices. When my mom was in college she worked at an Italian restaurant, where she got the recipe for this bread. Now it's a staple in our family and something my siblings and I will pass down to our children. It is so good it defies description. I can't tell you how many missionaries have walked away from our house begging for this recipe. Thanks, Mom! We love you!

Amelia Mandrake
Milwaukee City Branch
Milwaukee Wisconsin North Stake
Whitefish Bay, Wisconsin

Bleu Cheese Biscuits

3 pkgs. refrigerated biscuits

¾ C. butter

4 oz. crumbled bleu cheese

Lightly grease 9 x 13-inch pan. Cut biscuits in fourths and arrange in pan. Melt butter in saucepan and add bleu cheese until melted, stirring constantly (you can also use the microwave). Pour butter mixture over biscuits. Bake at 375 for 20 minutes or until biscuits are brown and butter is absorbed. Makes 15–20 servings.

This recipe was given to me by a special friend many years ago. I always get requests for this recipe whenever I serve them.

Lanita Wimer
Black Forest Ward
Colorado Springs Colorado East Stake
Colorado Springs, Colorado

Easter Bread

1½ Tbsp. dry yeast
1 C. warm water, divided
1½ C. sugar, divided
1 tsp. salt
¼ C. butter

1 C. milk, scalded
6 eggs
2 tsp. vanilla
8 C. flour

Soften yeast in ½ C. warm water and 2 Tbsp. sugar. In a separate bowl, combine remaining water, remaining sugar, salt, and butter in scalded milk. Cool to lukewarm. Mix with yeast mixture. Add eggs and vanilla. Add flour a little at a time, and knead until dough falls off hands (about 10 minutes). Let rise in a warm place until double in size (about 1 hour). Punch down. Split into 3 greased loaf pans and let rise for about 45 minutes in a warm place. Bake at 350 for 20–30 minutes. *Note:* Make sure not to add flour all at once. The flour amount is approximate, and you may need more or less, depending on weather conditions. Makes 3 loaves.

Patrick Flanagan
Prairie 8th Ward
Prairie Utah Stake
West Jordan, Utah

After I got married, my wife and I talked about traditions from our families that we would like to pass on to our children. One that I especially enjoyed was that every Easter for breakfast my mom would make boiled eggs, polish sausage, and this Easter Bread. Our first Easter together my wife was able to try the bread and became a fan. When we asked my mother where the recipe came from, we learned that her grandmother had memorized the recipe before she came to the United States from Poland. Eating this bread on Easter is now a tradition we carry on with our children.

Choco-Dot Pumpkin Bread

2 C. flour

2 tsp. baking powder

1 tsp. baking soda

½ tsp. salt

1½ tsp. cinnamon

½ tsp. ground cloves

¼ tsp. allspice

¼ tsp. ginger

1½ C. sugar

4 eggs

1 16-oz. can pumpkin (2 C.)

¾ C. oil*

1½ C. bran flakes

1 C. semi-sweet chocolate chips

1 C. nuts, chopped (optional)

*You can substitute applesauce for part or all of the oil; I prefer half oil and half applesauce. In a medium bowl, combine dry ingredients and set aside. In a large mixing bowl, beat eggs until foamy. Add pumpkin, oil, and bran flakes, and mix well. Let stand for about 5 minutes. Add dry ingredients and mix only until blended. Stir in chocolate chips and nuts. Pour batter into 2–3 large loaf pans or 6 mini loaf pans coated with cooking spray. Bake at 350 for 45–60 minutes or until toothpick comes out clean. Time depends on loaf size and oven. Cool completely before removing from pan. Slice and enjoy! Be careful, this is addicting! We often eat it warm right out of the pan. Makes 2–3 large loaves.

MaraLee Judd
Warrenton 2nd Ward
Centreville Virginia Stake
Warrenton, Virginia

Growing up, I always saw my mom bake. As the oldest of ten children, I learned to cook out of necessity, and I love to do it. My mom loved teaching me, and I loved spending time with her. Breads have always been her specialty. Our favorite was this Choco-Dot Pumpkin Bread—a recipe she got from her mom. Each Christmas we cleaned out food cans and cooked the bread in them; then we wrapped them in plastic wrap and put a Christmas bow on top. My mom has always been one of the most giving people I know. When we were young, we asked why she gave so much food away, and she said we always need to give what we can to others. We never had a lot of money, so we gave the gift of food. I vowed I wanted to be just like her when I grew up. I knew that I was making progress when my own children asked me one day why I always gave away so much bread. What a great day that was! I now teach my children to bake, and this recipe is one of their favorites as well. I will be eternally grateful to my mom for teaching me how to love baking, but I am even more grateful for her example of thinking of others and giving what you can.

Grandma's Yummy Rolls

2 pkgs. dry active yeast

1¼ C. warm water, divided

3 eggs, well beaten

½ C. shortening

½ C. sugar

4½ C. flour

3 tsp. salt

Soften yeast in ¼ C. warm water. In a separate bowl, combine eggs, shortening, sugar, 1 C. warm water, 2½ C. flour, and salt; add softened yeast. Beat until smooth. Add remaining flour to make a soft dough, blending well. Cover and allow to rise until double. Punch down and place in refrigerator overnight. Three hours before baking, roll out by dividing dough in half. Roll each half into a rectangle ½ inch thick. Spread with butter. Roll up jelly roll style and cut into 1-inch slices (or shape into Parker House rolls). Place in greased muffin tins, cut-side down. Cover and allow to rise three hours before baking at 400 for 12–15 minutes. Makes 36 rolls.

Alysia Duke
Quantico Ward
Woodbridge Virginia Stake
Montclair, Virginia

These fantastic rolls were always a holiday treat at Grandma McMullin's home. They were my favorite part of Christmas and Thanksgiving dinners. Even though she isn't with us for these holidays anymore, we still make her rolls and remember the familiar and comforting smells and tastes of Grandma McMullin's kitchen.

Anna's Banana Nut Bread

1 C. sugar
½ C. margarine or butter
2 eggs
3 bananas, mashed
¼ tsp. salt

1 tsp. baking soda dissolved in 1 Tbsp. warm
 water
2 C. flour
¾ C. walnuts, chopped

Cream margarine (or butter) and sugar together. Add eggs and mix well. Stir in mashed bananas, mixing well. Add salt. Stir in baking soda and warm water mixture, stirring well. Mix in flour and stir in nuts. Put batter into two small well-greased loaf pans. Bake at 325 for 45–50 minutes or until loaves test done with a toothpick. Cool on wire rack. When cool, wrap in aluminum foil. My friend calls this "gourmet" banana bread because it is so moist and flavorful. Makes 2 small loaves.

Deanna Larsen
Eastridge 5th Ward
Draper Utah Eastridge Stake
Sandy, Utah

Some of my earliest memories are of "helping" my wonderful mother, Anna Ekins, cook. When I was four years old, my mother gave me an apron with my name on it. While growing up, I spent many hours in the kitchen with my mother learning how to cook. We especially had fun baking. I loved that she taught me to make some of my Grandma's Czechoslovakian recipes for foods like rozky and zazvorniky. Even as a teenager, I remember coming home from school to the aromas of freshly baked white or cinnamon bread along with her yummy banana bread and cookies. It was very rare to have store-bought bread or commercial cookies in our house. I am so glad that my mother had the patience to teach me to cook. Not only was it fun, but it gave us opportunities to do something together and talk. I am grateful for the time she spent with me, for the fun we had, and for all the dirty dishes she washed for me. She passed away much too young, but I will always have precious memories of the time we spent together. I have tried to make baking fun for my children, and I'm looking forward to spending more time in the kitchen with my grandkids.

Kansas Wheat Dinner Rolls

2 C. lukewarm water
¾ C. oil
2 Tbsp. honey
½ C. sugar

2 pkgs. yeast (2 Tbsp.)
2 eggs
4 C. flour (I use part white, part whole wheat)
2 tsp. salt

Mix all ingredients in a bowl with electric mixer for 3 minutes. Gradually add as much as 3 C. additional flour. Mix thoroughly. May be kneaded. Let rise. Punch down. Turn out on lightly floured surface. Cut into 32 pieces. Place on greased baking pans, either close together or spread apart. Let rise for 30 minutes or until double. Bake at 375 for 15 minutes. Dough may also be used for cinnamon rolls. *Note:* This recipe is from the Kansas Wheat Commission. Makes 32 rolls.

Linda Lindquist
Columbus Branch
Lincoln Nebraska Stake
Osceola, Nebraska

My mom taught me just about everything I know. As the oldest child, I got plenty of practice helping around the house, garden, and barnyard. My first attempt at baking was a cake mix. I don't remember what I did wrong, but it didn't turn out well. Mom simply said, "I didn't know a cake mix could fail." That didn't help my ego, but I tried again, and this time it came out okay. Mom taught me how to garden and how to preserve the produce we grew. We worked side by side, and I never wanted to disappoint her. Mom had one specialty, and that was making double-crust fruit pies. Of course, she learned how to make pies from her mom, and I suppose it went back for countless generations in that manner. My grandma made pie for my grandpa just about every day. Luckily, I have a daughter who loves to cook, and it has been fun to pass the art of pie baking down to the next generation.

Carolyn's Homemade Bread

3 qts. milk
½ C. butter (not margarine)
½ C. honey
3 Tbsp. salt

2 Tbsp. dry yeast
10 C. whole wheat flour
4 C. unbleached white flour

In a large pan, bring milk to a boil; add butter and honey. Cool to lukewarm and add salt, yeast, and whole wheat flour. Mix well. Knead, using about 4 C. white flour to knead. Let rise until double, punch down, and let rise again. Shape into 10 loaves and place in pans. Let rise about 15–20 minutes; bake at 350 for about 50–60 minutes. Makes 10 loaves (I usually make half a recipe). *Note:* You can vary the ratio of white and wheat flour you use to make it more predominantly wheat or white bread. It seems to always come out good no matter the ratio!

Jana McGettigan
Jordan North 8th Ward
Jordan Utah North Stake
West Valley City, Utah

My mom always made bread when I was growing up, and since there were ten children, she usually made this ten-loaf bread recipe two or three times a week. There's nothing better than a hot slice of homemade bread slathered with butter! The year I graduated from high school, my mom decided that before I went off to college, I needed to learn how to make bread. So she had me make her recipe EVERY DAY (okay—not Sundays) for the whole summer! By then, there were only five of us at home, and I knew we would never eat that much bread, so I asked her what we'd do with all the bread. She said, "We'll give it to the neighbors!" More than twenty-five years later, I've just recently started making bread again!

Buttery Breadsticks

1 Tbsp. yeast
1½ C. warm water
2 Tbsp. sugar

½ tsp. salt
3 C. flour
½ C. butter

Preheat oven to 350. Dissolve yeast in warm water. Let it stand until foamy. Add sugar, salt, and flour; mix well. Knead until smooth and elastic. Let dough rise for 10 minutes. Melt butter and pour into a baking sheet. Roll out dough into a rectangle about ¼-inch thick. Cut into 1 x 4-inch strips using a pizza cutter. Roll each piece in butter (covering all sides) and arrange in the baking sheet. Sprinkle with garlic salt or Parmesan cheese. Let rise 15–20 minutes. Bake for 15–18 minutes. Makes 12 breadsticks.

Kimberly Gleason
Green Park Ward
Willow Park Utah Stake
Lehi, Utah

These breadsticks always remind me of childhood dinners (and lunches and snacks)! During my early teen years, these breadsticks were a comforting staple. I was rarely home for dinner due to ballet classes and rehearsals, so my mom would save a few and bring them for me to eat while she drove me home. These were very informal and nontraditional dinners, but I am so grateful for that time. Over the course of eight years, my mom and I spent more than 900 hours talking (and eating) in the car.

Perfection Rolls

2 pkgs. dry yeast
¼ C. lukewarm water
1 C. shortening
1 C. sugar
2 eggs

2 tsp. salt
1 C. boiling water
1 C. cold water
6½–7 C. flour

Dissolve yeast in lukewarm water. Set aside. Using electric mixer, cream shortening and sugar. Add eggs, salt, and boiling water. Add cold water and yeast mixture. Sift in half of the flour and mix with mixer. Add rest of the flour and mix by hand. Place dough in greased bowl. Brush top of dough with shortening. Cover and let rise 2–3 hours or until doubled in size. If you live in a dry and arid climate, cover the dough with a warm, moist cloth while the bread rises; in more humid climates, use a dry cloth. Form rolls, place in greased pan, and cover. Let rise for 1 hour. Place pan of rolls in cold oven. Bake at 400 for 25 minutes. Makes 9–12 servings.

Lilia Bullock
Cameron Ward
Fayetteville North Carolina West Stake
Cameron, North Carolina

These are hearty rolls that are meant to fill you up. My mom got this recipe from my great-grandmother; she tried to teach me the recipe when I was sixteen, but at the time, I wanted nothing to do with baking. When I later got interested in cooking, Mom no longer remembered the recipe. She passed away shortly after that, and I was saddened to think that she took the recipe with her to her grave. Imagine my joy not long after that when I was looking through her ward cookbooks and came across her recipe! I could now pass on her tradition of baking these rolls to my own family. I have baked them for my brothers, and we all agree that the rolls are as good as we remember.

Potato Puff Buns

6 C. warm water

1 C. powdered milk

4 Tbsp. instant yeast

1 C. shortening

1 C. sugar

2 C. mashed potato flakes

4 eggs, beaten

2 Tbsp. salt

Flour

Combine all ingredients but flour; stir in enough flour to make a soft dough. Knead on speed 1 in a bread machine or with an electric mixer for 5 minutes. Let rise until double in size. Roll out for cinnamon rolls or dinner rolls. Let rise again. Bake at 350 for 20–25 minutes. Makes 5–6 dozen dinner rolls or 3–4 dozen cinnamon rolls.

One of my mother's favorite traditions is her famous cinnamon rolls that she gives out each year to her neighbors for Christmas. All of her neighbors look forward to them each year because they love them so much. It's a special memory, because my mom puts so much of herself into each gift she gives. She used to own a shop called Ilene's Bosch Kitchen Center, where she taught cooking classes. We did not have a lot, but my mom gave the best she could—something I LOVE and appreciate about my mom.

Heather Leishman
Paradise 2nd Ward
Paradise Utah Stake
Paradise, Utah

Alan's Favorite After School Days Rolls

1 pkg. dry yeast

½ C. sugar

5 C. sifted flour

½ tsp. salt

½ C. shortening

Butter

Dissolve yeast and sugar in 1½ C. lukewarm water. Sift flour and salt into a bowl. Cut in shortening until crumbly. Stir in yeast mixture until flour is moistened. Chill, tightly covered, overnight. Knead on floured surface for 5 minutes; shape as desired. Place on greased baking sheet. Brush with butter. Bake at 350 for 20 minutes or until golden brown. Makes 2 dozen.

My mom made these rolls often, and our family seemed to eat them by the dozen. Many days my brother Alan and I returned from school to hot rolls. Talk about a yummy treat to come home to!

Christina Marcano
Dry Creek Ward
Lehi Utah South Stake
Lehi, Utah

Wixom Family Rolls

5–6 C. all-purpose flour (I use Gold Medal or
  Martha White)

2 pkgs. yeast

½ C. sugar

1 tsp. salt

2 C. whole or low-fat milk (not skim)

1 egg

A large kitchen mixer makes these rolls SO much easier! Put half the flour in the bowl with the yeast, sugar, and salt; stir with a spoon to blend. Heat 2 C. milk in the microwave for 1 minute 40 seconds to 2 minutes. It should be warm like a baby's bottle. If it's too cold, it won't activate the yeast; if it's too hot, it will kill the yeast. Crack the egg into the milk and mix. Add the milk/egg mixture to the flour mixture and stir vigorously with a spoon until everything is wet. Using the dough hook, mix on low to medium speed until the dough is smooth and you don't see any lumps. Slowly add the remaining flour, ½ C. at a time, blending well each time, until the dough is smooth and has no lumps. (*Note:* Don't rush this process; I often walk away and do other small things while each portion of flour is being blended. Take it slow—you want the dough as smooth as silk!) Once all the flour has been added and the dough is smooth, use cooking oil or butter to grease the dough lightly on all sides (you want the dough to rise smoothly without ripping away from the bowl). Cover with plastic wrap and put in a warm place free of drafts. Let rise 30–45 minutes, or until doubled in size. Once the dough has risen, grease your hands, roll pieces of dough into balls, and drop them into greased muffin tins. Let rise in a warm place until doubled in size. Bake at 400 until very lightly browned (watch carefully, because they cook very quickly; mine take 4–5 minutes). After baking, brush lightly with salted butter. (If you are watching your fat intake, you can eliminate the butter; instead, cover rolls with a paper towel and foil to let the rolls "sweat" and soften). Makes 24 servings.

My wife encouraged me to submit this roll recipe because it was the one thing she begged my mom for when we got married. When I was young, my mom used to cater; of all the wonderful things she made, these rolls became the most requested item. I wanted to share them with everyone, since we think they are just awesome. Happy Mother's Day, Mom!

Steven Wixom
Champions Ward
Klein Texas Stake
Houston, Texas

{ SIDE DISHES }

The goodness of home is not dependent on wealth, or spaciousness, or beauty, or luxury. Everything depends on the Mother.

{ G.W.E. Russell }

Homemade Garden Salsa

10 qts. tomatoes (just more than half a canning kettle)

5 green bell peppers, chopped

8–10 jalapeno peppers, chopped (use gloves while chopping!)

11 medium onions

4 C. celery, chopped

6 cloves garlic, chopped, or ¾ tsp. garlic powder)

2 tsp. paprika

¾ C. sugar

1 C. vinegar

2 Tbsp. pepper

½ C. salt

4 tsp. cumin

¼ C. fresh cilantro (don't add more, no matter how big a batch)

Scald and peel tomatoes. Dice all vegetables, including tomatoes, and put in large cooking pot. Add seasonings and simmer 1 hour. Place in sterile jars, and process in a hot water bath 15 minutes. Makes about 21 pints.

Erin Haskell
Battle Creek 9th Ward
Pleasant Grove Utah East Stake
Pleasant Grove, Utah

All throughout my childhood my family had a garden. At the end of each summer we made homemade salsa. My siblings and I gathered in the kitchen, where tomatoes were being steamed, and waited for an assignment from my mom. With her wearing gloves to handle the jalapeno peppers (which added a sense of spicy danger to our salsa), we spent an hour or so together peeling and dicing tomatoes, chopping up celery and bell peppers, shedding many a tear over the onions, and pouring them all together into the biggest silver pot we had. The smell of the tangy simmering vegetables filled the whole house, making our mouths water while we waited to dip a tortilla chip into the pot for a first taste. The crinkle of the chip bag, the small splash of salsa when a chip was dunked into it, the anticipated journey to the mouth, and the satisfying crunch into the world's best salsa are the delicious memories that contribute to my mom's homemade salsa recipe. We weren't just making salsa—we were enjoying the reward at the end of a summer of hard work pulling weeds and watering plants. Through this, my mom taught us that "you reap what you sow."

Mom's Famous Baked Beans

2 large cans pork and beans
½–1 lb. uncooked bacon, diced
1 large onion (or more), chopped
1 green pepper (or more), chopped

1 C. brown sugar
1½ C. ketchup
2 tsp. Worcestershire sauce

Mix all ingredients and pour into a 3-quart roasting pan or casserole dish. Bake at 325 for 3 hours. Makes 8–12 servings.

It doesn't get much better than Mom's baked beans. Our family has fond memories of the aroma of Mom's baked beans cooking. Whenever we go to Mom's house for dinner, as soon as her front door is opened, the smell makes everyone perk up and say "Aahhh, that smells so good." This delicious recipe makes our family Easter dinner something to look forward to each year.

RaeAnn Jarvis
Park 4th Ward
West Jordan Utah Park Stake
West Jordan, Utah

Portuguese Cod Cakes

4 potatoes
10 oz. salted cod (presoaked about 7 hours)
3 eggs

1 small onion, very finely chopped
2 Tbsp. parsley, finely chopped
Oil for frying

Boil potatoes in their skins so they do not absorb water. Peel and mash the potatoes well. In the meantime, simmer cod in boiling water 20 minutes. Discard bones and skin, and flake it as much as possible until it resembles threads. Mix flaked cod with the potatoes and add the eggs. Stir in the onions and parsley. Taste and add a little salt if necessary, but the mixture should be salty enough from the salted cod. The mixture should be quite stiff; if a spoon stuck in the mixture stands up on its own, it's ready. If the mixture seems too dry, add a tablespoon or two of milk. Allow the mixture to cool completely before frying. When cool, use two spoons to form the cakes so that they resemble eggs. Dip in hot oil and cook until nicely browned on all sides, turning a few times. Remove each cake with a slotted spoon and drain on paper towels. Makes 4 servings. *Note:* You can substitute tuna or chicken for the cod; the cakes will taste different, but are just as good.

Sara Moreira
Ermesinde Branch
Porto Norte Portugal Stake
Valongo, Portugal

Aunt Michelle's Veggies

1 onion, diced

2 Tbsp. butter

3 C. broccoli, cut into bite-size pieces

3 C. cauliflower, cut into bite-size pieces

1 8-oz. can sliced water chestnuts

4 carrots, thinly sliced

¾ C. water

1 C. mayonnaise

2 C. cream

1 C. Parmesan cheese, grated

2 C. cheddar cheese, shredded and divided

In large saucepan, cook onions in butter until tender. Add broccoli, cauliflower, water chestnuts, carrots, and water. Cover and steam until tender. In a large bowl, mix mayonnaise, cream, Parmesan cheese, and 1 C. cheddar cheese. Fold in to veggie mixture, being careful not to mash veggies. Pour into a 9 x 13-inch pan. Top with remaining 1 C. cheddar cheese. Bake at 350 for 45 minutes or until golden brown. Makes 8–10 servings.

Sara Moreira
Ermesinde Branch
Porto Norte Portugal Stake
Valongo, Portugal

My family loves these vegetables, and it's a tradition to have them on Thanksgiving. Aunt Michelle is my sister-in-law. She is an amazing cook and a wonderful mother. I know if my own mother were still alive she would love these veggies. She has been gone for twenty-seven years now, and I miss her dearly. She was such a great cook. I wish I could call her and have her teach me how to make her homemade chicken noodle soup, homemade bread, and homemade potato salad. Those are what I miss the most. My mother was an amazing woman; I remember coming home from school and the house smelling like fresh-baked bread or cookies. I can't wait to see her again. I hope she will be able to make me some chicken noodle soup and fresh bread. As a mother I love it when my children call me to find out how to make something they loved when they were at home.

Carne en Polvo (Colombian Powdered Beef)

1 lb. flank steak

2 cloves garlic, crushed

2 scallions, chopped

½ C. onion, chopped

½ tsp. ground cumin

Salt and pepper to taste

5 C. water

Place the flank steak in a plastic bag and add the garlic, scallions, onion, cumin, salt, and pepper. Refrigerate for about 2 hours. In a medium pot, place the flank steak and water; bring water to a boil. Reduce heat to medium-low and cook for about 1 hour, or until the beef is cooked. Remove the beef from the water and set aside to let it cool. Cut the beef into chunks and place in a food processor. Process until the beef is finely shredded and is a powdered consistency. It is a bit bland if you it eat alone, but it is great as part of the *Bandeja Paisa*. My mother sometimes mixes this with *Hogao* (tomato and onion sauce) and serves it over white rice, which is delicious. Makes 4–6 servings.

Arroz Blanco (White Rice)

2 C. long-grain white rice, rinsed

4 C. water

1 Tbsp. olive oil

1 tsp. salt

In a medium pot, place the rice, water, oil, and salt. Bring to a boil for 30 seconds; reduce the heat to low and cook for 15–20 minutes or until the water is absorbed and the rice is tender. Remove from heat and let sit for 5 minutes before serving. Makes 4–6 servings.

Hogao (Tomato and Onion Sauce)

3 Tbsp. vegetable oil

2 C. fresh tomatoes, chopped

1 C. scallions, chopped

1 clove garlic, minced

1 tsp. ground cumin

¼ tsp. salt

¼ tsp. ground pepper

¼ C. fresh cilantro, chopped

In a large saucepan, heat oil; add the tomatoes, scallions, garlic, and cumin. Cook gently for 10 minutes, stirring until softened. Reduce heat to low; add salt, pepper, and cilantro. Cook for additional 10 minutes, stirring occasionally until the sauce has thickened. Check and adjust the seasoning. This is wonderful as a dipping sauce or a topping. It can even be used as the beginning of other recipes. There are many versions of this sauce in Colombia. I think this recipe—my mother's—is the best. Makes 2 cups.

Frijoles Paisas (Paisa Pinto Beans)

Beans:

3 C. pinto beans

½ lb. pork hocks

6 C. water

½ green plantain, cut in ¼-inch cubes

1 C. carrots, shredded

½ tsp. salt

Guiso:

3 Tbsp. vegetable oil

2 C. tomatoes, diced

1 Tbsp. onions, chopped

¼ C. scallions, chopped

¼ tsp. salt

1 clove garlic, minced

¼ C. cilantro, chopped

¼ tsp. ground cumin

Wash the beans and soak overnight in cold water. Drain. Place in a large pot with pork hocks and 6 C. water. Bring to a boil, then cover and reduce the heat to medium-low. Cook the beans until almost tender, approximately 2 hours. While the beans are cooking, prepare the *guiso*. In a large skillet, heat the vegetable oil over medium heat; add the tomatoes, onions, scallions, ¼ tsp. salt, garlic, cilantro, and cumin, and cook for 10–15 minutes. When the beans are almost tender, add the *guiso*, plantain, carrots, and ½ tsp. salt. Cover and cook for another hour or until the beans are fully cooked. (Add additional water as necessary). Makes 10 servings.

Tajadas de Platano (Fried Sweet Plantains)

2 very ripe large plantains

½ C. vegetable oil

Peel the plantains and cut on the diagonal into ½-inch-thick slices. In a large pan, heat the oil over medium-high heat. Add the plantain slices in a single layer, and cook about 2 minutes on each side. Remove the plantains with a slotted spoon and transfer to a plate lined with paper towels. Sprinkle with salt. Serve warm. Makes 6 servings.

My mom's best recipe is actually a *number* of recipes that together make my favorite meal—*Bandeja Paisa*, a huge meal that includes many dishes. I have eaten this meal my entire life, and it is one of my favorites. *Bandeja Paisa* includes *Carne en Polvo, Frijoles Paisas, Arroz Blanco, Hogao, Tajadas de Platano, Colombian chorizo*, avocados, *chicharron*, and fried eggs. With so much food each person gets a platter. The platter holds some of each dish with a fried egg right in the middle on top of everything, with a bowl of the *Frijoles Paisa* and a bowl of the *Hogao* to the side. My mother is a master at making this meal; I get hungry just thinking of this delicious feast!

Julieta Arturo Sandoval
Las Villas Ward
Soacha Stake
Bogota, Colombia

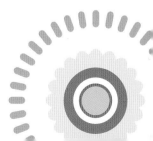

New Potatoes and Peas

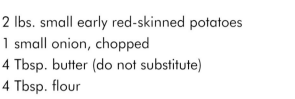

2 lbs. small early red-skinned potatoes

1 small onion, chopped

4 Tbsp. butter (do not substitute)

4 Tbsp. flour

1 tsp. salt

½ tsp. pepper

2½ C. milk, half-and-half, or a combination

½ C. of the water the potatoes are boiled in

4 C. shelled fresh peas (about 6 lbs. unshelled peas) or 2 10-oz. pkgs. frozen peas

In a medium-large saucepan, cook scrubbed unpeeled potatoes in boiling salt water for 15–20 minutes or until tender. Drain all but ½ C. of the water; set aside. In the same saucepan, sauté the onions in the butter. Blend in flour, salt, and pepper. Stir in milk and remaining potato water and heat until sauce thickens, stirring constantly. Add potatoes and peas and heat through. Makes 16 ½-cup servings. *Note:* You can add 8 slices partially fried crumbled bacon to the sauce as you heat it. You can also use ½–1 C. canned milk for part of the milk.

Sheree Fabian
Skiatook Branch
Tulsa Oklahoma Stake
Skiatook, Oklahoma

This is one of my mom's favorite recipes. She made it for her birthday every year when we were kids; since her birthday is June 29, it was the time of year when the new potatoes are the most tender and the peas are so fresh. My mother is now in her eighties and is legally blind, so my youngest sister has kept the tradition going by inviting our mother to her home for New Potatoes and Peas every year on her birthday. It was hard to write the recipe down, because it is one of those recipes that we made by looking at it. Does that look thick enough? Does it look like it has enough potatoes or peas? Does it need a little more salt or pepper? So feel free to adjust the recipe so that it looks and tastes right to you.

Singapore Noodles

10 oz. dried rice vermicelli

1½ lb. raw shrimp

2 Tbsp. cooking oil, divided

2 cloves garlic, finely chopped

1 lb. pork loin, cut into strips

1 large onion, cut into thin wedges

1 Tbsp. mild curry powder

½ lb. green beans, cut into small diagonal
  pieces

1 large carrot, cut into fine matchsticks

1 tsp. castor sugar (finely ground sugar)

1 tsp. salt

1 Tbsp. soy sauce

½ lb. bean sprouts, scraggly ends removed

Salt and pepper to taste

Sugar to taste

Spring onion (green onion), cut into fine strips
  (for garnish)

Soak the vermicelli in boiling water for 5 minutes or until it becomes soft; drain. Devein and peel the shrimp, then chop the shrimp meat. Pour 1 Tbsp. cooking oil in a wok and heat it; when it is hot, add the shrimp, garlic, and pork. Stir-fry for 2 minutes or until meat is just cooked; remove from the wok. Reduce the heat to medium and heat another 1 Tbsp. oil. Add the onion and curry powder and stir-fry for 3 minutes. Add the beans, carrot, sugar, and salt. Sprinkle with a little water and stir-fry for 2 minutes. Add the vermicelli and soy sauce to the wok; toss with 2 wooden spoons. Add the bean sprouts and pork mixture, and season with salt, pepper, and sugar to taste. Toss well before serving; use spring onion as garnish. Makes 6 servings.

Ruth Pangan
Singapore Tagalog 3rd Ward
Singapore Stake
Singapore

I was so lazy about learning how to cook when I was still at home with my mom in the Philippines. I remember my mom always told me that I needed to learn to cook in preparation for having my own family. Now I am in Singapore and I am learning to cook, but I'm not with my mom. I love her and I miss her.

Yummy Rice Pilaf

¼ C. butter or margarine

1 medium to large bell pepper, coarsely chopped

1 medium to large onion, coarsely chopped

1 C. fresh mushrooms, sliced, or small can sliced mushrooms, drained

2 C. uncooked long-grain rice

½–1 tsp. dried thyme leaves (use the smaller amount the first time if you are not sure your family likes the flavor of thyme)

4 C. water

2 bouillon cubes

Preheat oven to 350. Melt butter in skillet over medium heat. Add bell pepper, onion, and mushrooms, and sauté for 3–5 minutes. Add rice and thyme; stir well. Meanwhile, in a separate pan, bring water to a boil. As soon as water is boiling, add bouillon cubes and stir until the cubes are mostly dissolved. Pour into veggie mixture and stir until well combined. Transfer to 1.5-quart casserole dish with lid. Cover and bake at 350 for 40–45 minutes or until liquid is absorbed and veggies rise to the top. Remove lid and stir once before serving. Makes 8 ½-cup servings, but don't count on it actually serving 8, because people will want seconds. *Note:* When I make this as a side dish for beef, I use beef bouillon; as a side dish for chicken, I use chicken bouillon; and as a side dish for pork or fish, I use vegetable bouillon. You use any vegetables, based on your family's likes and dislikes. You can adjust recipe for a larger group by adding another ¼ C. rice and ½ C. broth per serving and by cooking a little longer. If you are short on time, you can increase the oven temperature to 375 and bake 30–35 minutes for original recipe amounts. If you have a small family, you can cut recipe in half, use a 1-quart dish, and bake 30–35 minutes.

Jaime Gillies
Broadneck Ward
Annapolis Maryland Stake
Arnold, Maryland

As a child, I was notorious for going to great lengths to avoid eating my veggies. From pretending to go to the bathroom just to spit them in the toilet to wrapping them in a napkin and tucking them away in my father's coat pocket for safekeeping, I proved to be quite the challenge to my mother! However, she ultimately won the battle with this recipe, which incorporates the perfect blend of rice, vegetables, and seasoning. Now eating my veggies has never been more delicious!

Yorkshire Pudding

½ C. butter (can use drippings from beef roast)

4 eggs

2 C. milk

2 C. flour

1 tsp. salt

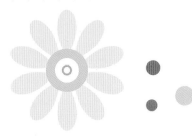

Put the butter in a 13 x 9-inch baking pan, and place the pan in a 425-degree oven to melt. In a large bowl, mix eggs, milk, flour, and salt until smooth. When the butter has melted, pour the batter over the melted butter and return the pan to the oven right away. Make sure there is space above the pan, because the Yorkshire pudding will be tall. Bake 25 minutes until the pudding is puffed up and beginning to brown a bit. Remove from oven and show it to your family for a round of "Oohs" and "Aahhs." Cut into pieces and serve immediately; excellent with roast beef. Makes 10 servings—fewer if you have boys!

Nona Springer
Dallas 1st Ward
Monmouth Oregon Stake
Dallas, Oregon

My missionary son was riding his bike through Deanna Buxton's neighborhood. She saw him and asked what his favorite homemade dish was; he replied, "Yorkshire Pudding!" This dish has become a family favorite since before my missionary was born. We had become "homeless" due to an unscrupulous individual, so my husband and I and our three small children—ages two, three and a half, and five—took up residence in an RV behind the home of our friends. We learned how to make Yorkshire pudding from their mother, who learned it from her mother-in-law. It's an old English favorite that came about during the potato famine. It provided a starch to eat with the meat during hard times. It became a blessing in our lives when we experienced our own "famine" of sorts, and we will remain forever grateful to our friends who provided us with shelter and food in our time of need.

Sweet Potato Surprise

4 large sweet potatoes

½ C. cream

½ C. maple syrup

1 bag large marshmallows

3 C. crushed cornflakes

Oil for deep-frying

(recipe continued on next page)

(Sweet Potato Surprise, continued)

Clean, peel, cube, and boil sweet potatoes until tender, about 20–25 minutes. Mash until smooth with an electric mixer. Slowly add cream and syrup (you may not need it all). One by one, cover each marshmallow with the mashed sweet potatoes, then roll in crushed cornflakes. Deep-fry in oil until golden. Serve hot. The marshmallow will be runny, so be careful. Makes 12 servings.

This is a recipe my grandmother used to make when my mother was a little girl, and it is a favorite of everyone in my family except for me—and that's only because I don't like sweet potatoes!

Julie Slaughter
Caribou Ward
St. John New Brunswick Canada Stake
Presque Isle, Maine

Apple Yams

1 ½ lb. yams

1 Tbsp. butter

½ tsp. cinnamon

¾ lb. tart apples, peeled, cored, and sliced

6 shakes of salt

1 Tbsp. honey

2 tsp. fresh lemon juice

Cut the unpeeled yams into 1½-inch chunks. Cook the yams in salted water until tender. Remove from pan and let cool until able to handle. Peel and put in bowl; mash. While yams are cooking, prepare apples. Let a medium-sized skillet heat for about 30 seconds over medium heat; add butter and let it melt. Swirl to coat pan. Sprinkle in the cinnamon, then add the apples. Stir and cook until the apples are very soft. Add apples to mashed yams. Add salt, honey, and lemon juice and mash to desired consistency—smooth or chunky, whatever your family likes. Makes 4–5 servings. Note: If desired, you can substitute applesauce for the apples.

Bryan McCall
Pittsburgh 4th Ward
Pittsburgh Pennsylvania North Stake
Pittsburgh, Pennsylvania

My mom found this recipe while I was serving my mission. When I came home, she fixed it, thinking it would be a treat for me—but I don't like yams. Even though I was an adult, she put a spoonful on my plate and insisted that I try them. I had to admit that I really enjoyed them. Everyone in my family loves this dish.

Candied Carrots

1 2-lb. pkg. carrots
1 tsp. salt
1 tsp. sugar

½ C. butter
½ C. packed brown sugar

Peel and slice carrots. Place in pan and cover with water. Add salt and sugar. Bring to boil, reduce heat to medium, and boil gently for about 20 minutes or until carrots are very soft. Pour into colander to drain. In the same cooking pan, heat butter and brown sugar until melted and bubbly. Immediately pour carrots back into pan. Stir to coat. Makes 6 servings.

Lani Buxton
Battlecreek 10th Ward
Pleasant Grove Utah East Stake
Pleasant Grove, Utah

My mom, Deanna Buxton (author of this book and actually many others), is definitely the most excellent lady. I like to call her Bob. You know how when your nose is stuffed up, "Mom" sounds like "Bob"? That's where I got it. Bob always has something to make or someone to take care of or something to be fixed—and she always has hungry people to feed. Bob goes to extreme lengths to make sure my family is not hungry. This recipe has always been a gem to us. I don't know where she got it, but, oh, does it hit the spot. I remember when I got baptized, we came home to a most delightful feast—but we could all smell something burnt. The carrots had not been taken off the burner, so they . . . got crusty. We were all a little disappointed, but Bob was the saddest of all. She was really looking forward to giving us those top-notch carrots. Nevertheless, dinner was abundant and satisfying. Everyone loves Bob, but especially me. I love you, Bob!

Fried Green Tomatoes

2–3 large green tomatoes

¾ C. cornmeal

¼ C. flour

1 tsp. sugar or equivalent sugar substitute

Dash of salt

Dash of pepper

2 Tbsp. (approximate) canola oil

Slice green tomatoes into ¼-inch slices. Mix cornmeal, flour, sugar, salt, and pepper in a flat-bottomed dish. Pour oil into cast-iron skillet over medium heat (if you don't have a cast-iron skillet, any other type will work). When oil is hot enough (almost smoking), dip both sides of tomato slices into the cornmeal mix to cover as well as you can, then carefully place into hot oil. Cook on both sides until brown, approximately 1–2 minutes on each side. Drain on paper towels. Makes 4–6 servings . . . never enough! *Note:* You can use 1 C. boxed cornbread mix in place of the cornmeal and flour.

Susan Casdorph
Charleston 1st Ward
Charleston West Virginia Stake
South Charleston, West Virginia

My mother-in-law, Doris Casdorph, made these for me when I was dating my husband, and I absolutely adore them. Now, almost three years later, I could eat my weight in fried green tomatoes if my stomach could hold 'em!

Chili Sauce

8 qt. tomatoes, quartered (Roma tomatoes are the best)

3 C. onion, ground

2 scant qt. sugar

1 scant C. flour

½ C. salt

2 Tbsp. dry mustard

2 Tbsp. black pepper

1 tsp. ground cloves

2 tsp. cinnamon

1 tsp. ginger

⅓ oz. red food coloring

1 qt. vinegar, divided

Wash tomatoes and blanch in hot water for 5 minutes. Tomato skin should slide off. Put skinned tomatoes in large bowl and mash with a potato masher. Pour mashed tomatoes into a large kettle. In a large bowl, mix all dry ingredients. Add dry ingredients, red food coloring, and all but 1 C. vinegar to mashed tomatoes. Bring to a boil. Stirring constantly, cook over medium-high heat for 2½ hours, stirring constantly. Stir in 1 C. vinegar 20 minutes before bottling, and continue to cook. Bottle in pint jars. The mixture is hot enough that you shouldn't have to process in boiling water. Just put the lids and rings on the bottles. We love to put this sauce on roast beef and meatloaf, and my son-in-law loves it on scrambled eggs. Makes about a dozen pints.

Sue Heaton
Sunset Heights 3rd Ward
Sunset Heights Utah Stake
Orem, Utah

As long as I can remember, it has been a tradition to get together every year on October conference Saturday and make Chili Sauce with all of the girls. We double the recipe and have two kettles going. We take turns stirring the pot, since it has to be stirred constantly. Afterwards, we divide the pints up. After we have cleaned up and the men have gone to the priesthood session, the women and children go out to dinner. It has been a great tradition, and it is now going on in my family with my daughters and daughters-in-law; we grow our own Roma tomatoes, and the girls really look forward to it. This is one of our favorite recipes in a cookbook that I compiled of my mother's best recipes. I had a book of my grandmother's recipes that was given to me when I was first married; it was fading, so I entered all the recipes on the computer along with all of my mother's recipes so they could be preserved and passed down to our families. Each member of the family was so excited about the project that they all contributed recipes. It was a labor of love that ended up becoming a book of 125 pages. We named the book *When the Thompsons Meet They Eat!*

Copper Pennies

2 lb. carrots, cut into ¼-inch slices
1 green pepper
1 large onion
1 10.75-oz. can tomato soup
1 C. sugar
½ C. oil

1 C. apple cider vinegar
1 tsp. mustard
½ tsp. pepper
½ tsp. salt

Steam carrots until tender; do not overcook. While carrots are cooking, chop green pepper and onion. In a separate saucepan, combine soup, sugar, oil, vinegar, mustard, pepper, and salt. Stir and heat until sugar dissolves. Drain carrots and stir in green pepper, onions, and sauce. Put a lid on the pan and let sit until it has cooled down. Put in refrigerator. This is always better when it has been in the refrigerator overnight. Makes 8–10 servings.

Lannette Kirkland
Apopka Ward
Leesburg Florida Stake
Apopka, Florida

My father grew 600–700 acres of carrots, and my mother was always finding new ways to fix carrots. This particular recipe was given to her by one of her sisters-in-law. We have a very large family, and all of us love this dish!

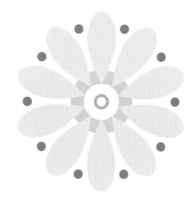

Pepian

10 ears corn
1½ C. cold water
3 Tbsp. rendered bacon fat or olive oil
2 small onions, finely chopped
3 cloves garlic, minced
1 tsp. coarse sea salt
2 tsp. cumin

½ tsp. freshly ground black pepper
2 jalapeno peppers, minced
4 oz. Panela cheese, diced into ⅛-inch pieces
2 Tbsp. red wine vinegar
½ bunch fresh dill, leaves only

(recipe continued on next page)

(Pepian, continued)

Slice the whole kernels from 5 ears of corn and set them aside in a bowl. Slice the kernels from the remaining 5 ears of corn and place them in a blender with water. Blend until completely smooth; then press the liquid through a fine sieve, pressing down on the skins to get all the juice. Discard the skins and set the mixture aside. In a heavy saucepan, heat the bacon fat over medium heat. Add the onions and cook for 4–5 minutes, stirring occasionally, until softened but not browned. Add the garlic, salt, cumin, and pepper; cook for 2 minutes. Add the jalapeno peppers and cook for 2 more minutes. Add the whole corn kernels and cook for 5 minutes, stirring frequently. Add the pureed corn and reduce the heat to its lowest possible setting. Cook for 15–20 minutes, stirring and scraping the bottom of the pan occasionally to keep the mixture from scorching or sticking. Stir in the cheese and vinegar; cook for 5 more minutes. Sprinkle with dill and serve. Makes 6 servings. *Note:* Panela cheese is much like fresh mozzarella.

Ana Beatriz Garcia
El Roble Ward
Victorias Stake
Guatemala City, Guatemala

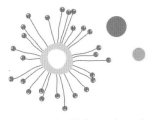

Cheesy Broccoli

3 bunches broccoli
2 Tbsp. lemon juice
½ C. mayonnaise

1 C. cheddar cheese, shredded
1 10.75-oz. can cream of chicken soup

Separate broccoli into florets and boil for 10 minutes. Drain and arrange in a greased baking dish. Combine lemon juice, mayonnaise, cheese, and soup. Pour over broccoli. Bake uncovered at 350 for 30 minutes. Makes 10 servings.

Hannah, Logan, and Wade Flanagan
Prairie 8th Ward
Prairie Utah Stake
West Jordan, Utah

Great-Grandma Peacock's Cheesy Broccoli is one of the first recipes our mom asked for after she got married. Grandma Peacock always made it at Thanksgiving time, and Thanksgiving isn't Thanksgiving without it! We don't like to eat our vegetables—but we love our Great-Grandma Peacock's Cheesy Broccoli.

Pansit Canton

½ C. onion, chopped

2 Tbsp. garlic, minced

4 Tbsp. cooking oil

½ lb. pork, sliced in small pieces

4 C. chicken broth (from boiled breast), divided

1 chicken breast, cooked and shredded

½ C. Chinese sausages, sliced

½ lb. shrimp, shelled and deveined

2 C. snow peas (sitsaro)

2 C. cabbage, sliced into strips

1 C. celery, sliced

1 carrot, diced

1 C. cauliflower florets

12 oz. pansit canton noodles (Chinese wheat noodles), divided

¼ C. sliced scallions

4 Tbsp. soy sauce

1 Tbsp. sesame oil

Salt and pepper to taste

In a big pan or wok, sauté the onions and garlic in oil. Add sliced pork, and sauté until cooked. Stir in 2 C. chicken broth and add the shredded chicken, sliced Chinese sausages, shrimp, snow peas, cabbage, celery, carrot, and cauliflower. Simmer for about 10 minutes or until vegetables are cooked. Add the remaining 2 C. chicken broth and the pansit canton noodles. Let simmer until noodles are soft. Add the scallions, soy sauce, sesame oil, and salt and pepper to taste. Serve hot. Makes 6–8 servings.

Ronalee Hopkins
Dubai 1st Ward
Manama Bahrain Stake
Dubai, United Arab Emirates

Hi! Just call me Rona. I am from the Philippines, happily married, a first-time mum, and working in Dubai. My mum is in the Philippines right now. I love it when she cooks all my favorite foods, especially pansit—which she cooks every morning. I've been away from my mum for four years, and really miss her. I never learned how to cook pansit or any kind of food until I got married in April 2009. Now my husband is always asking me to cook Filipino food for him. I am thankful for my mum, because even though she is always busy, anytime I need a recipe, I just phone her and she helps. I love my mum so much and really miss her; I hope she'll be able to come here soon to see her first grandchild!

{ SOUPS }

Children are the anchors that hold a mother to life.

{ Sophocles }

The Three Little Bears Clam Chowder

2 slices bacon, diced

1 large onion, diced

4 stalks celery, diced

2½ C. butter (no substitutions)

1½ C. flour

8–10 C. water

1 12-oz. can evaporated milk

2 medium potatoes, diced

Sprinkle of nutmeg

Sprinkle of thyme

1 tsp. salt (or to taste)

⅛ tsp. white pepper (or to taste)

1 10-oz. can chopped clams

Cook bacon, onion, and celery until onion is transparent. Add butter (you read right: 5 sticks of butter—no substitutions!). Stir until melted. Stir in flour. Cook and stir for about 2 minutes over medium heat. Stir in water and milk to make a smooth soup. Add potatoes and spices. Drain clam broth into the soup. Cook for about 15 minutes, until potatoes are tender. Stir in clams and simmer 10 minutes longer. Serves 2 adults and 3 little bears.

Elisabeth Gagon
Battlecreek 10th Ward
Pleasant Grove Utah East Stake
Pleasant Grove, Utah

My oldest child, Victor, wants to go to France to cooking school and become a famous chef. I think he wants to be a chef because when he was a little boy he was always hungry. Vita (Victor) is from Nakhodka, a small village in Russia. When we found him, he was living in an orphanage in Vladivostok, Russia; he was two and a half years old and weighed twenty pounds. Every day for lunch and dinner the children in the orphanage ate vegetable broth with a piece of bread. Vita doesn't remember his life in the orphanage, but he does love soup. If I ask my children what they want for dinner, he always asks for soup. This clam chowder recipe is Vita's favorite soup; it is delicious and filling. It is called The Three Little Bears Clam Chowder because I have three children. We also found Dar'ya, our second child—a daughter we call Dasha—in the Vladivostok orphanage. Eventually we adopted our third "little bear," Roman—a boy we call Roma—from Petropavlovsk, Kazakhstan. I feel blessed to have been able to participate in this amazing journey of finding these children and creating our eternal family together with Heavenly Father and my husband.

Cho's Chicken Fat-Noodle Soup

Soup:
4 large chicken breasts
3 Tbsp. chicken bouillon paste, divided
1 tsp. salt
3 tsp. poultry seasoning, divided
4 tsp. Mrs. Dash seasoning, divided
2 C. celery, chopped
1 large onion, chopped
1 qt. water

Salt and pepper to taste
Noodles (purchased or
    see recipe below)

Noodles:
4 C. flour
4 tsp. olive oil
4 eggs
1½ tsp. salt

Soup: In a medium pot, combine chicken with just enough water to cover the chicken, 1 Tbsp. chicken bouillon paste, 1 tsp. salt, 1 tsp. poultry seasoning, and 2 tsp. Mrs. Dash seasoning. Bring to a boil and cook until chicken can be pulled apart easily (about 20 minutes at full boil). Take chicken out of pot; save broth. Cool chicken in a bowl of cool water or refrigerator until you can handle it. Add celery and onion to broth. Once chicken is cooled, pull into small bite-size pieces and add to broth. Add 1 qt. water, 2 Tbsp. chicken bouillon paste, 2 tsp. poultry seasoning, and 2 tsp. Mrs. Dash seasoning to broth. Bring to a boil and add noodles. Salt and pepper to taste, then cook until noodles are soft and flavors have mixed, about 30–60 minutes.

Noodles: In a large bowl, mix all ingredients; knead until dough is pliable enough to roll out. If the dough is not pliable enough, carefully add a few drops of water at a time until you can roll the dough out but it is still somewhat stiff. Roll the dough out onto an oiled counter with an oiled rolling pin. Roll sheets of noodles to $1/16$ of an inch thickness, then slice into long strips and drop into boiling soup. Makes 8–12 servings.

Bean Daughters
Sunset Heights 8th Ward
Sunset Heights Utah Stake
Orem, Utah

Ma Bean—my mother—is known as "the Good Fairy," delivering her food to help mend hearts, comfort the sick, celebrate a marriage, or recognize family togetherness. She is always aware of someone in need and sees to it that they are recognized. Even when we were younger she realized the need to be a good mother to our friends, and she welcomed them warmly into our home (which is how she became known as Ma Bean). No one left our house empty-handed; each went home with a bag full of love! This chicken noodle soup provides comfort, which is what best describes our mom. That's why friends and family want to be in her home—to feel the comfort she provides with her love and her fabulous food.

Gentse Waterzooi

1 whole chicken
Salt
Pepper
Parsley sprigs
Thyme sprigs
1 bay leaf
6 C. chicken broth

2 leeks
1 small bunch celery
2 onions
4 cloves
2 large carrots
1 C. cream
Parsley, chopped (for garnish)

Rinse chicken inside and out; season with salt and pepper inside and out. Tie the parsley and thyme sprigs together with the bay leaf; tuck the bundle inside the chicken. Place chicken, breast side up, in a large pot. Add enough chicken broth (about 6 C.) to cover chicken. Add the green part of the leeks, the leaves of the celery, one peeled onion, and the cloves. Simmer for 25 minutes. Remove the chicken to cool, and pour the broth through a sieve. Return the sieved broth to the pot. Chop the white part of the leeks, the celery, and the second onion. Slice the carrots. Add the leeks, celery, onion, and carrots; cook 25 minutes longer, or until the vegetables are tender. Pull the chicken meat from the bones and return chicken pieces to the pot. Simmer for 5 minutes. Once the soup is heated through, stir in the cream. Sprinkle with parsley and serve with boiled potatoes. Makes 4 servings. *Note:* If you want thicker soup, make a roux with melted butter and flour; stir into the simmering broth and let thicken before you add the cream.

Danny Mycek Daneman
Brugge Branch
Ghent Flemish Region
Ghent, Vlaanderen
Belgium

This is a typical dish from my city, Ghent; it's simple to make, and everyone in Ghent likes it. What used to be a typical dish for poor people has now become one of Belgium's specialties of choice. The way most prepare it is far from the way poor people eat. Every cook makes a little different version; this is my mom's recipe, and I think it is best.

Mexican Meatball Soup

2 Tbsp. olive oil

2¾ C. onions, chopped and divided

4 garlic cloves, minced and divided

2 small bay leaves

5 14.5-oz. cans beef broth

1 28-oz. can diced tomatoes in juice

½ C. chunky tomato salsa (medium-hot)

½ C. fresh cilantro, divided

1 lb. lean ground beef

¼ lb. bulk pork sausage

6 Tbsp. yellow cornmeal

¼ C. whole milk

1 large egg

½ tsp. salt

½ tsp. pepper

½ tsp. ground cumin

½ C. long-grain white rice

Salt and pepper to taste

Heat oil in a heavy, large pot over medium-high heat. Add 1¾ C. onions, 2 garlic cloves, and bay leaves; sauté 5 minutes. Add broth, tomatoes with juices, salsa, and ¼ C. cilantro; bring to boil. Cover and simmer 15 minutes. Meanwhile, in a medium bowl combine ground beef, pork sausage, cornmeal, milk, egg, salt, pepper, and cumin with remaining 1 C. onions, 2 garlic cloves, and ¼ C. cilantro. Mix well. Shape meat mixture by generous tablespoonfulls into 1–1¼-inch balls. Add rice and meatballs to soup and bring to boil, stirring occasionally. Reduce heat, cover, and simmer until rice and meatballs are tender, stirring occasionally, about 20 minutes. Season to taste with salt and pepper. Ladle soup into bowls and serve. Makes 8–10 servings.

Louise Phelps
Groton Ward
Providence Rhode Island Stake
Ledyard, Connecticut

Aji de Gallina

2 lb. skinless, bone-in chicken breast halves

1 onion, coarsely chopped

2 carrots, chopped

2 cloves garlic

2 qt. water

1 12-oz. can evaporated milk

1 loaf white bread, crusts removed and cubed

½ C. grated Parmesan cheese

¼ C. walnut pieces

1 tsp. vegetable oil

2 cloves garlic, minced

1 onion, chopped

2 tsp. aji amarillo chile paste

2 tsp. ground turmeric

4 hard-cooked eggs, sliced

¼ C. kalamata olives, pitted and quartered

(recipe continued on next page)

(Aji de Gallina, continued)

In a large saucepan, combine chicken breasts, onion, carrots, and 2 cloves garlic. Pour in water and slowly bring to a simmer over medium-high heat. Skim off the foam that forms on top, then cover, reduce heat to medium-low, and simmer until the chicken is tender, about 30 minutes. Remove chicken to a plate and allow to cool. Strain the chicken stock and discard the vegetables. Pour evaporated milk and ½ C. chicken stock into the bowl of a blender. Add bread cubes and puree until smooth. Add Parmesan cheese and walnuts; puree until smooth. Shred the cooled chicken and discard the bones. Heat vegetable oil in a large saucepan over medium heat. Stir in minced garlic and minced onion; cook until the onion has softened and turned translucent, about 5 minutes. Stir in shredded chicken and aji amarillo chile paste until heated through. Pour in bread puree and cook until hot, stirring frequently. Add more chicken stock if needed to keep soup from getting too thick. Season with turmeric and simmer for 5 minutes more. Serve garnished with hard-cooked egg slices and sprinkled with kalamata olives. Makes 12 servings.

My mom is everything to me. She is the mother of six, including me. She is a great cook; you can't imagine the great food she makes! Peru is beautiful. It would be great if you came to see it—I promise you won't regret it!

Alexandra Magdiel Zegarra Sabaducci
La Molina Ward
La Molina Stake
Lima, Peru

Hotchpotch

2 lb. beef cutlet (or other kind of meat)
Vegetable oil
6 C. water
2 onions
1 head cabbage
2 tsp. salt, divided

2 carrots, sliced
1 turnip, sliced
2 lb. potatoes
1 Tbsp. oil
Pepper to taste
Parsley, chopped (for garnish)

Brown the meat in oil on both sides. Add water and whole onions. Cut the cabbage into sections and add to the water and onions. Simmer over low temperature for 30 minutes. Add 1 tsp. salt, sliced carrots, and sliced turnip. Simmer for another 10 minutes. Cut the potatoes in half and place in the pan on top of the vegetables. Add 1 tsp. salt and pepper to taste. Simmer for another 20 minutes or until all of the ingredients are soft. To serve, sprinkle with parsley. Makes 8 servings.

Piret Luik
Tartu Branch
Estonia District
Tartu, Estonia

Baked Potato Soup

⅔ C. butter

⅔ C. flour

6 C. milk

4 C. baked potato cubes

1 bunch green onions, sliced

1½ C. cheddar cheese, shredded

1 C. sour cream

1 12-oz. can evaporated milk

1 lb. mushrooms, sliced

6 slices bacon, cooked and crumbled

Salt and pepper to taste

Melt butter, add flour, and slowly stir in milk. Cook and stir until thickened. After mixture thickens, add remaining ingredients; serve and enjoy. Makes 4 servings.

Alyssa Lloyd
Ephraim 2nd Ward
Ephraim Utah 1st Stake
Ephraim, Utah

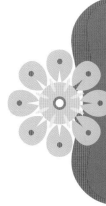

The best thing in the world is a mother's cooking, but for me it's the best thing in the universe. Having a mom like mine is unheard of because she is for sure one of a kind. Two years ago I left for college—both a nervous and exciting thing for my whole family. Before I left, my mom told me that someday I would realize how much I would miss her cooking. That day came the first week I was in college when I realized I then had to cook for myself. I wanted nothing more than my mama's cooking back. Baked Potato Soup is one of my favorite things she makes. If there was room, I'd share everything she ever cooked, because it's all my favorite. Nothing compares to my mom!

Ukranian Borscht

½ C. dry pinto beans

1 pork chop with a bone

1 qt. water

1½ C. beets, peeled and julienned

1½ C. carrots, peeled and julienned

¼ C. cider vinegar

1 onion, cut into 2-inch chunks

2 large or 4 small potatoes, peeled and cut into
   1-inch cubes

1 large stalk of celery, chopped fine

1 or 2 sprigs of fresh parsley or ½ tsp. dried
   parsley

½ small head of cabbage, shredded

1 qt. water

2 Tbsp. vinegar

1 Tbsp. sugar

2 tsp. chopped sweet red pepper

2 tsp. salt

2 or 3 cloves of garlic, pressed fine

1 8 oz. can tomato sauce

1 medium onion, chopped

1 Tbsp. oil

1 tsp. paprika

½ tsp. dried oregano

1 bay leaf

1 tsp. dried basil

Soak beans overnight and rinse. In a large pan, put pork in small amount of water and bring to a boil; pour off the water. This keeps the soup from having "scum" on it. Add 1 qt. water and the soaked pinto beans to the meat; boil for 1½ hours. Remove the beans and set aside. Add the beets, carrots, vinegar, onion chunks, potatoes, celery, and parsley to the soup. Bring to a boil and boil gently for about 5 minutes. Reduce heat to medium-high and simmer until vegetables are tender-crisp (about 5 minutes). Add all remaining ingredients to the soup. Remove pork chop from the soup, remove the pork from the bone, chop the pork into very small pieces, and stir the pieces into the soup. Put the pinto beans in the soup. Cook for just a few more minutes until the cabbage is tender-crisp. Serve with sour cream. The soup can also be refrigerated or frozen and served later. Makes 12 servings.

Anna Fowler
Provo Peak 4th Ward
Provo Utah East Stake
Provo, Utah

My mother, Alice Rampton, has always been a wonderful example of charity and unconditional love. She always taught me and my siblings to love one another and to extend a helping hand to our neighbors. She also strived to open our eyes and understanding to the different countries and cultures around us. We'd often have exchange students live with us and had people from different countries over for dinner. As "empty nesters," my parents help with special-needs orphans in the Ukraine, traveling annually to the Ukraine as co-chairs of the TOUCH Project (Take One Ukrainian Child's Hand). When they go to the Ukraine, they love to eat the famous borscht soup. This recipe for authentic borscht soup is from the kitchen of a Ukrainian friend.

Budaatai Khuurga (Mongolian Stew)

½ lb. beef
1 C. rice
1¼ C. water
1 tsp. salt
⅓ C. oil, divided
2 onions, cut in half rings

2 cloves garlic, minced
½ C. carrots, julienned
½ C. slivered green beans
½ C. cabbage, shredded
½ C. bell peppers, sliced
Salt and pepper to taste

Cut the beef into thin strips. Put rice, water, salt, and 1 Tbsp. oil in a pan and bring it to a boil. Simmer 10 minutes or until the water level is below the rice. Leave the pan on the stove, but turn off the heat for 10 minutes if you have an electric stove; if it is gas, maintain a very small flame. In a separate pan, sauté the onions, garlic, carrots, and green beans in the remaining oil. When the carrots begin to soften, add the cabbage and bell peppers. Add the meat and cook and stir until beef is cooked through. Season to taste with salt and pepper. Add the rice mixture and stir to thoroughly combine. Arrange and decorate on plates. Makes 4 servings. *Note:* Traditionally, we make this stew with mutton, but other types of meat—such as beef—work just as well. Mongolians consider fat meat to be of higher quality, but there's no problem using western-style lean meat.

Odgerel Bumandalai
Sansar Ward
Bayanzurkn District
Khoroo 1, Ulaanbaatar, Mongolia

I learned to cook from my mom when I was five. The first thing I learned was how to make dough. When I was ten, I cooked my first meal, and I was delighted, because I thought I could then cook delicious food just like my mom. My mom taught me cooking methods one by one, starting with small things like how to peel potatoes and other vegetables, and I watched my mom to learn how to cook different kinds of foods. I like to cook, and when I have free time, I like to try new recipes.

Granny's Fishhead Soup

6–8 cups water

2 salmon heads

½ C. macaroni or rice

1–2 potatoes, diced

½ medium onion, chopped

1 tsp. salt

2 ribs celery, sliced

Combine all ingredients and boil 20 minutes or until done. Makes 4 servings.

Zoanne Anderson
Bear Mountain Ward
Anchorage Alaska Chugach Stake
Chugiak, Alaska

My Granny, Lena Venes Laraux, was born in 1902 or 1904 outside of Bethel, Alaska, far out in the tundra. In 1922 she married a French Canadian, and together they raised eight children. Granny was embarrassed about her English, yet she was very witty and had an excellent sense of humor. She was the hunter in the family, often tying the dogs to the sled in the winter and going out all day with her shotgun or .22 rifle. She'd come home loaded down with rabbits, ptarmigan, and spruce hens. None of the meat was wasted. Internal organs, heads, bone marrow, and feet were considered delicacies. Fur and feathers were used to make warm clothing and blankets. Pelts are not displayed on walls in Native homes, neither are faces or paws of the animals worn on fur hats or wraps. Animals have dignity. They are respected and appreciated for giving their lives for our sustenance. We do not hunt for sport, but to sustain our families. This soup had a wonderful aroma, and when I was small I used to beg Granny to let me have some. Considering the richness of the fishheads, she would always say, "You're too little." Finally when I was twelve or so, I was deemed old enough to eat this soup with her. It really did taste as delectable as it smelled. It seems like when I make it, it's never quite as good as Granny's Fishhead Soup.

Chicken Pot Pie Soup

1 C. onion, chopped

1–2 C. carrots, chopped

1 C. celery, chopped

1 large garlic clove, minced

1 Tbsp. olive or canola oil

¼ C. flour

½ tsp. dried oregano

¼ tsp. dried thyme

¼ tsp. poultry seasoning

2 32-oz. boxes chicken broth

4 C. potatoes, diced and peeled

1 tsp. salt

2 C. deli rotisserie chicken, shredded or torn in thick chunks

2 C. uncooked yolk-free wide noodles

1 12-oz. can evaporated milk

1 C. frozen peas

In a Dutch oven or soup kettle, sauté the onion, carrots, celery, and garlic in oil for 5 minutes or until tender. Stir in the flour, oregano, thyme, and poultry seasoning until blended; sauté 1 minute longer. Gradually add broth, potatoes, and salt; bring to a boil. Reduce heat; cover and simmer for 15–20 minutes or until potatoes and carrots are tender. Stir in the chicken and noodles; simmer for 10 minutes or until noodles are tender. Reduce heat. Stir in the milk and peas; heat through (do not boil). Makes 13 servings.

Alexia Hinkley
Palmyra Ward
Palmyra New York Stake
Palmyra, New York

This is my favorite comfort soup. My grandma made this for my mom when she was little, and my mom always made it for me—especially in the fall and winter when it was cold outside. I now make this for my husband. I love sitting out on the back deck eating this soup when the weather is chilly. It is perfect comfort food, and looks just like the inside of a chicken pot pie . . . hence its name. Enjoy!

Ham Chowder

1½ lb. potatoes, peeled, cooked, and drained
½ C. onion, chopped
½ C. celery, chopped
3 Tbsp. margarine
1 14.5-oz. can chicken broth
2 C. half-and-half (can use skim milk)

1 C. ham, cooked and diced
¼ C. fresh parsley, minced
½ tsp. salt
⅛ tsp. freshly cracked pepper
¼–½ C. cheddar cheese, shredded (optional)

Cube potatoes and set aside. Sauté onion and celery in margarine until tender. In blender, combine half of the potatoes and the onion and celery mixture with ¼ C. chicken broth. Blend until smooth. Add remaining chicken broth and blend. Pour mixture into saucepan; add half-and-half, remaining potatoes, ham, parsley, salt, and pepper. Bring just to boiling point, reduce heat, and simmer 10 minutes, stirring occasionally. Top with cheese if desired. Makes 6 servings. *Note:* This recipe is easily doubled and tripled.

This chowder is the reason we have ham for the holidays. It is wonderful. One recipe is never enough for our family.

Denae McCall
BYU 232nd Ward
BYU 22nd Stake
Provo, Utah

Italian Tomato Macaroni Soup

6 C. water
2 pkgs. onion soup mix
2 15-oz. cans Italian stewed tomatoes
2 Tbsp. Worcestershire sauce

1 lb. ground beef, browned and drained
1 C. ketchup
2 C. macaroni
Salt and pepper to taste

This is a quick, easy soup that can be tossed together in short order. Put all the ingredients in the pot, bring to boil, and cook until the noodles are tender. Serve with dip-type sandwiches. Makes 12 servings.

Max Finch
Sterling Ward
Alaska Soldotna Stake
Sterling, Alaska

Nettie loved soup, and labored over the stove making many types and varieties of favorite soups. One day she said she just loved the soup at Juniper Takeout in Logan, Utah, so she thought about what the soup there tasted like and put the ingredients in a pot. Within half an hour we had the best soup she ever made. It's much better than Juniper's, and so fast and easy to make. It's even good chilled.

Chicken and Cheese Tortellini Florentine Soup

1 32-oz. carton chicken stock + carton of water

1 14.5-oz. can diced tomato with green chiles

2 8-oz. cans tomato sauce

1 15-oz. can white beans, drained

1 15-oz. can black beans, drained

1 15-oz. kidney beans, drained

2 10-oz. cans white chicken meat, drained and shredded

1 tsp. dried basil

1 tsp. dried oregano

1 tsp. dried parsley

2 bay leaves

1 env. dry taco seasoning

1 10-oz. pkg. frozen spinach, thawed and drained

Salt and pepper to taste

2 tsp. olive oil

2 C. baby carrots, sliced

1 medium yellow onion, chopped

2 gloves garlic, crushed

1 C. salad macaroni

1 13-oz. pkg frozen cheese tortellini

Parmesan cheese, grated (for garnish)

In a large stock pot, combine chicken stock, water, tomatoes, tomato sauce, beans, chicken, basil, oregano, parsley, bay leaves, taco seasoning, spinach, salt, and pepper. Pour olive oil into a frying pan; sauté carrots, onion, and garlic until vegetables are soft and onions are transparent. Add to stock pot. Simmer on medium heat for 1 hour. Add salad macaroni and cheese tortellini and simmer for additional 20–30 minutes until macaroni and tortellini are al dente. Remove bay leaves before serving. Sprinkle with Parmesan cheese, and serve with garlic bread or bread sticks. Makes 10–12 servings. *Note:* This soup can also be made in a slow cooker; add the macaroni and tortellini during the last hour of cooking.

Janet Pratt
Regal Country Ward
Kanesville Utah Stake
West Haven, Utah

I am the mother of four wonderful children—Megan, Austin, McCall, and Kylee. I love to cook but do not follow recipes well. I love to "doctor" recipes to my liking, something I learned from my wonderful mother. She rarely used recipes; she just added "a little of this, and a little of that" to come up with delicious meals for her large family! My mother was a wonderful cook, and we four girls learned often joke that we don't know how to cook small meals, because we learned to cook for "our army" of eight while growing up. My mother is gone now—she passed away in October 2005—but I often think of her when I am cooking, and often make things I learned from her. I came up with this recipe for Chicken and Cheese Tortellini Florentine Soup one cool autumn evening when I wanted to make something warm and comforting for my family—much like some of the meals my mother used to make for me.

Porotos Granadas (Chilean Bean Stew)

1 yellow onion, chopped

1 Tbsp. olive oil

2 C. butternut squash or pumpkin, cubed

1 15-oz. can great Northern or navy beans, rinsed and drained

1 C. frozen lima beans

3 C. chicken stock

2 C. fresh or frozen corn kernels

2 Tbsp. fresh basil, chopped

1 banana pepper, chopped

Cook onion in oil until clear and soft. Stir the squash and both kinds of beans into the pot. Pour in chicken stock. Cover and cook until the squash is tender and beginning to break apart, 30–45 minutes. Stir the corn and basil into the stew. Cook for 10 more minutes. The stew should be fairly thick. Serve in bowls and sprinkle with chopped banana pepper. Makes 6 servings.

I love my mom with all my soul, and I can testify of my mom and the love that she has for me. The truth is that my mom does everything to keep my family going. Everything that I am is for her. I am who I am because of her. I love her so much.

Diego Perez
Centinela Ward
San Fernando District
San Fernando, Chile

Mom's Clam Chowder

2 C. potatoes, peeled and chopped

2 C. water

2 Tbsp. onion, minced

¼ tsp. pepper

1 tsp. salt

1 7.5-oz. can clams

1 qt. half-and-half

4 Tbsp. flour

5 slices bacon, cooked and crumbled

1 Tbsp. butter

Cook potatoes in water until tender. Add onion, pepper, salt, and clams. In a medium bowl, combine the half-and-half and flour. Add to soup. Cook and stir until thickened. Add bacon. Top with butter. Makes 6–8 servings.

My mom made this on cold wintry days and served it with garlic toast. It is really easy!

Lisa McIntyre
Cheyenne Ridge Ward
Lone Mountain Nevada Stake
Las Vegas, Nevada

Chicken Enchilada Soup

3–4 boneless, skinless chicken breasts

1 Tbsp. extra-virgin olive oil

1–3 tsp. seasoned salt

½ C. onion, diced

1 clove garlic, minced

4 C. chicken broth

1 C. masa harina (Mexican corn flour)

3 C. water

1 15-oz. can mild red enchilada sauce

1 10-oz. can mild green enchilada sauce

16 oz. processed American cheese loaf
   (Velveeta)

1 tsp. salt

1 tsp. chili powder

½ tsp. cumin

Sour cream, cheddar cheese, green onions,
   tortilla strips (garnish)

In a large stockpot, sauté chicken in olive oil and seasoned salt on medium or medium-high heat until cooked thoroughly and lightly browned on both sides. Remove chicken from pot, but do not drain the pot; shred chicken and set aside. Add onions and garlic to remaining drippings in pot. Sauté for about 2 minutes on medium-low to medium heat, taking care to not burn the garlic or onions. Add chicken broth to pot. In a separate small bowl, whisk masa harina with 2 C. cold water until mixture is smooth. Add flour mixture to pot; stir. Add remaining 1 C. water, enchilada sauces, cheese, salt, chili powder, and cumin. Stir mixture constantly with wire whisk until cheese is melted and mixture comes to a boil. Add chicken to pot, reduce heat, and simmer 30–40 minutes, stirring occasionally. Serve soup warm garnished with sour cream, cheddar cheese, sliced green onions, and tortilla strips. Makes 8 servings.

Ashley Rencher
Westland Ward
Columbus Ohio Stake
Galloway, Ohio

My mom is my best friend—always has been, and always will be. She is such an example to me in so many ways. My mom had a rough childhood; her own loving mother passed away two weeks after my mom turned eleven, and she was raised in less-than-ideal circumstances. She was introduced to the Church as a teenager, but was unable to be baptized until she turned eighteen. My mom set a goal for herself to marry in the temple to a worthy priesthood holder and returned missionary, and I'm in awe at the generations she has now affected because of her faith, dedication, and commitment to the gospel. My three siblings and I had a childhood my mother never had. We have known nothing but love and warmth in our family; we have been so incredibly blessed. I became a first-time mom in late 2009. My mom was able to fly out for my son's birth and to help me and my husband adjust to life with a newborn. It's crazy, but so fun. I only hope that I can be half as good a mom to my new son as my mom was and is to me.

Aztec Chicken Soup

2 29-oz. cans tomatoes

1½ C. salsa

3 large chicken breasts, cooked and diced

1 15-oz. can cannelloni beans

1 15-oz. can kidney beans

1 C. zucchini, seeded and sliced

1 C. onion, diced

1 C. celery, diced

1 15-oz. can corn

1 C. green pepper, diced

1 C. potato, diced

2 Tbsp. olive oil

5 cloves garlic, diced

1 C. chicken stock made from bouillon paste

2 C. water

Cilantro to taste

Combine all ingredients. Simmer for 30 minutes on stove top or all day in slow cooker on low. Makes 8 servings.

Robin Wardle
Battlecreek 10th Ward
Pleasant Grove Utah East Stake
Pleasant Grove, Utah

My mother, Mary Lou, was a great cook. She made delicious soups and stews, always with a clear tomato broth like the one in Aztec Chicken Soup. I created this recipe with her soup as my model. She made wonderful "country" food! Her biscuits were lighter than air, her gravy tasted like heaven, and her pineapple upside-down cake put a smile on all of our faces! She taught dancing her whole life. When I was a child, my mom had 300 students in and out of our house every week. Our house was always full of activity and fun . . . and little girls in black leotards and pink tutus. We used to do lots of shows in our area west of Chicago. When she passed away, we had a variety show at her funeral. She wore a cute little pink crocheted hat over her bald head and a pretty pink dress. I just know she loved her last show!

Maggie's Green Chile Stew

1 3 to 4-lb. pork roast, cut into bite-size pieces

3 medium onions, diced

16 cloves garlic, chopped

¼ C. cooking oil

3 8-oz. cans mild green chiles with juice, sliced into strips

2 5-oz. cans hot jalapeno peppers, or to taste

3 29-oz. cans diced tomatoes with juice

1 Tbsp. salt

2½ .5-oz. bottles of cumin (less if you don't want it spicy)

1½ qts. water

1 env. pork gravy mix

1 C. flour

2 C. water

Brown the pork, onions, and garlic in oil in a large pot. Add remaining ingredients except the gravy mix, flour, and water. Simmer for at least 3–4 hours, adding water as needed. Stir as needed to keep from scorching. Combine gravy mix, flour, and 2 C. water. Mix well and add to pot, stirring constantly until thickened. Serve and enjoy. Makes 20 servings. *Note:* We serve this with flour tortillas and refried beans. Serve with milk or soda pop to cut the heat. You can also top this soup with cheese, sour cream, chopped tomatoes, or chopped onions.

Maggie Haley
Three Peaks Ward
Enoch Utah Stake
Cedar City, Utah

I first started to make this soup at Halloween. We set up a Green Chile Stew bar for our sons and their friends while we checked the candy after they'd been trick-or-treating. As my husband and I sent each of our five sons into the mission field over the years, each time we asked what they wanted when they came home, and every one said, "Mom's Green Chile Stew with burritos and all the fixings." It's now tradition to have a family party with all the kids and grandkids and the Green Chile Stew.

Pork Bone Soup

4 qts. water

1 lb. roast pork bones (*siew chee guat* in Cantonese)

2 white radishes, cut into chunks

2 carrots, cut into chunks

1 lb. mushrooms, sliced

½ tsp. white pepper

Salt to taste

(recipe continued on next page)

(Pork Bone Soup, continued)

Bring water to a boil. Stir in all remaining ingredients except salt and bring to a boil again. Reduce heat and simmer for 4 hours. Skim off any fat or oil that comes to the surface of the soup. Season to taste with salt. Makes 4 servings. *Note:* If you can't find roast pork bones in your area, you can substitute fresh pork bones or ribs. Or if you roast a chicken, turkey, or pork at home, save the bones and use them to make this soup. Store the roast bones in the freezer for use in soups later.

It is impossible to get to know the Church in China. The nearest meeting to me is in Shanghai, which is at least two hours away by bus. I was blessed to learn about the Church from two members who were friends of mine at school in Bangkok, and I was baptized there. Even though it has been difficult to attend church in China, I am going to try my best. I am the only member of the Church in my family.

Xia Chen
Suzhou Branch
Shanghai China International District
Changshu, China

Grandma Jean's Instant Noodle Soup

1–2 pkg. chicken-flavored ramen noodle soup

1 10.75-oz. can cream of mushroom soup

1 15-oz. can green beans with liquid

1 15-oz. can corn with liquid

Cook ramen noodles according to package directions. Open can of soup and use a fork to break up any lumps in the soup. Add soup and canned vegetables to ramen noodles and stir until blended. If needed, add a soup can of water or milk. Stir on stove top until desired temperature. Makes 4–8 servings. *Note:* You may use any kind of cream soup and any vegetables to suit your taste.

Connie Caldwell
Glines 4th Ward
Glines Utah Stake
Vernal, Utah

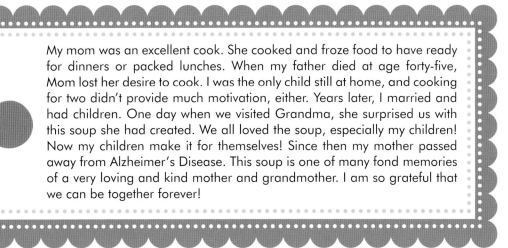

My mom was an excellent cook. She cooked and froze food to have ready for dinners or packed lunches. When my father died at age forty-five, Mom lost her desire to cook. I was the only child still at home, and cooking for two didn't provide much motivation, either. Years later, I married and had children. One day when we visited Grandma, she surprised us with this soup she had created. We all loved the soup, especially my children! Now my children make it for themselves! Since then my mother passed away from Alzheimer's Disease. This soup is one of many fond memories of a very loving and kind mother and grandmother. I am so grateful that we can be together forever!

White Chili

2½ C. water

1 tsp. lemon pepper

1 tsp. ground cumin

3½ C. chicken breast

1 C. onion, chopped

1 clove garlic, minced or crushed

2 Tbsp. butter

2 19-oz. cans white corn (can use frozen corn)

2 4-oz. cans diced green chiles, undrained

2 15-oz. cans white beans, undrained

2–3 Tbsp. lime juice

Bring water to a boil with the lemon pepper and ground cumin. Add raw chicken and cook 20–28 minutes. Remove chicken and cut into bite-size pieces. Put chicken back into water. In a frying pan, cook onion and garlic in butter until tender; add to soup. Stir in corn and green chiles. Bring to a boil. Add beans and lime juice. Cook until heated through. Or, as my mom says, "Just throw it all in at the same time. It still tastes good!" This chili is delicious served with chips, sour cream, and cheese. Makes 8 servings.

Megan Anderson
University 3rd Ward
University 1st Stake
Salt Lake City, Utah

Our mom, Jocelyn Meacham, is the best cook in the world. She is a nationally known chef and has inspired many to become magical in the kitchen. She's always creating something new and has passed this wonderful talent on to all four of her marvelous daughters. Oh, wait . . . who are we kidding? To be completely honest, our mom is far from all of this. She is a cook, but I wouldn't quite call her a chef. She's just a normal mother and housewife who cooks fast, easy dinners to satisfy her six children along with her hubby, two sons-in-law, and two grandsons. We count down the days until we can all gather around the table together and dive in to her wonderful Sunday dinner. The two of us that are married can always call and count on our mom to know a yummy, quick recipe we can make for our families. She is amazing and a true idol in our eyes. Our mother is always putting others before herself. All four of us, as her daughters, pray we can be the mother to our children that she has been to us, and that we can pass on the wonderful characteristics she has shown. We love you, Mom—you're the best. XOXOXO—Cassie, Mallory, Megan, and Paige

{ SALADS }

Youth fades; love droops; the leaves of friendship
fall: A mother's secret love outlives them all.

{ Oliver Wendell Holmes }

Strawberry Spinach Salad

Salad:

10 oz. baby spinach

10 strawberries, sliced lengthwise

2 chicken breasts, boiled and shredded

¾ C. sliced almonds

½ C. Feta cheese, crumbled

¼ C. dried cranberries

1 C. mandarin oranges

½ C. pistachios

Homemade Poppy Seed Dressing:

¾ C. mayonnaise

3 Tbsp. vinegar

½ C. sugar

⅓ C. whole milk

3 Tbsp. poppy seeds

Salad: Combine all ingredients and serve with Homemade Poppy Seed Dressing.

Homemade Poppy Seed Dressing: Combine all ingredients in a jar. Cover and shake until well blended. Refrigerate immediately. Makes 8 servings.

Robert McBride
Westland Ward
Columbus Ohio West Stake
Galloway, Ohio

Some of the greatest experiences I have enjoyed with my mom have happened as we prepared for Sundays. I wish I could attribute that to the Sabbath Day, but I think the real reason is because of the huge feast she prepared for after church. It all started Saturday evening with mom attempting to convince us that helping peel and cut potatoes and carrots would be fun. After a while the convincing turned into threatening. Nonetheless, each Sunday morning we left for church surrounded by wonderful aromas. The table setting became predictable: jelly in a small dish with a special spoon, salt and pepper shakers at both ends of the table, butter, and the always-classic, slightly chilled water with half-frozen ice cubes, all because Dad took too long to make the gravy. In the end Mom never seemed to fail. Whether it was roast beef, turkey, or ham, the dinner was perfect. Rarely was she thanked enough, nor did anyone make a true effort to help, yet Mom's loving service never stopped. Though I am away with my own family and have endured life's ebbs and flows, I have no doubt that if we arrive on a Sunday afternoon the same smells, taste, and love will welcome me again.

Raspberry Lemony Jell-O

1 large pkg. raspberry gelatin (Jell-O) (can use any flavor)

1 small pkg. cook-and-serve lemon pudding (NOT instant)

1½ C. cream

1 C. milk

⅓ C. powdered sugar

1 small pkg. instant cheesecake pudding (or lemon, vanilla, white chocolate)

Prepare raspberry gelatin according to package directions. Set aside. Cook lemon pudding according to package directions. Stir into the liquid raspberry gelatin. Pour into a 9 x 13-inch pan. Chill until firm. Meanwhile, make the topping by combining the cream, milk, powdered sugar, and instant pudding mix. Whip until thick. Spread on top of set gelatin/pudding mixture. Makes 12 servings.

My mom was a Jell-O queen. We had to have Jell-O every Sunday for dinner, but Mom thought it was blasphemy to serve "plain" Jell-O; it at least had to have fruit in it. Well, I feel the same way. My kids wouldn't know what to do if there was not Jell-O with our Sunday dinner. It just wouldn't be Sunday! Mom died a few years ago and I miss her terribly, but when I found this recipe, I knew it was one she would have loved.

Shelly Whitnah
Sunset Heights 2nd Ward
Sunset Heights Utah Stake
Orem, Utah

Corn, Tomato, and Basil Salad

2 large fresh tomatoes or 2 lb. cherry tomatoes

1½ C. fresh corn or frozen corn, blanched and drained

8 fresh basil leaves, torn into small pieces

Balsamic vinegar

Extra-virgin olive oil

Chop tomatoes or cut cherry tomatoes in half. In a large bowl, combine tomato, corn, and basil. Drizzle with balsamic vinegar and olive oil to taste. Stir. Makes 2–3 servings.

Shawnnee Miranda
Weston 1st Ward
Boston Massachusetts Stake
Natick, Massachusetts

Bean Salad

3 C. beans (any variety you enjoy; I use red
kidney beans)

1 small onion, diced

2 Tbsp. grape seed oil

¼ C. malt vinegar

Combine all ingredients. This is even better when it has been allowed to sit for half an hour. It is great at parties or barbecues. Makes 8–10 servings.

Laura Russell
Gosford Ward
Newcastle Australia Stake
Springfield NSW Australia

Tomato Cucumber Summer Salad

1 large cucumber

6 ripe red tomatoes

½ sweet onion, chopped

2 Tbsp. dill weed

2 C. sour cream

1 C. mayonnaise

1 Tbsp. vinegar

Salt and pepper to taste

Slice cucumbers and cut tomatoes into wedges; add the rest of the ingredients and stir to combine. Refrigerate until chilled. Makes 6 servings.

Natalee Binning
Bellingham Singles Ward
Bellingham Washington Stake
Bellingham, Washington

This summer salad is so good with fresh veggies from the garden. My mom makes this all through the summer. It's her favorite recipe that she got from her grandma, who fled Poland during the war and immigrated to Ontario, Canada. She and my great-grandpa had a 100-acre apple orchard and a huge garden. My mom says there were always great aromas coming from her kitchen and that she was the best cook. Mom is also a good cook, and she loves to cook when we bring friends home. She is always taking a meal or treats to someone she knows!

Chicken Rice-a-Roni Salad

1 pkg. chicken rice and pasta mix (Rice-a-Roni)

1 tsp. chicken bouillon or stock base

2 lg. chicken breasts, cooked and diced

2½ C. mayonnaise or Miracle Whip

1 green pepper, diced

4 lg. stalks celery, diced

2 oz. slivered almonds

Ripe olives, chopped

6 hard-boiled eggs, chopped or sliced (for garnish)

Prepare the chicken/rice mix according to package directions, except add bouillon or chicken stock base to the water. Cool; add remaining ingredients except eggs. Mix well. Add eggs as a garnish or decoration. Chill for at least one hour. Makes 8 servings.

This salad was served at a Relief Society birthday party in my mother's ward (East Carbon Ward) several years ago. She has served it to family many times since then, and I have taken it to many pot-luck lunches at work. The men in our family are big fans of this salad. It is especially pretty served on a lettuce leaf.

Leslie Keele
Carbonville Ward
Helper Utah Stake
Helper, Utah

Sour Cream Dill Potato Salad

5 lbs. red potatoes

1 C. dill pickle, finely chopped

1 C. onions, finely chopped

1½ C. celery, diced

6 hard-boiled eggs, chopped

4 oz. pimientos, chopped

1 C. sour cream

1 C. salad dressing (Miracle Whip)

1½ C. mayonnaise

2 tsp. dry dill weed

1 tsp. white pepper

1 Tbsp. salt

Clean, boil, and cut up potatoes with skin on; place in large mixing bowl. Add the pickle, onions, celery, eggs, and pimientos. In a separate bowl, combine sour cream, salad dressing, mayonnaise, dill weed, pepper, and salt; add to potato mixture and stir in gently until all is well blended. Best if refrigerated for several hours before serving. Makes 20 servings.

Christine Price
Heritage Ward
San Antonio Texas Stake
San Antonio, Texas

Banana Salad

6 C. iceberg lettuce, torn

2 bananas

⅔ C. salad dressing (Miracle Whip)

6 Tbsp. milk

2 tsp. apple cider vinegar

1 Tbsp. sugar

⅛ tsp. celery seed

⅛ tsp. celery salt

Salt and pepper to taste

Place torn lettuce in a large bowl. Slice bananas and arrange over salad. In a small bowl, combine salad dressing, milk, vinegar, sugar, celery seed, and celery salt. Whisk until smooth. Add salt and pepper to taste. Pour over salad and mix well. Serve immediately. Makes 6 servings.

David Buxton
Battlecreek 10th Ward
Pleasant Grove Utah East Stake
Pleasant Grove, Utah

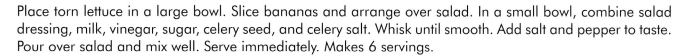

I don't recall having a "favorite" meal growing up. Just about everything my mother put on the table was delicious, and I never had to worry that dinner might be something I was going to dread. She made liver about once every two or three years, as if to give our taste buds one more chance to overhaul their preferences. Even on those rare occasions, she always served a full meal, and there were plenty of other flavors to drown out the pasty, nasty liver. When I was a newlywed, I once asked my wife, Deanna—the second dream cook of my life—if she would make a banana salad. She had never heard of such a thing, so I directed her to my mother. Deanna loved it immediately and serves it to our family quite often. It's such a simple but yummy side that complements just about any meal. Every time I eat Banana Salad, I'm reminded of my mother's tasty repertoire and her consistent diligence in putting a delicious, well-rounded meal on the table so we could enjoy dinner as a family every evening.

Mary Lynn's Chicken Salad

4 chicken breasts

1½ tsp. seasoned salt (to taste)

1½ C. red grapes, halved

½ C. mayonnaise

½ C. cream (no substitutes)

1 Tbsp. butter

½ C. slivered almonds

Boil chicken breasts until done; cool in refrigerator or freezer. Once cool enough to handle, cut into cubes. Place cubed chicken in salad bowl and toss with seasoned salt. Add grapes. In small bowl, mix mayonnaise and cream; pour mixture over chicken and grapes. Mix well. In a small saucepan, melt butter; add slivered almonds and stir until browned. Add buttered nuts to salad just before serving. Makes 8 servings.

My mom created this chicken salad and has made it often for our family. My dad loves chicken salad, and he was spending too much money going to the deli every day while he was in school, so my mom tried to mimic the deli's chicken salad. This was the result, and it has been a favorite in our home. I still have friends I grew up with who call and ask me for "that chicken salad with the grapes" recipe. I love you, Mommy! Thanks for gracing us with your culinary masterpieces for the past twenty-five years!

Jenika Reed
Morgan Park Ward
Chicago Illinois Stake
Chicago, Illinois

Grandma's Blueberry Salad

Salad:

2 C. boiling water

1 large box cherry gelatin (Jell-O)

1 20-oz. can blueberries with juice (not pie filling)

1 20-oz. can crushed pineapple with juice

Topping:

1 8-oz. cream cheese

1 C. sour cream

⅓ C. sugar

Walnuts, crushed (optional, for garnish)

Boil water and pour into a pan or dish. Add Jell-O and mix well. When Jell-O has completely dissolved, stir in blueberries and pineapple with juices. Let chill. When Jell-O is firm, make topping by combining cream cheese and sour cream; mix well. Add sugar and mix well. Spread on top of Jell-O. Sprinkle with crushed walnuts if desired. Makes 20 servings.

Natalie Sinks
Glines 5th Ward
Glines Utah Stake
Vernal, Utah

Oriental Chicken Salad

Salad:

4–6 C. chicken, cooked

2 pkg. ramen teriyaki noodles, crumbled

¼ C. sliced almonds

¼ C. sesame seeds

4 green onions, chopped

2 16-oz. bags coleslaw (shredded cabbage)

Dressing:

¾ C. salad oil

¼ C. plus 2 Tbsp. white vinegar

¾ C. sugar

2 packs of seasoning from the ramen noodles

¾ tsp. pepper

1 tsp. salt

2 tsp. accent

In a large bowl, combine all salad ingredients. In a separate bowl, combine all dressing ingredients well; pour over salad. Stir to thoroughly coat all ingredients and serve! Makes 4–6 servings.

Cassie Mark
Sharon Park 6th Ward
Sharon Park Utah Stake
Orem, Utah

I love this salad. Better yet, my husband LOVES this salad! I serve this as our only dinner dish, and we are completely satisfied. I have two little boys that I love cooking for. Although they are still pretty young (one is still nursing and the other just likes the chicken), I can't wait to make them home-cooked meals for the rest of their lives. These two boys, along with my husband, are what bring me to the kitchen . . . otherwise, to be perfectly honest, I don't think I'd have anything to do with it. I love to make them smile and fill their bellies. It makes me feel accomplished as a mother and a wife. You boys are my life. I love you.

Cornbread Salad

1 9 x 9-inch pan of cornbread (leftover
    cornbread is perfect!)
4 strips bacon, crisply cooked and crumbled
1 can red kidney beans, drained and rinsed

1 medium green pepper, diced
2 green onions, including tops, chopped
1 medium tomato, diced
Mayonnaise

Crumble cornbread into a large bowl. Add bacon, kidney beans, green pepper, green onions, and tomato. Toss. Add mayonnaise by the tablespoon to taste. Remember: You can always add more, but you can't take any out! Salad should be moist but not soupy. Makes 10–12 servings—more if you use more cornbread!

Susan Casdorph
Charleston 1st Ward
Charleston West Virginia Stake
South Charleston, West Virginia

This recipe was given to me by my mother-in-law, Doris Casdorph. She has used it for years. It is one of my husband's favorite recipes. When asked how much of everything to use, she said she didn't really know because she cooks like her mother cooked: with dashes, globs, and pinches! This is as close to a measured recipe as we can get.

Orange Jell-O Salad

3 C. water

1 small pkg. orange gelatin (Jell-O) (can use any flavor)

1 small pkg. instant vanilla pudding

1 small pkg. cook-and-serve tapioca pudding

8 oz. whipped topping (Cool Whip)

1 can mandarin oranges, drained (or any fruit)

In a medium saucepan, boil 3 C. water. Add the Jell-O, vanilla pudding, and tapioca pudding. Stir well (I use a whisk to get all the lumps out). Cook until bubbly. Cool completely, then add cool whip and oranges. Mix well and refrigerate until ready to serve. Best when made the day before serving. Makes 8–10 servings. *Note:* You may use any flavor of Jell-O and fruit to get lots of variety.

I have always loved my mom's cooking. Even when things were tight, she could always put together a great meal with very little money. It is always a treat to eat one of her meals. She always makes all sorts of wonderful salads for our family get-togethers. When we are headed to grandma's house for dinner, my kids always hope that she will bring this Orange Jell-O Salad. And because you can use any flavor of Jell-O and different kinds of fruit, it is always a fun surprise to see which flavor it will be.

Thad Kress
Cottonwood Ward
Ucon Idaho Stake
Idaho Falls, Idaho

Raspberry Nut Jell-O Salad

1 large pkg. raspberry gelatin (Jell-O)

2 C. boiling water

1 21-oz. can raspberry pie filling

1 small can crushed pineapple, with juice

1 C. pecans, chopped (optional)

1 8-oz. pkg. cream cheese

½ C. sugar

1 tsp. vanilla

1 C. sour cream

(recipe continued on next page)

(Raspberry Nut Jell-O Salad, continued)

Dissolve Jell-O in 2 C. boiling water. Add pie filling, pineapple, and nuts (if desired). Pour into a 9 x 13-inch pan. Chill until set. Beat cream cheese, adding sugar and vanilla. Beat well. Add sour cream gradually (it's very important to add it gradually). Spread over the set Jell-O. Chill several hours before serving. Makes 12 servings.

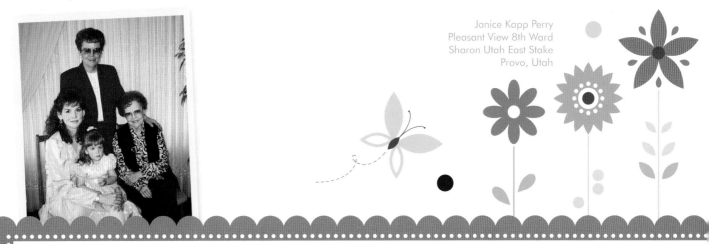

Janice Kapp Perry
Pleasant View 8th Ward
Sharon Utah East Stake
Provo, Utah

My talented mother is Ruth Saunders Kapp. I grew up on a small farm in Oregon, and we enjoyed lots of basic good meals consisting of meat, potatoes, and garden produce. Mom made sure we had nice healthy meals, but she also made time to develop many talents and interests that would serve her well. She passed away in 1991, and somehow this recipe fell into my possession. It has been such a hit at get-togethers that I rarely make any other Jell-O recipe. Mother was widowed very early when Dad died at fifty-seven. It could have been a very lonely and sad twenty-one years as a widow, but the talents she had developed gave a focus to her life and enabled her to serve others. Mom and Dad had played piano and drums in a dance band, and she continued this after he passed away (with me playing drums in his place). She was the heart and soul of a Senior Citizen Fun Band that toured northern Utah; she accompanied singers of all kinds; she wrote musicals that were performed; she crocheted booties for every new baby in her ward for decades; she made quilts for all of her grandchildren—there was no end to her talents! When Dad died she served a full-time mission in Jackson, Mississippi, after which she became an avid genealogist, researching more than 40,000 names for temple work. While I was caring for her at the end of her life I noticed ten pennies on the windowsill above her kitchen sink, and I asked her if she would like me to put them away. She said, "Not yet. Those are my service pennies—they start out on the left side of the window in the morning, and as I perform acts of service I move them to the right side by evening." She was almost bed-bound by that time, and I asked how she could perform acts of service. She told me she could call people in the ward who were sick and try to cheer them up, she could write a short note to a missionary, she could still swing her legs off the side of the bed and type a few more names for temple work on her portable typewriter. I marveled at her positive attitude and felt that she had come up with the perfect "recipe" for a happy, fulfilling life.

Mahana Jell-O

1 16-oz. container cottage cheese
1 20-oz. can crushed pineapple
2 C. pecans, chopped
1 large pkg. lime gelatin (Jell-O)

1 large pkg. lemon gelatin (Jell-O)
4 C. boiling water
½ gal. vanilla ice cream

In two 9 x 13-inch cake pans, divide the cottage cheese, pineapple, and nuts in half. Arrange evenly into bottom of each pan. In a separate pan, dissolve both boxes of Jell-O in the 4 C. water. Add ice cream until melted. When ice cream is melted, pour equally over the cottage cheese, pineapple and nut mixture in both pans. Let set and then you have Mahana Jell-O. Makes 24 servings.

When I was young, my mother made this Jell-O. Because the salad was really not pretty to look at, my younger sister, Melva, named it Mahana ("You Ugly") Jell-O. It is one of our family's favorites.

Thora Eager
Cedar Hills 2nd Ward
Cedar Hills Utah Stake
Cedar Hills, Utah

Blueberry Jell-O

Jell-O:
1 6-oz. pkg. black cherry gelatin (Jell-O)
3 C. boiling water
1 21-oz. can blueberry pie filling
1 20-oz. can crushed pineapple, with juice

Topping:
1 8-oz. pkg. cream
   cheese, softened
2 C. sugar

Dissolve Jell-O in boiling water. Add pie filling and pineapple; mix well. Put in a 9 x 13-inch cake pan or a large bowl; refrigerate until firm. Combine topping ingredients and pour over firm Jell-O. Refrigerate until topping is firm. Makes 12 servings.

My mother-in-law and I have joked about this recipe for years because we have made it for so long. We even got to the point where we used cans of blueberry pie filling to trade for other items.

Lori Lind
Lolo Ward
Stevensville Montana Stake
Florence, Montana

Michigan Salad

Salad:

6–8 C. mixed greens

½ C. pecans or walnuts, toasted

½ C. bleu cheese, crumbled (can use gorgonzola)

½ C. dried cherries

1 Granny Smith apple, cored and cut into matchsticks

Raspberry Vinaigrette:

½ C. vegetable oil

½ C. raspberry wine vinegar

½ C. white sugar OR 1/3 C. pure maple syrup with 1 T. sugar

2 tsp. Dijon mustard

½ tsp. dried oregano

¼ tsp. ground black pepper

In a large bowl, combine all salad ingredients. In a jar with a tight-fitting lid, combine vinaigrette ingredients. Shake well. Use to dress salad. Makes 8 servings.

Maureen Cannan Bringhurst
Rochester Ward
Grand Blanc Michigan Stake
Rochester Hills, Michigan

Broccoli Salad

3–4 heads broccoli florets, bite-size pieces

1 small red onion, diced

1 C. craisins or raisins

1 lb. bacon, fried crisp and crumbled

1 C. toasted, shelled sunflower seeds

1½–2 C. mayonnaise

½ C. sugar (or more!)

4 Tbsp. red wine vinegar

Mix broccoli, onion, craisins, bacon, and sunflower seeds. In a separate bowl, mix mayonnaise, sugar, and vinegar. Pour over broccoli mixture. Chill at least 2 hours. Makes 10–12 servings.

Susan Arbuthnot Gough
Calgary 4th Ward
Calgary Alberta Stake
Calgary, Alberta
Canada

{ MAIN DISHES }

The future destiny of the child is always the work
of the mother.

{ Napolean Bonaparte }

Mom's Best Lasagna Ever

1 lb. lean ground beef
1 Tbsp. olive oil
1 tsp. hot pepper flakes
2 cloves garlic, minced
1 13-oz. can tomato paste
2–3 Tbsp. sugar
Salt and pepper to taste

1 28-oz. can whole tomatoes
1 medium onion, chopped
½ C. Parmesan cheese, grated, plus 3 Tbsp.
1 16-oz. container cottage cheese
2 C. sharp cheddar cheese, shredded
2 C. mozarella cheese, shredded
1 pkg. oven-ready lasagna noodles

In a skillet, brown ground beef; set aside. In large saucepan, combine oil and hot pepper flakes. Cook about 1 minute. Add garlic and cook for another minute. Add tomato paste and 2½ cans water. Bring to a boil, then reduce heat to a simmer. Add sugar to desired sweetness and salt and pepper to taste. Process tomatoes in food processor until smooth and add to saucepan. Add onion. Cook for about 30 minutes, until sauce starts to thicken. Add ½ C. Parmesan cheese and ground beef. Cook another 10 minutes. Cool 10 minutes. Place small layer of sauce in a 9 x 13-inch casserole dish. Place 5–6 lasagna noodles in casserole dish. Cover with sauce. Sprinkle half the cheddar and mozarella cheese over sauce. Place another 5–6 noodles over this layer. Spread sauce over noodles and top sauce with the cottage cheese. Spread evenly. Place another layer of 5–6 noodles and spread with the remaining sauce. Top with remaining cheddar and mozarella cheese and sprinkle with 3 Tbsp. Parmesan cheese. Bake at 350 for about 1 hour, or until bubbly and noodles are soft. Allow to cool before cutting. Makes 12 servings.

Angela Nelson
Kennebecasis Valley Ward
Saint John New Brunswick Canada Stake
Sussex, New Brunswick
Canada

I remember always being in the kitchen with my mom while she cooked, mainly because I wanted to be the one to lick the spoon! I learned to make most of my mom's recipes just by being in the kitchen and watching her do her magic. Most of my memories of my mom involve her cooking and baking and me smelling the great aromas. Mom always cooked from scratch, and every meal was delicious. We were spoiled as kids from all her baking and great meals, and even to this day I can't have a meal without following up with something sweet. I love to cook and bake, and I thank my mom for her great example in loving to cook for her family. This was always one of my favorites, and now my kids love it too. Hopefully they will love to cook and bake when they have their own families!

Pepper Steak

1 lb. beef chuck or round, fat trimmed

¼ C. soy sauce

1 clove garlic

1½ tsp. fresh ginger, grated, or ½ tsp. ground ginger

¼ C. vegetable oil

1 C. green onion, thinly sliced

½ C. red bell pepper, cut into 1-inch squares

½ C. green bell pepper, cut into 1-inch squares

2 stalks celery, thinly sliced

1 Tbsp. cornstarch

1 C. water

2 tomatoes, cut into wedges

Cut beef across the grain into ½-inch-thick strips. In a medium bowl, mix soy sauce, garlic, ginger, and beef. Set aside. Heat the oil in a wok or large pan. Add the beef mixture and cook over high heat until beef is browned. Simmer over low heat for 30 minutes until beef is tender. Add the vegetables and cook over high heat for 10 minutes. Combine the cornstarch with water and add to the pan. Stir and cook until the sauce thickens. Stir in the tomatoes and cook through. Makes 4 servings.

Susan Silvestre
Desert Breeze Ward
Lakes Nevada Stake
Las Vegas, Nevada

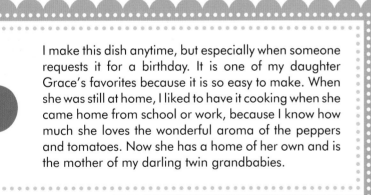

I make this dish anytime, but especially when someone requests it for a birthday. It is one of my daughter Grace's favorites because it is so easy to make. When she was still at home, I liked to have it cooking when she came home from school or work, because I know how much she loves the wonderful aroma of the peppers and tomatoes. Now she has a home of her own and is the mother of my darling twin grandbabies.

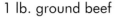

Healthy Hearty Meatloaf

1 lb. ground beef
1 C. zucchini, chopped
1 C. yellow squash, chopped
1 C. carrots, grated
1 onion, chopped
1 egg

1–2 C. oatmeal
1 10.75-oz. can cream of mushroom soup
1 15-oz. can diced stewed tomatoes
2 8-oz. cans tomato sauce
1 Tbsp. seasoned salt

Mix all ingredients in large bowl. Fill loaf pans ½ full for faster cooking. Cook at 350 for 45 minutes. I freeze the extra loaves for later dinners. This is super yummy and healthy. Makes 12 servings (I usually use 4 pans).

Janelle Anusiem
River Grove 3rd Ward
Provo Utah Central Stake
Provo, Utah

Chicken-Fried Chicken

Boneless, skinless chicken breasts (1 per person)
Flour

Salt and pepper to taste
Buttermilk
3 C. peanut oil

Pound chicken breasts flat between sheets of plastic wrap. In a bowl, combine flour, salt, and pepper. Dip chicken pieces into the flour mixture, shake excess flour from the pieces, dip into the buttermilk, then dip into the flour mixture again. Fry in heated oil for about 2½ minutes per side or until golden brown. Cooking time depends on the thickness of the breast. Serve with mashed potatoes and country gravy.

Linnita Proctor
Hunter 15th Ward
Hunter Utah East Stake
West Valley City, Utah

Holupkis (Cabbage Rolls)

1 large onion, chopped

½ green pepper, chopped

3 stalks celery with leaves, chopped

1 large carrot, chopped

¼ C. butter or bacon grease

2 lb. ground beef

1 egg

1 C. long-grain rice, cooked

1 tsp. pepper

1½ tsp. garlic salt

1 lg. head cabbage, cored, parboiled, and leaves separated

1 46-oz. can tomato juice

Sauté all chopped vegetables in butter or bacon grease until tender (bacon grease is more flavorful). Remove from heat and stir in ground beef, egg, cooked rice, pepper, and garlic salt; combine everything until mixed well. Cover the bottom of a 6- or 8-quart Dutch oven with a few cabbage leaves. For remaining cabbage leaves, place 2 heaping tablespoons of mixture (less if leaf is smaller) on leaf, roll up, and tuck in the ends. Place side by side in pan, then layer as needed. Pour tomato juice over top. Place any remaining cabbage leaves on top to keep Holupkis from burning. Cover with lid and bake at 350 for 1½ hours. Reduce heat to 300; bake an additional 2–3 hours or until cabbage is tender. Turn off oven and let Holupkis sit in oven, covered, for as long as an hour after the heat is turned off. These are even better the next day! Makes 8 servings.

Katia Tishnya
Cherkassy Tsentrainy Branch
Ukraine District
Cherkassy, Ukraine

I joined the Church when I was a teenager, and my mother and grandmother later joined the Church. I have returned from my mission to Russia and was married last October. We first had to have a civil ceremony in the Ukraine, then we joined our district's temple trip so we could be sealed in the temple. We rode a train across the Ukraine, switched to a bus to cross Poland, and then rode another bus to get to the temple in Frieberg, Germany. I was happy to do this to be sealed for eternity.

Sweet and Sour Beef

1 lb. stew beef

3 Tbsp. oil

1 large onion, cut in wedges

Flour

1 C. beef broth

½ C. ketchup

¼ C. vinegar

¼ C. packed brown sugar

1 tsp. mustard or Worcestershire sauce

Salt and pepper

Brown beef in oil; remove meat from pan. In same pan, sauté onions in the oil. When onions are tender, sprinkle enough flour over onions to soak up the oil. In a bowl, combine beef broth, ketchup, vinegar, brown sugar, and mustard or Worcestershire sauce. Mix well. Add sauce mixture and beef to onions in skillet. Salt and pepper to taste. Stir and cook until meat is tender (1–2 hours). We like to serve this over mashed potatoes. Makes 4–6 servings.

This is my mother's recipe. It's wonderful on a cold evening—very much a comfort food. I had my mom write the recipe down so I could make this dish; she has been making it for so many years that she just throws everything in and cooks.

Margo McCall
Pittsburgh 4th Ward
Pittsburgh Pennsylvania North Stake
Pittsburgh, Pennsylvania

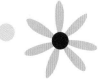

Eye of Round Beef Roast

1 eye of round roast (note weight)

4 cloves of garlic, slivered

Salt to taste

Black pepper (I use at least 3-4 Tbsp.)

1 stick butter (room temperature)

1 env. dry au jus gravy mix (or any brown gravy)

Cut slits in roast on all sides and push slivers of garlic into holes. Salt and pepper the roast (I usually put salt and pepper on waxed paper and roll the roast in it). Put the roast in a black iron skillet and spread the stick of softened butter over the roast like icing. Sprinkle gravy gravy mix over butter. Leave uncovered and put into preheated 475-degree oven. Bake 4 minutes per pound for medium-rare, 6 minutes per pound for medium-well. (You will be able to adjust the doneness after experimenting with the time per pound.) Set a timer; when the timer goes off, turn off oven. DO NOT OPEN THE OVEN DOOR. Leave the roast in the oven for at least 3–4 hours to cool and finish cooking. DO NOT PEEK! When you take the roast out of the oven, take the meat out of the pan, add a little water to the drippings, and make gravy. Makes 3–4 servings per pound of roast.

Hessie Maud Snodgrass
Clinton Ward
Jackson Mississippi Stake
Clinton, Mississippi

Pollo Grande Quesadillas

Quesadillas:

4 boneless, skinless chicken breasts, diced

1 large sweet onion, coarsely diced

5–10 Tbsp. oil, divided

Fajita seasoning to taste

2 bell peppers (any color), very coarsely chopped

8 oz. mushrooms, sliced (optional)

Jalapeno Cheese Sauce:

4 oz. Neufchatel cheese

¼ C. fat-free sour cream

½ tsp. garlic

¼ C. milk

2–5 Tbsp. pickled jalapeno peppers, seeds removed

For assembly:

10–12 tortillas

12 oz. cheese (Monterrey Jack or cheddar), shredded

In a frying pan, fry chicken and onions in 1–2 Tbsp. oil and fajita seasoning to taste until chicken is cooked and onions are tender. In a separate pan, fry peppers in 1–2 Tbsp. oil until crisp-tender, adding the mushrooms to the peppers during the last 4–5 minutes of frying, if desired. In a blender, puree all Jalapeno Cheese Sauce ingredients. To assemble, layer one half of each tortilla with chicken mixture, peppers and mushrooms, 2 Tbsp. shredded cheese, and 1–2 Tbsp. Jalapeno Cheese Sauce. Fold over the other half of the tortilla, enclosing all of the filling. On a griddle or pan lightly brushed with the remaining oil, fry the quesadilla until the tortilla is light brown and the cheese inside has melted. Makes 10–12 servings.

Amy O'Brady
Idaho Falls 26th Ward
Idaho Falls Idaho Central Stake
Idaho Falls, Idaho

My mom—mother of six and feeder of many—is an amazing cook. One of my greatest goals is to become as good a cook as my mom. While attending college in Rexburg, Idaho, my roommates and I cooked Sunday dinner for one another. When it was my turn to cook, my mantra was, "Be like Mom!" Now, as an adult and mother of four, I am lucky to live only a mile away from Mom. We like to get together for "cooking" days to experiment with new recipes. She is especially good at helping me figure out all of the ingredients to our favorite restaurant recipes. This recipe is an exceptionally good imitation of a dish from my favorite Mexican restaurant.

Huushuur (Mongolian Fried Meat Pies)

Crust:

2¼ C. all-purpose flour

½ tsp. salt

¾ C. warm water

For filling and frying:

2 garlic cloves

1½ tsp. salt

1 lb. ground fatty lamb shoulder

1 C. onion, minced

2 scallions, minced

¼ C. water

6–8 C. vegetable oil

In a large bowl, stir together flour and salt; stir in warm water until a dough forms. Transfer to a floured surface and knead briefly. Form into 16 balls, each about 1½ inches. Cover with the inverted large bowl; let stand at room temperature 1–2 hours. While you wait for the dough, make the filling. Mince and mash garlic to a paste with salt; mix in the lamb, onion, scallions, and water. Preheat oven to 250. Roll out 1 ball of dough into a 3- to 4-inch round on a floured surface with a floured rolling pin. Put about 2 Tbsp. filling on one side of the dough, flattening the filling slightly, and fold the other half over the filling to form a half-moon. Press edges together to seal, forcing out air. Starting at one end of curve, fold edge over in triangles (each fold should overlap previous one), pressing as you go and pressing last fold under (this will help seal). Repeat with remaining dough and filling. Meanwhile, heat 1½–2 inches oil to 350 in a deep 4- to 5-quart heavy pot. Fry pies, 4 at a time, until golden and meat is just cooked through, about 6 minutes. Transfer to paper towels to drain. Return oil to 350 before frying each batch. Keep pies warm on a baking sheet in oven. Makes 16 meat pies.

This is my favorite Mongolian food. I have watched my mother and helped her make Huushuur since I was very small. My mother can make these little half-moon-shaped pies very rapidly in her very experienced hands. I am learning the same art from her.

Odgerel Bumandalai
Sansar Ward
Bayanzurkn District Khoroo 1
Ulaanbaatar, Mongolia

Our Favorite Glazed Meatloaf

2 eggs, beaten
2/3 C. milk
2 tsp. salt
1/4 tsp. pepper
3 slices bread, torn into pieces
1 onion, chopped

1 carrot, shredded
1 1/2 C. cheese, shredded
2 lbs. ground beef
1/4 C. ketchup
1/4 C. packed brown sugar
1 Tbsp. mustard

Combine eggs, milk, salt, pepper, and bread; mix well. Add onion, carrot, cheese, and ground beef, mixing well with your hands. Form into a loaf in the center of a 13 x 9-inch greased baking dish. Bake at 350 for 1 hour 15 minutes. Combine ketchup, brown sugar, and mustard. Remove meatloaf from the oven and drain off all liquid. Spread ketchup mixture evenly over meatloaf, and put meatloaf back in oven for 15 minutes. Makes 10–12 servings.

Heidi Miller
Texarkana Ward
Shreveport Louisiana Stake
Ashdown, Arkansas

This meatloaf recipe was one that my mom got in a ward cookbook when she lived in Hawaii in the early seventies. It was always my favorite dish, because most of the time she served baked potatoes with it, and I love baked potatoes! My mom was the BEST meatloaf maker! When I got married and began submitting recipes to ward cookbooks, I always submitted this recipe as my own. It's my husband's favorite, as well as that of our seven children. When I moved next to my in-laws in 2005, I made this meatloaf for our family one night and invited my in-laws for dinner. My father-in-law couldn't get enough of it, and my mother-in-law asked me for the recipe. Let's face it: I've had her meatloaf before, and it was dry and boring. I gave her my recipe, and she often tells me that when she makes it, it just doesn't taste as good as mine. Every year, I make my meatloaf for my father-in-law on his birthday.

Mom's Special Chicken

2 C. lemon-lime soda

1 C. soy sauce

1 C. vegetable oil

2 tsp. garlic powder or 1 tsp. crushed garlic

2 tsp. horseradish

2 lb. boneless, skinless chicken or turkey breast

In a large bowl, combine soda, soy sauce, oil, garlic, and horseradish. Add chicken or turkey, and marinate for at least 4 hours; overnight is even better. You can cook it however you want; we usually grill it, and enjoy that best, but it's also really good baked. I've even fried it in olive oil when I didn't have time to bake it. Makes 4–8 servings. *Note:* This recipe is best when prepared with fairly thin chicken breasts, but works with any type of chicken or turkey.

My mom, Judy Porritt, created a tradition that on our birthdays all of us children got to design our own dinner—all of it, down to what we wanted to drink, and when we wanted to have it served. For my birthdays, I have requested this kind of chicken for years. I've considered other things, but I always come back to "Mom's Special Chicken" with mashed potatoes, salad, and cake for dessert. Even the smell of this chicken reminds me of my birthday and my mom. It probably always will.

Stephanie Jarman
11th Ward
Salt Lake City Utah Central Stake
Salt Lake City, Utah

"Veal" Parmesan

1-lb. sirloin tip steak, frozen

1 egg

1½ Tbsp. water

½ C. bread crumbs

½ C. Parmesan cheese

3 Tbsp. oil

½ C. water

Salt and pepper to taste

3 8-oz. cans tomato sauce

1 tsp. marjoram

⅓ C. onion, minced

1–1½ lb. mozzarella cheese

(recipe continued on next page)

("Veal" Parmesan, continued)

Partially thaw steak in microwave to make it easier to cut; cut into pieces approx 1½ inches x 2½ inches. Further slice these to ⅛-inch thick. Break egg into cereal-size bowl; stir in 1½ Tbsp. water. In a separate bowl combine bread crumbs and Parmesan cheese. Dip steak pieces into egg mixture and then into bread crumb mixture. Fry in oil to keep from sticking. After turning once, add ½ C. water, salt and pepper to taste, and cover with lid. While steak simmers, make sauce: in medium pan, combine tomato sauce, 4 cans water, marjoram, and minced onion. Sauce will be thin. Bring to a boil. While both pans heat, slice mozzarella cheese. Layer simmered steak into baking pan (I use just larger than 9 x 13), place mozzarella cheese on top, and pour sauce over steak. Bake at 375 for about 40 minutes. Serve over cooked angel hair or regular spaghetti. Great with garlic bread. Makes 8–10 servings.

I don't recall a single birthday in my family where this was not the meal of choice! With seven children in my family, we had it at least nine times a year—sometimes more if grandparents were in town around their birthday. Since I have been away from home attending college, I haven't been able to pick my birthday dinner. This summer when I went home I made sure to learn how to prepare this family favorite, and am excited to know that I can have it on my birthday this year!

Marci Krumperman
Nauvoo 1st Ward
Nauvoo Illinois Stake
Nauvoo, Illinois

Hot Chicken and Rice Casserole

4 C. chicken, cooked and cubed
1 dozen eggs, hard-cooked and diced
4 C. celery, chopped
8 tsp. onion, minced
2 tsp. salt

8 C. cooked rice
1 10.75-oz. can cream of chicken soup
3 C. mayonnaise
Rice krispies, cornflakes, or crushed Ritz
    crackers

In a large bowl, combine chicken, eggs, celery, onion, salt, and rice. In a separate bowl, combine soup and mayonnaise. Stir into chicken mixture and pour into a large greased casserole pan. Crumble cereal or crackers on top and bake at 375 for 30 minutes. Makes 20 servings.

Leslie Day
Danville Ward
Lexington Kentucky Stake
Danville, Kentucky

My mom—Peggy Cornett from the Danville Ward in Lexington, Kentucky—is always doing charitable acts of kindness, whether in church or for family and friends. This casserole is one of the main dishes she makes to take whenever a family is in need of a meal. I am thankful for my mom's example in showing Christlike love to those in need.

Krebinetter

Krebinetter:

2 lb. ground pork

Salt and pepper

2 Tbsp. butter

3 lb. potatoes

Sauce:

2 Tbsp. wheat flour

2 Tbsp. butter

2 C. beef broth (from bouillon)

Browning sauce

Shape the meat into 6–8 patties. Season with salt and pepper. Cook the patties on a pan with 2 Tbsp. butter for 4–5 minutes on each side. Boil the potatoes until tender. To make the sauce, make a roux of flour and 2 Tbsp. butter. Add the beef broth and cook and stir until thickened. Add salt, pepper, and browning to taste. Serve patties on a plate with potatoes and the gravy poured over the top. We like to serve it with beetroot and gherkins. Makes 6 servings.

Mille Norgaard
Randers Branch
Aarhus Denmark Stake
Randers, Denmark

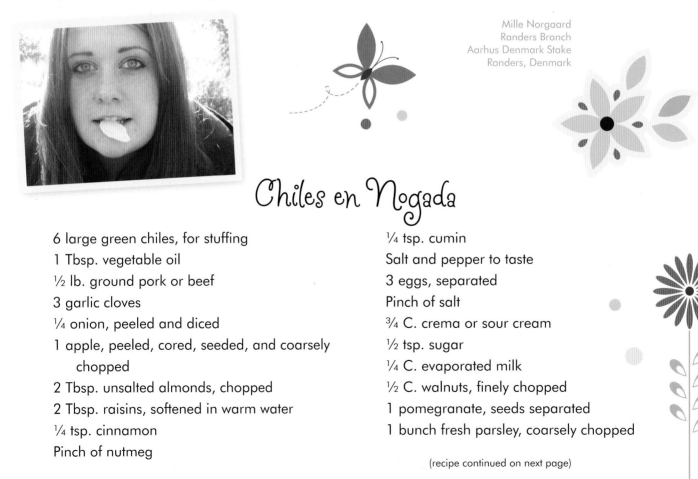

Chiles en Nogada

6 large green chiles, for stuffing

1 Tbsp. vegetable oil

½ lb. ground pork or beef

3 garlic cloves

¼ onion, peeled and diced

1 apple, peeled, cored, seeded, and coarsely chopped

2 Tbsp. unsalted almonds, chopped

2 Tbsp. raisins, softened in warm water

¼ tsp. cinnamon

Pinch of nutmeg

¼ tsp. cumin

Salt and pepper to taste

3 eggs, separated

Pinch of salt

¾ C. crema or sour cream

½ tsp. sugar

¼ C. evaporated milk

½ C. walnuts, finely chopped

1 pomegranate, seeds separated

1 bunch fresh parsley, coarsely chopped

(recipe continued on next page)

(Chiles en Nogada, continued)

Roast the chiles and remove the skins and seeds. In a large pan, heat the oil over medium heat. Add the pork or beef and brown until nearly done. Add the garlic, onion, apple, almonds, raisins, cinnamon, nutmeg, cumin, and salt and pepper, and cook for about 5 minutes. Stuff the chiles with equal portions of the stuffing. In a large bowl, beat the egg whites until they form stiff peaks. Fold in the egg yolks and a pinch of salt. Dip each stuffed chile in the egg mixture and fry until golden brown. In a medium bowl, mix the crema, walnuts, sugar, and evaporated milk. Pour over the freshly cooked chiles and sprinkle with pomegranate seeds and parsley. Makes 6 servings.

This is my favorite thing to eat. We eat this for special occasions like Independence Day—it has a GREEN chile, WHITE sauce, and RED pomegranate, which are the colors of the Mexican flag. My mother makes this dish for me; I love it, and I love her.

Amado Daruich
Valle del Sol Ward
Valsequillo Stake
Puebla, Coahuila
Mexico

Three-Cheese Enchiladas

1 8-oz. pkg. cream cheese
2 C. cheddar cheese, shredded
2 C. mozzarella cheese, shredded

1 C. salsa
1 pkg. flour tortillas
Extra cheese and salsa for topping

Mix the cheeses and salsa and spoon into tortillas. Roll up enchilada-style and place in a pan. Cover with salsa and extra shredded cheese. Bake at 350 for 35–45 minutes, or until the cheese in the enchiladas is melted. Makes 8 servings.

Krystal Brockholt
Heatheridge 9th Ward
Orem Utah Heatheridge Stake
Orem, Utah

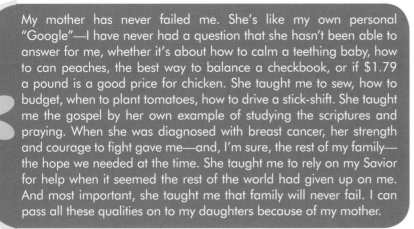

My mother has never failed me. She's like my own personal "Google"—I have never had a question that she hasn't been able to answer for me, whether it's about how to calm a teething baby, how to can peaches, the best way to balance a checkbook, or if $1.79 a pound is a good price for chicken. She taught me to sew, how to budget, when to plant tomatoes, how to drive a stick-shift. She taught me the gospel by her own example of studying the scriptures and praying. When she was diagnosed with breast cancer, her strength and courage to fight gave me—and, I'm sure, the rest of my family— the hope we needed at the time. She taught me to rely on my Savior for help when it seemed the rest of the world had given up on me. And most important, she taught me that family will never fail. I can pass all these qualities on to my daughters because of my mother.

Chicken Fricassee

1 whole chicken

2 14.5-oz. cans chicken broth

1 medium onion, diced

4–5 ribs celery, diced

2 C. carrots, sliced

1 tsp. salt

1 tsp. pepper

1 tsp. onion powder

6 Tbsp. flour

6 Tbsp. butter

4 C. milk

Remove fat and skin from chicken. Place chicken in a pot; add chicken broth plus enough water to cover the chicken. Add onion, celery, carrots, salt, pepper, and onion powder. Bring to a full rolling boil, then reduce heat and cook for 1–1½ hours. Remove chicken from the broth. Let chicken cool and then pull the meat off the bones. Cut into cubes or shred in large chunks. Put the chicken back into the broth. In a separate saucepan, combine flour and butter to make a roux. Stirring constantly, slowly add milk. After the roux thickens, add to the chicken broth. Bring to a boil for 1 minute. Serve fricassee over mashed potatoes or wide egg noodles. Makes 12 servings.

Sherrie Hunter, Debbie Danielson, Joi Lynn Fenton
Pleasant Grove 1st Ward
Pleasant Grove Utah Stake
Pleasant Grove, Utah

June Berry Fenton loved to cook, and Chicken Fricassee is a family favorite. She made this dish when her grandkids came from Phoenix and when she went to Phoenix to visit them. Her grandkids in Utah also love the dish. June returned home to Heavenly Father in June 2009. When we heard about this cookbook, we knew that her Chicken Fricassee had to be submitted. We asked June's husband, Don, where the recipe came from, and he said his mom used to make it for him. All these years we thought it came from June's family. June had taken a dish her husband loved, learned how to make it herself, and carried on the tradition. This ultimate comfort food has been passed on to at least four generations in our family. Since June passed away, we have tried to write down her recipes, but it has been difficult: she didn't have recipes—she just knew how to cook. We—her daughters, Sherrie and Debbie, and her daughter-in-law, Joi Lynn—get together and try to get the recipes just right so we can teach our sons and daughters how to cook like Grandma June.

Nacatamales

6 C. masa harina

1 C. shortening

1 Tbsp. salt

½ C. sour orange juice (*naranja agria*)

4–5 C. chicken broth

3 lb. pork roast, cubed

Salt and pepper

¾ C. rice, soaked in water for 30 minutes

12 banana leaves, cut in 10 x 10-inch pieces

½ lb. potatoes, peeled and sliced

1 onion, sliced

2 bell peppers, sliced

2 tomatoes, sliced

1 bunch mint

12 10 x 10-inch pieces of foil

In a large bowl, blend masa harina, shortening, and 1 Tbsp. salt to a mealy texture. Add the orange juice and enough chicken broth to make a soft, moist dough. It should be a little firmer than mashed potatoes. Use an electric mixer at medium-high speed and beat for 2–3 minutes to incorporate some air into the masa and make it fluffier. Cover the bowl and set the masa aside to rest for at least 30 minutes. Season the pork with salt and pepper. Drain the rice. Assemble all the filling ingredients and assembly items on a large table or work surface. Gather family and friends to help in an assembly line. Lay out a banana leaf square with the smooth side up. Place 1 C. masa in the middle of the banana leaf and, using wet hands, spread it out a little. Put about ½ C. pork on top of the masa and sprinkle 1–2 Tbsp. rice over the pork. Lay 1–2 slices potato on top of the pork and then top with 1–2 pieces onion, 1–2 pieces pepper, and a slice of tomato. Top it all off with a few mint leaves. Fold the top edge of the banana leaf down over the filling. Bring the bottom edge of the banana leaf up over this. Then fold in both sides to make a rectangular package. Be careful not to wrap it too tightly or the filling will squeeze out. Flip the package over so it is seam side down. Set the *Nacatamale* in the middle of an aluminum foil square and wrap the foil tightly around the *Nacatamale* the same way you wrapped up the banana leaf. Set aside and repeat with the remaining ingredients to make 10–12 *Nacatamales*. Add 2–3 inches of water to a *tamalera* or pot large enough to hold all the *Nacatamales*. (You may have to use two pots if you don't have one big enough to hold the *Nacatamales* in one batch.) Place a rack in the bottom or toss in enough wadded-up aluminum foil to hold the *Nacatamales* mostly out of the water. Add the *Nacatamales* and bring to a boil over high heat. Cover tightly, reduce heat to low, and steam for 3–4 hours. Add more water as needed to keep the pot from boiling dry. Remove the *Nacatamales* from the pot, take off the aluminum foil, and serve hot. Each diner opens the banana leaf on his or her own *Nacatamale* before eating. Makes 10–12 servings.

Rebeca Chavez
Las Mercedes Ward
Bello Horizonte Stake
Managua, Nicaragua

German Chicken Doner

⅓ C. olive oil

2 tsp. oregano

1 tsp. sweet paprika

1 tsp. salt

Pepper

2 cloves garlic, crushed

Juice from 1 lemon

2 lb. chicken thighs

½ C. hummus

½ C. yogurt

4 rolls or pita breads

Lettuce, shredded

Tomato, sliced

Cucumber, sliced

Preheat barbecue or oven to 350. In a large bowl, combine oil, spices, garlic, and lemon juice. Add chicken and thoroughly coat in marinade. Cook chicken at 350 for about 1 hour, basting occasionally with remaining marinade, until browned and cooked through. In a small bowl, combine hummus and yogurt. Cut chicken from the bone in very thin slices. Pile chicken onto long roll or stuff into pita. Serve with shredded lettuce, tomato, cucumber, and yogurt-hummus mixture. Makes 4 servings.

I am currently serving in the town of Langen, which is close to the city of Frankfurt. I love German foods, from Bratwurst to Doners. Doners are really popular in Germany; they are actually a Turkish food, but the Germans have adopted them and love them. I miss my mom's cooking, but I really do love the food in Germany.

Elder Sean Whitnah
Langen Branch
Germany Frankfurt Mission
Langen, Germany

Nacatamales are popular steamed corncakes from Nicaragua. They are similar to Mexican tamales but are larger, filled with meat and vegetables, and steamed in banana leaves. *Nacatamales* are special-occasion food and are most often served as a Sunday morning meal or at Christmas, weddings, and other large celebrations. Of course, the ones my mother makes are the best. Banana leaves can be found in the frozen section of many Latino and Asian markets. If they aren't available in your area, you can use a double layer of aluminum foil alone. You won't get the extra flavor the banana leaves add, though. In Central America, *Nacatamales* are usually wrapped in banana leaves alone and tied like a package with twine or the spines from the banana leaves. If you can't find sour orange juice *(naranja agria)*, substitute the juice of 1 orange and 2 limes.

Sweet and Sour Glazed Ham

⅓ C. rice vinegar

4 Tbsp. packed brown sugar

1 Tbsp. ketchup

1 tsp. soy sauce

2 tsp. cornstarch

4 tsp. water or pineapple juice

10 lb. ham

1 20-oz. can pineapple rings

In a small saucepan, combine vinegar, brown sugar, ketchup, and soy sauce. Bring to a boil. Combine cornstarch and water or pineapple juice. Stir into saucepan and cook, stirring constantly, until thickened. Pour over ham and refrigerate overnight. Before baking the ham, place pineapple rings on the ham. Bake at 275 for 5–6 hours. Makes 10–12 servings.

Julie Slaughter
Caribou Ward
St. John New Brunswick Canada Stake
Presque Isle, Maine

My dad was a young man during the Depression, and he worked for a grocer who accepted chickens as trade for groceries. My dad's job was to kill and pluck the chickens to be sold. As a result, he can't stand fowl of any kind, and he won't eat chickens or turkey, so we have to have a ham at every holiday. This is a nice, easy ham recipe that is always enjoyed.

Sesame Chicken

2 lb. boneless skinless chicken breasts

1 egg

3 Tbsp. flour

2 Tbsp. cornstarch

2 Tbsp. water

1 tsp. salt

2 tsp. vegetable oil

¼ tsp. baking soda

¼ tsp. white pepper

1 C. sugar

1 C. chicken broth

¾ C. vinegar

2 tsp. dark soy sauce

Sprinkle chili powder

1 tsp. vegetable oil

1 clove garlic, minced

½ C. water

¼ C. cornstarch

Vegetable oil

2 Tbsp. sesame seeds

(recipe continued on next page)

(Sesame Chicken, continued)

Cut chicken into pieces. In a bowl, beat egg. Add flour, 2 Tbsp. cornstarch, 2 Tbsp. water, salt, 2 tsp. vegetable oil, baking soda, and white pepper. Put in a gallon-size bag; put chicken pieces in the bag. Seal bag and refrigerate for 20–30 minutes. In a saucepan, combine sugar, chicken broth, vinegar, dark soy sauce, chili powder, 1 tsp. vegetable oil, and garlic; bring to a boil. In a measuring cup, stir together ½ C. water and ¼ C. cornstarch. Stir cornstarch mixture into the saucepan. Cook, stirring constantly, until thickened. Remove from heat; keep warm. Heat small amount of vegetable oil in a wok or skillet. Fry the chicken pieces until done. When done, drain chicken on paper towels, and place in warm oven. Once all chicken is cooked, place on a platter. Pour warm sauce over the chicken. Sprinkle with sesame seeds. Makes 12 servings.

Heidi Miller
Texarkana Ward
Shreveport Louisiana Stake
Ashdown, Arkansas

Sweet and Sour Sauce

1 C. sugar
⅔ C. pineapple juice
½ C. vinegar
½ C. water

½ C. ketchup
1 Tbsp. soy sauce
¼ C. cornstarch
¼ C. water

Combine sugar, pineapple juice, vinegar, water, ketchup, and soy sauce in a pot and cook over medium heat. Let sugar dissolve and bring to a light boil. In a small bowl, combine cornstarch and water; mix well so that there are no lumps. Pour cornstarch mixture into boiling pot and stir for 1 minute. You can also add pineapple chunks or chunks of bell pepper. Makes about 3 cups.

Nancy King
Desert Valley Ward
Desert Ridge Arizona Stake
Mesa, Arizona

I love my mother. Now being a mother myself, I know of the many sacrifices she made and continues to make for me. It is true that a mother's love never ends. This Sweet and Sour Sauce reminds me of my childhood and the love and safety I feel from my mother. She would make it gallons at a time because all five of her children would practically drink it. Thanks, Mom, for the best Sweet and Sour Sauce—and for being my mom.

Apricot Chicken

1 C. cooked white beans (cooked in chicken noodle soup)
2 small chicken breasts, chopped
1 onion, diced (I used dried onion)
1 env. French onion soup mix

1 tin apricots, most of them blended to make nectar
1 handful TVP (textured vegetable protein), cooked chickpeas, or raw red lentils

Place all ingredients into a microwave bowl or saucepan. Stir to combine, and cook until chicken is cooked. Serve on cooked rice with greens on the side. Makes 5–6 servings.

Laura Russell
Gosford Ward
Newcastle Australia Stake
Springfield NSW
Australia

My mum, one of fifteen children, had to leave school at an early age to look after her younger brothers and sisters. She always encouraged everyone to go to school, specialized courses, TAFE, or college and to study, telling all to never give up. When my dad was on overseas assignments, I remember curling up in my mum's bed with her, my sister, and my two brothers while mum told us stories or read to us. She has read to all my children and told them stories of her childhood. She continued to serve all her life and loved to do family history. She lost her battle with cancer in April 2006, and I lost my best friend. She loved her Heavenly Father, and served Him all the days of her life. She is truly missed.

Fish Tacos

Fish:
1 C. fish batter mix
1 C. water
Dash salt
3 lb. halibut
Vegetable oil for deep-frying

Taco Shells:
18 corn tortillas

Slaw:
½ head cabbage, thinly
    sliced
3 tomatoes, chopped
3 green onions, sliced
Juice from 1 lime
Salt and pepper to taste

Chipotle Lime Tartar Sauce:
1–1½ canned adobe chipotle
    peppers
1½ C. mayonnaise
1 Tbsp. onion, chopped
2 Tbsp. pickle relish
Juice of ¼ lime
Dash of salt, garlic salt, and
    pepper

Fish: In a medium bowl, combine batter mix, water, and salt. Cut fish into bite-size pieces, dip pieces in the batter, and fry until golden brown.

Slaw: In a large bowl, combine cabbage, tomatoes, and green onions. Add lime juice, salt, and pepper to taste.

Chipotle Lime Tartar Sauce: Into a blender, put desired amount of chipotle peppers (depending on how spicy you want the tartar sauce), mayonnaise, and onion. Blend until well incorporated. Stir in pickle relish and lime juice. Season with salt, garlic salt, and pepper.

Taco Shells: Deep-fry tortillas in same oil used to fry the fish. As each tortilla fries, use a large spoon to press the middle of the tortilla to make a taco shell shape; fry until golden brown, about 30 seconds.

To assemble, load taco shell with halibut, slaw, chipotle lime tartar sauce, salsa, limes, and salt. Makes 5–7 servings.

Emerson Croxton
BYU–Idaho 10th Ward
BYU–Idaho 2nd Stake
Rexburg, Idaho

Chicken Tetrazzini

1 10-oz. pkg. very thin spaghetti noodles
6 Tbsp. butter
¾ C. cream

5 chicken breasts, cooked
Garlic salt
½ C. Parmesan cheese

Boil and drain noodles. In a frying pan, toss noodles with butter and cream. Chop chicken; stir in to cream. Salt to taste with garlic salt. Toss until warm. Add Parmesan cheese and toss lightly. Makes 6–8 servings.

Miriam Housley
Battlecreek 10th Ward
Pleasant Grove Utah East Stake
Pleasant Grove, Utah

My mom used to make Chicken Tetrazzini every time someone in our ward got sick or injured. She would make this gigantic batch and split it between our family and theirs. Then she would always make me come with her to deliver it. I have never seen people so grateful to get a meal. Whether it was a new baby, a cold, or an accident, they all needed a hug and a warm meal. Seeing my mom smile and comfort all these families while delivering relief is a treasured memory for me.

(Emerson Croxton's Fish Tacos) I love my mother very much, and I grew up learning to cook at her side. I wanted to cook all the time when I was young, and my mom taught me what she knew and suffered through some of my culinary experiments. I have no specific memories to share, only years of bonding and growing closer to my mother over the stove. I have loved cooking for many years, and I think that's because I watched my mom serve so many people in our kitchen. I saw how she made other people happy through good food. I feel that food brings people together and makes them happy. I also feel that food tastes better when you have "the touch"—the ability to make food with love, which is really what my mom taught me: to love others and serve them in whatever way you can. Love is the greatest thing my mother taught me. I grew very close to my mom through cooking and being in the kitchen with her, and I would never trade those memories for anything. Love you, Mom, and thank you so much for teaching me to love and to cook.

Topside Beef

1 "square" topside or silverside beef roast

2–3 garlic cloves, cut into slivers

2 Tbsp. butter

2 Tbsp. oil

1 large onion, chopped

1 liter monis red grape juice (US equivalent, Martinelli's)

1 can creamed mushrooms or 1 can sliced mushrooms AND/OR

1 10.75-oz. can cream of mushroom soup

Soy sauce

Cornstarch for thickening

Spike roast with slivers of garlic. In a large frying pan, melt butter and oil; sear all sides of the roast. Remove roast from pan. Fry onion in same pan until onion is "glassy," adding more butter and oil if necessary. Place roast in a roasting pan; add onions, grape juice, and mushrooms (you can use canned mushrooms OR the mushroom soup OR both). The meat must be covered. If your roasting pan is too large, put the roast in a pouch of tin foil so that the liquid completely covers the meat. Cover and cook at 350 for 2–3 hours. Add soy sauce to taste (instead of using salt). Remove roast from sauce, shred the meat, and return meat to the roasting pan. Thicken sauce with mixture of cornstarch and water; the amount depends on how thick you want the sauce. Serve over rice, with a side of garden peas and fresh green salad. Makes about 8 servings.

Lesley Nell
Roodepoort Ward
Roodepoort Stake
Roodepoort, South Africa

My mother always made this when she had missionaries over for lunch on a Sunday. When I was no longer living at home, I made sure I wangled a lunch invite whenever I knew she was making this. Everyone would go back for seconds and thirds just because it tastes so good! My mom had ten children, and I think all would agree that this is her best recipe. We grew up calling it "Beef Stroganoff," but after making beef stroganoff in a high-school cooking class, I realized my mom's roast was not beef stroganoff. In 2004 I went back to South Africa to visit my mom while she was undergoing chemotherapy for her second round of breast cancer; I remember sitting on the edge of her bed and asking her the details of this recipe and other favorites. My mom died at age sixty-two of breast cancer. My name is Beverly Ledward, and though I grew up in South Africa, I now live in Herriman, Utah, and am a member of the Ledward Pioneer Ward. I put my mother's name on this recipe in her memory.

Hamburger Gravy

1 lb. ground beef
1 pkg. dry onion soup mix
3½ C. water
Salt and pepper to taste

Cornstarch or flour for thickening
1 10.75-oz. can condensed cream of
    mushroom soup (optional)

Brown ground beef; drain. Add onion soup mix and water. Mix well. Simmer for 15–20 minutes. Add salt and pepper to taste. Thicken to gravy consistency using cornstarch or flour mixed with a little water. Use as gravy over cooked, diced potatoes. *Optional:* Add can of cream of mushroom soup before thickening as gravy. Makes 6 servings.

Hamburgers in Gravy

1 lb. ground beef OR 5 preformed beef patties
1 10.75-oz. can French onion soup
1 C. water

1 10.75-oz. can cream of mushroom soup
1 C. water
Salt, pepper, garlic powder to taste

Shape ground beef into patties. Fry until browned. Drain grease. Add French onion soup and water. Simmer for 15–20 minutes. When patties are completely cooked, add cream of mushroom soup and mix well. Serve with potatoes. Makes 5–6 servings.

As a child, I loved these recipes, and they conitinue to be a favorites of mine. My mother made them frequently. My dad is German, and he wasn't a happy camper without a meal of meat and potatoes. He didn't like rice or noodles! This was always a challenge to my mother, who loved noodles and casseroles. Now that I'm a mom of five boys and two girls, keeping them full is a challenge—but they all love these recipes! I usually double or triple the recipes, and they can be made quickly. At one time we had fifteen children living with us—our own, as well as foreign exchange students and a few friends of our children. It was nice to feed them something yummy and filling. Now three of my children are married with families of their own; five have served missions, and our sixth just received his call to serve in the Nagoya Japan Mission. That leaves just one more, our sixteen-year-old, to serve.

Betty Pearson
Dry Creek Ward
Lehi Utah South Stake
Lehi, Utah

Barbecue Beef

6- to 8-lb. beef roast

1 onion, sliced

Seasoned salt

1 onion, chopped

2 Tbsp. oil

2 Tbsp. cornstarch

2 C. water (or juice from cooking the meat)

1 C. ketchup

1 pt. chili sauce

1 tsp. onion salt

1 Tbsp. Worcestershire sauce

1 Tbsp. chili powder

1 tsp. paprika

½ tsp. pepper

4 Tbsp. vinegar

½ C. brown sugar

¼ tsp. ground allspice

2 Tbsp. prepared mustard

Place the beef roast in a large pan or slow cooker; cover with onion slices and sprinkle with seasoned salt. (I put the frozen roast in a slow cooker and cook it on low for about 12 hours. I do this a day ahead and refrigerate the beef.) Remove the beef from the pan; slice, trimming off all the fat. To prepare the barbecue sauce, sauté chopped onions in oil. Blend cornstarch in the water. Add cornstarch mixture, ketchup, and chili sauce to sautéed onions. (Use a chili sauce that is mainly tomato sauce with some spices, but not one that is too spicy.) Stir in remaining ingredients. Simmer 15 minutes. In a deep casserole dish, layer sliced beef and sauce, ending with sauce on top. Cover and bake at 200 for at least 2 hours; the beef gets better the longer it cooks. Makes 24–32 servings.

Sister Jill Andersen
Mongolia Ulaanbaatar Mission
Ulaanbaatar, Mongolia

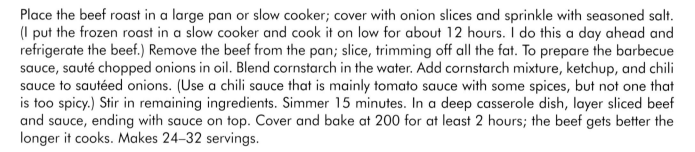

I am the mission president's wife, and we aren't really attached to a ward or a branch in Mongolia. We visit different ones each Sunday. We live in Ulaanbaatar and are in the Mongolia Ulaanbaatar Mission. We have two districts, one stake, and twenty-one units in Mongolia (three of the units are mission branches that are not in a stake or district). Mongolia is twice the size of Texas, and we have branches 1500 km to the west and 700 km to the east and 200 km to the north of Ulaanbaatar. The Church has been in Mongolia for sixteen years, and there are 9000 members. Our mission has 180 young missionaries and 14 senior missionaries. I do a huge amount of cooking, and it's a constant challenge to find recipes suitable for large numbers and to adapt them to the tastes and available ingredients where we serve. My mother-in-law, who also served as a mission president's wife, gave me this recipe. It is a family favorite that has also become a mission favorite. I serve it with a potato casserole, green salad, and various canned vegetables.

Italian Pasta

3½ C. flour
½ tsp. salt
3 large eggs, beaten

1 Tbsp. water
1 Tbsp. extra-virgin olive oil

Mix the flour and salt. Place the flour in a mound on a clean surface. Make a well in the center and add beaten eggs, water, and oil. Knead together by hand, just like bread dough, for about 15 minutes, until dough is stiff. Cover with plastic wrap and let dough stand for about half an hour. Roll the dough out with a rolling pin as thin as you can, or you can roll it through a pasta machine. Cut into desired shapes. To cook: In a large stock pot, place about 8 quarts of water; add salt and a little oil to the water. Bring water to a boil before adding pasta. Cook fresh pasta for about a minute, or until "al dente." Drain with a strainer and top with your favorite sauce; my favorite is Ham, Peas, and Tomato Cream Sauce (see recipe below). Makes 4 servings.

Ham, Peas, and Tomato Cream Sauce

2 Tbsp. butter
1 onion, chopped
2½ C. canned crushed tomatoes
1 tsp. salt
¼ tsp. freshly ground black pepper

½ C. cream
1 lb. cheese tortellini OR 1 lb. Italian Pasta
¼ lb. ham, diced into ¼-inch pieces
¾ C. frozen petite peas, thawed

In a large frying pan, melt butter over moderately low heat. Add the onion; cook, stirring occasionally, until onion starts to soften, about 3 minutes. Stir in the tomatoes with their juice, salt, and pepper. Simmer for 10 minutes. Add the cream and cook for 1 minute longer. Meanwhile, in a large pot of boiling, salted water, cook the tortellini until just done—about 4 minutes for fresh, 12 minutes for frozen. If using Italian Pasta, cook fresh pasta for 1 minute. Drain the pasta and add it to the pan with the sauce. Stir in the ham and peas and cook until warmed through, about 2 minutes. Makes 4 servings.

Sara Castellani
Nuernberg Ward
Nuernberg Germany Stake
Nuernberg, Germany

Norwegian Meatballs

2 lbs. ground beef

2 C. saltine cracker crumbs

Salt and pepper to taste

3 eggs

1 onion, chopped

3 10.75-oz. cans chicken and rice soup,
    drained; reserve broth for gravy

2 14.5-oz. cans chicken broth

2 Tbsp. cornstarch

In a large bowl, combine ground beef, cracker crumbs, salt, pepper, eggs, onions, and drained soup (reserve the broth). Using an ice cream scoop, make large meatballs. Brown meatballs in a large electric skillet. Remove meatballs from skillet and pour off grease. Stir in the reserved chicken broth and the 2 cans of chicken broth. Mix the cornstarch with a little water and pour into the broth using a wisk. Stir the gravy with the wisk, pulling up all the bits from the bottom of the skillet. When the gravy has thickened, place meatballs back in the skillet and cook at 350 for 1 hour. You can also put the meatballs and gravy in a casserole dish and bake in the oven at 350 for 1 hour. Serve with mashed potatoes. Makes 12–14 servings.

Lindsey Falk
Alta Vista Ward
Red Rock Nevada Stake
Las Vegas, Nevada

We had a great neighborhood growing up in Las Vegas. There were twenty-seven kids under the age of six in a cul-de-sac of twelve homes! One of our neighbors, who was from Minnesota, started making these Norwegian Meatballs whenever anyone had a baby. Soon my mom started making them as a regular dinner for us. They are a great comfort food, and they heat up the next day wonderfully! They make a lot, so you can feed your family and another family with one recipe. Now it's a tradition: whenever one of us has a baby, our mom makes us Norwegian Meatballs; we also take them to others who have had a baby or who have come home from the hospital. You will enjoy this great comfort food!

Real West Virginia Hot Dawgs

Hot Dawgs:
8 hot dogs, cooked—bun length if possible
8 hot dog buns, steamed
Mustard
Hot Dawg Sauce
"Cold" Slaw
3 Tbsp. onion, chopped

Hot Dawg Sauce:
½ lb. ground beef
1 8-oz. can tomato sauce
1 Tbsp. Worcestershire (or, as we say "What's-'is-here") sauce
1 tsp. chili powder
Dash pepper
Dash salt

"Cold" Slaw:
1 head cabbage, washed and shredded
2–3 Tbsp. salad dressing (Miracle Whip)
Splash apple cider vinegar
1 tsp. sugar or equivalent sugar substitute

Hot Dawgs: Steam buns by sprinkling water into the opened bag of buns, twisting the bag closed, and microwaving for 10 seconds. Place a cooked hot dog (grilled is best, but boiled will do) on a freshly steamed bun. Stripe dog with mustard, top with 2 Tbsp. Hot Dawg Sauce, then 1 Tbsp. slaw, and finish with 1 tsp. chopped onion.

Hot Dawg Sauce: Combine all ingredients in a small saucepan and cook over medium heat until the meat is done.

"Cold" Slaw: Place cabbage in a large bowl. In a small bowl mix salad dressing, vinegar, and sugar until smooth (should be the consistency of salad dressing). Taste! Add more of whatever you need to add. Remember: You can always add more, but you can't take any out, so add in small amounts! When it tastes right, pour mixture over cabbage and toss well. Makes enough for 8 hot dawgs plus extra slaw.

Patrick Casdorph
Charleston 1st Ward
Charleston West Virginia Stake
South Charleston, West Virginia

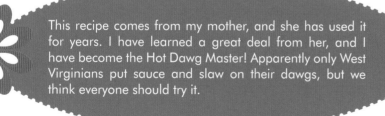

This recipe comes from my mother, and she has used it for years. I have learned a great deal from her, and I have become the Hot Dawg Master! Apparently only West Virginians put sauce and slaw on their dawgs, but we think everyone should try it.

Chicken Rolls

2 chicken breasts, cooked (can use canned chicken)

1 8-oz. pkg. cream cheese

½ 10.75-oz. can cream of chicken soup

2 tubes refrigerated crescent roll dough

Water or egg, beaten

1 C. Italian bread crumbs

Shred chicken. In a large bowl, combine chicken, cream cheese, and cream of chicken soup. Separate crescent rolls; put a spoonful of chicken mixture in the middle of each. Roll the crescent roll up to completely surround the chicken mixture. Dab the outside of each roll with water or egg and then roll in Italian bread crumbs. Bake at 350 for 15–20 minutes or until golden brown. Makes 16 servings.

Erika Howard
BYU–Idaho 37th Ward
BYU–Idaho 5th Stake
Rexburg, Idaho

This is just one of the fabulous recipes my mother has taught me to cook. As a child I helped her cook dinner for me and my brothers and sister; those were some of my favorite times, because I absolutely loved cooking. It was always a challenge to cook these chicken rolls in my family, because we love eating dough. We would be in the middle of making the rolls, and would look down to see that the dough was gone. We had to chase people away from eating it—but unbeknownst to us at that time, my mom was the biggest culprit. I think she ate more of the dough than anyone else. When we finally figured that out, we all had a good laugh. Luckily, we still had enough for dinner. My mother has been a great inspiration to me; she has always encouraged me to follow my dreams. Without her I would not be the person I am. I love my mom and all she has taught me. She is so funny, and when we get together as a family there is not a minute that we are not laughing. She has blessed my life and the life of my family.

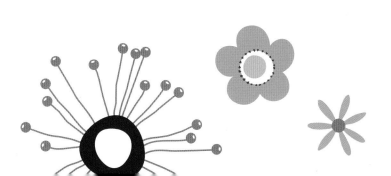

Empanadas de Horno

Dough:
6 C. flour
1 Tbsp. baking powder
4 Tbsp. shortening
¾ C. milk with dash of salt

Pino:
5 onions, diced
¼ C. oil
1 lb. ground beef
1 Tbsp. chili oil or chili powder
Oregano, salt, and pepper to taste
1 C. water
1 Tbsp. flour
2 eggs, hard-boiled
½ C. raisins
30 olives
Dab of milk
2 egg whites

Dough: In a large bowl, mix the flour and baking powder; add the shortening (do not melt it!) and work it into the flour mixture with a fork. Mix in the milk and salt. Knead until the dough is tender. Form dough into a long roll and divide into six servings. Roll out each portion into a thin layer 6 inches in diameter.

Pino: Brown onions in oil. Add meat and seasonings. Add the water and let simmer for 15 minutes. Sprinkle flour over all and stir in. Remove from heat and let cool. Place 2 tablespoons of Pino in each circle of dough. Add a slice of boiled egg, as many raisins as you'd like, and 5 olives. Wet the rim of dough with milk and fold over. Press closed. Paint with egg white. Using a knife, pierce the center of the pie. Bake at 350 for about 20 minutes, or until dough is browned. Makes 6 servings.

Karla Redfearn
French Creek Ward
Parker Colorado Stake
Parker, Colorado

I grew up in Santiago, Chile, and this is a famous recipe in Chile. What makes it so special to me is the tradition my family had of getting together to make this dish and share. I still remember the time my grandma, mom, and I spent in the kitchen and the patience they had to teach me. I'm still trying to get it right! So for me, it's the memories that make it so special, not just the taste.

Pennsylvania Dutch Onion Pie (Zwiebelkuchen)

Crust:

1½ C. flour

3 Tbsp. sugar

2 tsp. baking powder

¾ tsp. salt

⅓ C. shortening

1 egg

¼ C. milk

Filling:

2 Tbsp. bacon fat (or butter)

1½ C. onions, peeled and sliced

Pinch salt

2 eggs

1½ Tbsp. flour

2 C. milk

1–2 slices bacon

Pepper

Crust: Sift together flour, sugar, baking powder, and salt. Cut in shortening. In a small bowl, combine egg and milk; add to dry ingredients. Mix to form a soft dough. Roll out and line a 9-inch pie plate.

Filling: Melt fat in skillet; add onion and fry over moderate heat until translucent, stirring occasionally. Add just a pinch of salt. Spread onions in the bottom of pastry-lined pan. In a large bowl, beat eggs into flour. Add milk; pour mixture over onions in pan. Cut bacon into small squares and dot over all. Sprinkle with pepper. Bake on lower rack of 400-degree oven for 10 minutes. Reduce heat to 350 and finish baking until custard is set. Do not let filling boil. Makes 6–8 servings.

Kenneth Lee
Morrisville Pennsylvania Ward
Philadelphia Pennsylvania Stake
Levittown, Pennsylvania

Mom was proud of her German heritage, and a lot of her cooking showed that influence. However, Mom did not start making this recipe until her father came to live with us. Grandpop Frey claimed he didn't like onions—only when he knew that onions were in the food. This pie was the one exception, and he often asked Mom to make it for him. It wasn't long before the rest of the family was asking her for it as well.

Mom's Sweet Baked Pineapple Ham

1 C. maple syrup

1 C. orange juice

1 C. ginger ale

½ C. packed brown sugar

½ C. honey

1 10-oz. jar maraschino cherries, halved

1 10-lb. fully-cooked, bone-in ham

1 15.25-oz. can pineapple rings in juice, drained

Round wooden toothpicks

In a medium bowl, mix the maple syrup, orange juice, ginger ale, brown sugar, and honey. Stir in the juice from the maraschino cherries and half of the cherries. Score the outer edge of the ham with a sharp knife in a diamond pattern. Cuts should be about ¼-inch deep; this will allow the ham to soak up the juice. Place the ham into an oven bag, and carefully pour the juice mixture over it, keeping all of the juice in the bag. It may look like there is too much juice, but the ham will soak it up while baking. Place the pineapple rings on top of the ham; secure rings with toothpicks. Place a cherry in the center of each ring and secure the cherry with a toothpick. Tie the end of the bag closed and place in a large roasting pan. Let marinate overnight in the refrigerator. Before putting the ham in the oven, cut a few small slits in the top of the oven bag. Bake at 350 for 2½–3 hours (it may take longer, depending on the oven). The internal temperature should be 160 when the ham is done; be sure the thermometer is not touching the bone when taking the temperature. Remove ham from bag to a serving plate, and let stand for 10 minutes before carving. Makes 18 servings.

Claire and Ammon Mandrake
Bismarck Ward
Bismarck North Dakota Stake
Bismarck, North Dakota

We have made this ham every Easter, Thanksgiving, and Christmas for as long as I can remember. I have even made it for no particular holiday at all. I remember one time my mom accidentally dropped the ham on the floor, and our two little Yorkies just went crazy over it. As a result, my aunt ended up bringing us a ham that was already cooked. That was the holiday we didn't have our precious ham—and I think that's when we all realized how much we loved my mom's ham. None other has yet to compare. It's true—"you don't know what you've got 'til it's gone." This is a recipe that will be in our family for a long, long time.

Beef and Biscuit Casserole

1–1¼ lb. ground beef
½ C. onion, chopped
¼ C. green pepper, diced
1 8-oz. can tomato sauce
½ tsp. chili pepper
½ tsp. garlic salt

1 can country-style or buttermilk biscuits
1½ C. cheddar cheese, shredded and divided
½ C. sour cream
1 egg, slightly beaten

In a large frying pan, brown ground beef, onion, and green pepper. Drain. Stir in tomato sauce, chili pepper, and garlic salt. Let simmer while preparing dough. Separate biscuits into 10 pieces. Pull each apart into two layers. Press half the biscuit layers into the bottom of an ungreased 9-inch square pan. Remove meat from heat. In a small bowl, combine ½ C. cheddar cheese and sour cream. Stir into meat mixture. Spoon over dough. Arrange remaining biscuit layers on top, sprinkle with remaining cheese. Bake at 375 for 25–30 minutes until golden brown. Makes 4–6 servings.

Janet Gerla
Grand Forks North Dakota Ward
Fargo North Dakota Stake
Climax, Minnesota

My mom was a wonderful mother. She and my dad were married for thirty years and had three children, but my dad left when I was just eleven. My mom had to go back to work and worked hard to raise us children, and she did a remarkable job on her own. We lived on Long Island in New York at the time. She was always my Girl Scout leader and took us camping quite often. My mom was not afraid to take us anywhere. We did not have a lot of money, but we had a lot of fun. We ate a lot of casseroles! I fixed many after school while waiting for my mom to get home from work. Many years later, my dad came to visit me in Grand Forks, North Dakota. My mom had moved there to be closer to us, and we always had Mom over on Friday nights. My dad came one Friday night, and the next night he took Mom out to dinner. To make a long story short, they were remarried the following May! I have always been so proud of my mom and her willingness to forgive and forget. They have had a wonderful twenty years together, so far—the second time around. I have learned a lot from my mom's example!

Chicken with Glazed Pears

6 Tbsp. olive oil

6–10 chicken breasts, cut into bite-size pieces

Salt and pepper

Flour for dusting

2 large onions, thinly sliced

4 cloves garlic, thinly sliced

4 sprigs thyme

4 sprigs rosemary

1 lb. small red potatoes, halved

2 1/3 C. chicken stock, divided

4 Tbsp. butter

1/2 C. packed brown sugar

3 pears, peeled, cored, and cut into wedges

Heat olive oil in a Dutch oven or large pot over medium-high heat. Season chicken with salt and pepper. Place flour in a shallow dish and coat the chicken with flour, shaking off any excess. Add the chicken to the hot oil and brown on all sides. Once the chicken is browned all over, add onions and cook for 3–4 minutes, until softened. Add the garlic, thyme, and rosemary, and cook for another 2 minutes. Add the potatoes and cook until they begin to brown. Add 1/3 C. chicken stock and reduce for about 2 minutes. Stir in 2 C. chicken stock and bring to a boil. Stir well so that everything is mixed together. Cover and reduce the heat to medium and simmer for 45 minutes, or until the chicken is cooked through. While the chicken is cooking, make the glazed pears. In a skillet, combine butter and brown sugar. Place pears in the pan. Increase the heat to medium-high. Shake the pan to make sure all the pears are coated with the glaze. Cook until the fruit is easily pierced with a knife. Serve chicken and potatoes with some of the glazed pears on top. Makes 6–10 servings.

Audra Behling
Dutch Flat Ward
Ferron Utah Stake
Ferron, Utah

Kielbasa and Mushroom Penne

1 lb. dried penne pasta
1 lb. bulk kielbasa (or any smoked sausage)
2 Tbsp. olive oil
½ onion, chopped
2 garlic cloves, pressed
1 8-oz. package mushrooms, sliced

¼ tsp. salt
¼ tsp. pepper
1 C. heavy cream
½ C. Parmesan cheese, grated
1 C. mozzarella cheese, shredded

Cook penne in boiling salted water (2 Tbsp. salt for 6 qts. water) until al dente. Reserve ½ C. water from the pasta. Drain. Transfer pasta to a baking dish. Meanwhile, cook sausage in a skillet in oil, stirring occasionally. Add onion and garlic; cook until almost brown. Add mushrooms, and cook until mushrooms are golden. Add reserved pasta water, salt, pepper, and heavy cream; cook for 4 minutes. Pour over pasta, stir in cheeses. Broil about 5 minutes, or until golden brown in spots. Serve with a green salad. Makes 6 servings.

I made this recipe for my new husband the first week we were married. It was also the first meal my mom made for my dad thirty-one years ago in Brazil. I still love to ask my mom to make it any time I go to her house to visit.

Sandra Matthews
Pembroke Pines Ward
Ft. Lauderdale Florida Stake
Pembroke Pines, Florida

Empanadas Chilenas

2½ lb. beef roast
1 clove garlic
1 onion
3 cloves
1 carrot, chopped
1½ C. raisins
3 Tbsp. olive oil
1 onion, minced

3 tsp. oregano
3 tsp. cumin seed, crushed
2 Tbsp. ground chile
1 tsp. salt
¼ C. slivered almonds
1 C. black olives, sliced
¼ C. shortening
2 Tbsp. butter

3 C. flour
1 tsp. salt
½ C. plus 1 Tbsp. water
Canola oil for frying
2 Tbsp. sugar (optional)

(recipe continued on next page)

(Empanadas Chilenas, continued)

Cut meat in half; place in a heavy pot and cover with cold water. Add garlic, whole onion, cloves, and carrot. Simmer gently for 2 hours. When the meat is tender, turn off heat and let the meat cool in the broth until warm to the touch. Remove meat from the broth, but reserve the broth. Using a sharp knife, chop meat very finely; my mother puts the meat in a bowl and uses a chopper with a curved blade. In a small saucepan, barely cover the raisins with water. Bring the water almost to boiling, then turn the heat off and let the raisins soak in the hot water while you continue preparing the dish. In a large skillet, heat the olive oil; add the minced onion and cook until softened. Stir in the oregano and cumin and cook for another minute. Stir in the chopped beef, ground chile, and salt. Cook for 15 minutes, adding enough of the reserved broth to make the mixture wet but not soggy. Remove from the heat. Drain the raisins and stir them into the meat mixture. Add the almonds and olives. Taste, and add more salt, oregano, cumin, or chile powder, if desired. If the meat mixture seems a bit drier than you like, add more broth or some of the raisin water. Refrigerate overnight, or up to 3 days. Make the pastry: Using a large fork or pastry blender, cut the shortening and butter into the flour until crumbly. Stir the salt into the water. Drizzle the salt water slowly over the flour mixture, adding just enough to make a soft, pliable dough. Knead gently on a floured board for 1 minute. The dough should be nice and soft and smooth. Divide the dough into 24 little balls or 12 bigger balls. Keep covered in a bowl so they don't dry out. Roll each ball into a circle. Place ½ C. of the meat filling on half of the circle. Fold over the top half, pinching the edges; press with a fork to seal. If the edges don't get pressed together well enough to seal them, the filling will leak out when they are fried. In a deep skillet, heat 2 inches of canola oil. Fry the empanadas in the hot oil for about 1½ minutes; turn them over and cook for about another 1½ minutes. Drain on paper towels and sprinkle with sugar if you want. You can reheat them later in the oven by baking them at 350 for about 10 minutes. Makes 12 very large empanadas or 24 small turnovers.

My mom is a wonderful cook. She makes me these empanadas and *tortas fritas* (fried potatoes) and *arroz* (rice); she cares for me and loves me a lot. I have learned to make only a few things in the kitchen, and I cook only when my mom isn't here. I am seventeen, and in two years I will be a missionary. I hope to serve in the United States. I was baptized on June 8, 2008. My mom, Marcela Salas, was baptized three years ago.

Robert Hart Salas
Calle Larga Ward
Talca Stake
Talca, Chile

Mexican Pulled Pork Soft Tacos

1 medium onion, coarsely chopped

1 3.5- to 5-lb. boneless pork shoulder roast

1 medium red pepper, diced

1 medium green pepper, diced

1 15-oz. can jalapeno-flavored diced tomatoes

1½ tsp. garlic salt

1½ tsp. oregano or Italian seasoning

½ tsp. cayenne red pepper (optional)

1 4-oz. can diced green chiles (mild)

1 6-oz. can tomato paste

½ C. water

1 15-oz. can corn kernels, drained

1 15-oz. can black beans, rinsed and drained

Tortillas

In slow cooker layer chopped onion, pork roast, and sweet peppers. In medium bowl, combine all ingredients except corn, beans, and tortillas. Pour evenly over mixture in slow cooker. Cover cooker and cook on high 5½ hours. Add corn and beans during the last 30 minutes. Pull meat apart with two forks and place into warmed tortillas; top with cheese and lettuce if desired. Roll and pour liquid over tacos to smother them. Makes 8 servings.

Kiefer, Sawyer, and Carly Nunley
Emigration 6th Ward
Emigration Utah Stake
Salt Lake City, Utah

Cooking has always been a favorite pastime in our family. Our mother loves to cook, and we love to cook with her. Our sister has her very own knife and is very careful about how she uses it. She stirs, mixes, cuts, and kneads bread right along with our mother. Even we boys help in the kitchen because it seems like we are always hungry, and we have figured out that we can learn to cook things on our own. Our grandfather came from a family of sixteen children, and our mother is one of six children. Cooking in large quantities was normal for them, and they gathered for every occasion when our great-grandmother was alive. Now our grandmother is eighty-seven and unable to cook for everyone like she used to, but our mother not only cooks for her, but teaches us grandmother's specific favorite recipes so we can help cook for her.

Mom's Meatloaf

Meatloaf:

1 C. seasoned stuffing mix
(Stove Top)
Milk (enough to cover
stuffing)
1½ lb. ground beef
½ lb. sausage

1 egg
1 8-oz. can tomato sauce
½ medium onion, chopped
1 Tbsp. sage
Dash of pepper
1 env. onion soup mix

Topping:

1 C. ketchup
2 Tbsp. brown sugar
1 tsp. mustard

Place stuffing in bowl. Cover with just enough milk to moisten dry bread crumbs. Stir. Dump in the remaining meatloaf ingredients and mix with a spoon (or your hands). Press into a 9 x 13-inch pan (use an 8 x 8-inch pan if you prefer a thicker meatloaf). To make the topping, combine ketchup, brown sugar, and mustard, and spread over meatloaf. Bake at 375 for 1 hour (longer for the smaller pan). Makes 6 servings.

I wasn't always the biggest fan of my mother's meatloaf; I remember as a little girl watching her mush the ground beef and sausage together with her hands, and thinking it was slightly disgusting. As I grew older and my palate became more refined, I realized her meatloaf was actually quite delicious. Now that I live a distance away, Mom's Meatloaf is one of my husband's favorite dishes. I especially love making it just like she did . . . I even get my hands dirty!

Courtney Davis
Golden Gate Ward
San Francisco California Stake
San Francisco, California

Garden Supper

2 C. soft bread cubes
½ C. sharp cheddar cheese, shredded
2 Tbsp. butter, melted
1 C. peas or other vegetable, cooked
2 Tbsp. onions, chopped
3 Tbsp. butter
3 Tbsp. flour

1 tsp. salt
½ tsp. pepper
1½ C. milk
1 C. meat, cooked and cut up
1 large tomato, sliced (optional)

(recipe continued on next page)

(Garden Supper, continued)

Preheat oven to 350. Combine bread cubes, cheese, and melted butter. Spread half of the mixture in a greased 1-quart casserole. Top with vegetables. In a large saucepan, cook and stir onion in the 3 Tbsp. butter until tender. Blend in flour, salt, and pepper. Cook over low heat, stirring until mixture is bubbly. Remove from heat. Stir in milk; return to heat and bring to a boil, stirring constantly. Boil, stirring constantly, 1 minute. Stir in meat; pour over vegetables. Arrange sliced tomato on top. Sprinkle remaining bread mixture on top and bake uncovered 25 minutes. Makes 4 servings.

Sharon Swanger
Harrisburg Ward
Harrisburg Pennsylvania Stake
Harrisburg, Pennsylvania

Chicken Enchilada Casserole

4 chicken breasts

1 small onion, chopped fine

1 10.75-oz. can cream of mushroom soup

1 10.75-oz. can cream of chicken soup

1 soup can milk

1 4-oz. can diced green chiles

Salt and pepper

1½ C. cheese, shredded

1 dozen corn tortillas, torn in quarters

Cook chicken with onion in small amount of water. Cool and break into small pieces. Mix in remaining ingredients except cheese and tortillas, adding salt and pepper to taste. In large casserole dish, form layers of tortillas pieces, chicken mix, and cheese. Bake at 350 for 30–45 minutes. Makes 6–8 servings.

Tami Baker
Bear Canyon Ward
Albuquerque New Mexico Stake
Albuquerque, New Mexico

Chinese Noodle Hamburger Casserole

1 10.75-oz. can cream of mushroom soup

1 10.75-oz. can cream of chicken soup

1½ C. water

1 lb. ground beef

1 medium onion, chopped

1 Tbsp. soy sauce

¼ tsp. pepper

½ C. uncooked rice

1 C. peas

1 C. chow mein noodles

Combine soups and water. Stir in all remaining ingredients except chow mein noodles, and pour into greased casserole dish. Bake covered at 350 for 30 minutes; uncover and cook 30 additional minutes. Stir in chow mein noodles, cover, and continue baking for 15 additional minutes. Makes 6 servings.

Becki Kress
Cottonwood Ward
Ucon Idaho Stake
Idaho Falls, Idaho

My mom always loved to try different recipes, and this was one that she used to make quite often. I always thought my mom was the best mom and cook that there was, and I appreciate that she always put such love into the meals that she prepared for her family. It has become a goal of mine to do the same for my children!

Pork and Chicken Adobo

4 Tbsp. cooking oil or olive oil, divided

1 head garlic, minced (about 2 Tbsp.)

½ yellow onion, diced

1½ lb. pork, cut in cubes

1 lb. chicken, cut into pieces

2 C. water

½ C. soy sauce, divided

1 C. vinegar

1 tsp. paprika

5 laurel leaves (bay leaves)

2 Tbsp. cornstarch

3 Tbsp. water

Salt and pepper to taste

(recipe continued on next page)

(Pork and Chicken Adobo, continued)

In a big pan or wok, heat 2 Tbsp. oil; sauté the garlic and onions. Add the pork and chicken to the pan. Stir in 2 C. water, ¼ C. soy sauce, vinegar, paprika, and laurel leaves. Bring to a boil. Cover and simmer for 30 minutes or until meat is tender. Remove the pork and chicken from the pan. In a separate pan, heat 2 Tbsp. oil and brown the pork and chicken for a few minutes. Mix the browned pork and chicken back into the sauce; add cornstarch dissolved in 3 Tbsp. water to thicken. Add salt and/or pepper, if desired. Bring to a boil; simmer for an additional 5 minutes. Serve hot with the gravy and plain rice. Makes 8 servings.

Iris Denielle LaGuardia
Binangonan Branch
Manila Stake
Binangonan, Rizal
Philippines

Chicken and Broccoli Casserole

2 10.75-oz. cans cream of chicken soup
1 C. mayonnaise
½ C. milk
2 Tbsp. lemon juice

¼ tsp. curry powder
2 lbs. chicken, cooked and cubed
3 C. broccoli, steamed (can use frozen)
1 C. cheese, shredded

Combine soup, mayonnaise, milk, lemon juice, and curry powder. In a casserole dish, layer half the chicken, one-third of the sauce, and half the broccoli; repeat, finishing with the final third of the sauce. Top with shredded cheese. Bake at 375 for 15–20 minutes, until the edges are bubbly. Serve with rice or pasta. Makes 8 servings.

Kirsten Woodbury
Murray 33rd Ward
Murray Utah Parkway Stake
Murray, Utah

This was my favorite food as a child. I constantly asked my mom to make it. I loved helping her, and it was such an exciting day when I got to make it for my family for the first time. Now I have a nine-year-old daughter, and this is her favorite food too. It is such a fun thing to have her helping me in the kitchen now. Making this recipe is such a comforting ritual that it's much more than just about the meal itself.

Mongolian Beef

1 Tbsp. light soy sauce

1 Tbsp. red wine vinegar

½ tsp. ginger, freshly grated

1 Tbsp. peanut oil

1 lb. beef flank steak, sliced thin across the
     grain

4 C. peanut oil for deep frying

2 cloves garlic, sliced thin

4 green onions, cut in 1-inch pieces

1 tsp. hoisin sauce

¼ tsp. ground white pepper

Combine soy sauce, vinegar, ginger, and 1 Tbsp. peanut oil. Marinate cut meat in marinade for at least 15 minutes. Drain marinade well and separate meat into individual pieces. In a wok or deep pan, heat 4 C. peanut oil to 375. Add meat all at once and stir to separate. Remove after 1 minute and allow meat to drain. Remove most of the oil from the wok and heat again; add garlic and green onions, and toss for just a minute. Add hoisin sauce, white pepper, and meat. Toss until heated through. Makes 4 servings.

Odgerel Bumandalai
Sansar Ward
Bayanzurkn District Khoroo 1
Ulaanbaatar, Mongolia

In Mongolia, almost everybody learns how to cook at home; girls especially like to help their mothers, so we try to learn cooking at a little younger age. My mom is a microbiologist who works at Mongolian Academy of Science. I hope to follow her example and become a microbiologist as well.

Carrot Sandwich Filling

1 8-oz. pkg. cream cheese, softened
2 ½ C. carrots, finely grated
2 Tbsp. onion, grated
Pinch of salt

2 heaping Tbsp. sandwich spread (Kraft or Heinz)
1 loaf bread, sliced horizontally
Sweet gherkin pickles

Beat cream cheese until smooth; stir in carrots, onion, salt, and sandwich spread. Cut the crusts off the bread. Lightly butter each slice and spread with filling. On the short end, place pickles to fit. Roll and wrap 2 or three rolls in waxed paper. Place the rolls in a plastic bag and refrigerate overnight. Slice with a serrated knife in ¼-inch slices and arrange on a fancy plate. Makes enough filling for 1 loaf of bread.

Faye Williamson
Cambridge 1st Ward
Kitchener Ontario Stake
Cambridge, Ontario
Canada

My grandmother was the quilt coordinator for her church in a small town in Ontario. She organized the quilts for the ladies to do and also planned the luncheon. These little tea sandwiches were often served along with many other fancy sandwiches. Every summer she had a party for the grandchildren where she served these sanwiches with a variety of fillings. I was the only one who was fascinated with how they were made. I started making these for my ward when a friend's daughter got married. They became popular, and now I make them for a varity of activities. People usually make a face when they hear it is a carrot sandwich, but that attitude doesn't last long. I hope you enjoy them.

Rotisserie-Style Chicken

4 tsp. salt

2 tsp. paprika

1 tsp. onion powder

1 tsp. dried thyme

1 tsp. white pepper

½ tsp. black pepper

½ tsp. cayenne pepper

½ tsp. garlic powder

2 4-lb. whole chickens

2 onions, quartered

In a small bowl, mix salt, paprika, onion powder, thyme, white pepper, black pepper, cayenne pepper, and garlic powder. Remove and discard giblets from chicken if they weren't already removed. Rinse chicken cavity and pat dry with paper towel. Rub each chicken inside and out with spice mixture. Be sure to get under wings and skin; leave no stone unturned. Place 1 quartered onion into the cavity of each chicken. Place chickens in a resealable bag or double wrap with plastic wrap. Refrigerate overnight, or at least 4–6 hours. Preheat oven to 250. Place chickens in a roasting pan. Bake uncovered for 5 hours, to a minimum internal temperature of 180. Let the chickens stand for 10 minutes before carving. Makes 10 servings.

JonRyan Reed
Seaford Ward
Wilmington Delaware Stake
Millsboro, Delaware

My mom is amazing in everything she does. When it comes to food, my mom made sure we tried everything at least once. If we didn't like it, we didn't have to eat it, but we at least had to try it. Because of that I feel we grew up to love unique foods, and we developed an appreciation for all kinds of different flavors. My mom also raised eight boys, so even though money was tight, she really knew how to be creative with what food we had. I am forever thankful for her love as well as her culinary excellence. This fabulous chicken is cooked low and slow. It makes the meat literally fall off the bone while still retaining all the moisture. It tastes like those deli rotisserie chickens you get at the grocery store, but better. It's very easy and doesn't require a lot of preparation work. This is a family favorite in our house. For smaller families, simply half everything and use one chicken instead of two. Hope you enjoy it!

Lemon Artichoke Chicken

6 chicken breasts
Salt and pepper
¼ C. butter
2 C. chicken broth, divided
4 Tbsp. lemon juice
1 Tbsp. grated lemon rind
2 Tbsp. flour

⅓ C. broth (or water)
1 lb. fresh mushrooms, sliced and sautéed
1 14-oz. can artichoke hearts, drained and cut in half
Parmesan cheese, grated
6 thin pats butter

Sprinkle the chicken breasts with salt and pepper. In a skillet, melt butter; sauté chicken on all sides until golden brown. (The chicken doesn't have to be cooked through.) Place chicken in a greased baking pan. Add ¼ C. broth to the hot skillet with the lemon juice and rind. Deglaze the pan, getting all those juicy bits off the bottom of the pan. Add the remaining 1¾ C. broth. In a small bowl, mix the flour and ⅓ C. broth or water until smooth; add to the skillet and stir until slightly thickened. (Taste the sauce to make sure it's lemony enough; if not, add more lemon juice.) Spoon the sautéed mushrooms over the chicken, then pour the lemon sauce over everything. Bake uncovered at 350 for 30–45 minutes. Remove from oven; top with artichoke hearts. Sprinkle generously with cheese. Put a pat of butter on top of each chicken breast and bake until lightly browned. Makes 6 servings. *Note:* We often cook the breasts with oil, leave all the butter out, and omit the cheese on top, since our daughter is allergic to dairy products. That method makes it a little more healthy as well!

Matthew Brockholt
Heatheridge 9th Ward
Orem Utah Heatheridge Stake
Orem, Utah

I grew up in a home where my mother cooked all the time. I never had a desire to eat at friends' houses, and when I did, it was never as good as Mom's cooking (although I never said so out loud—my mom did teach me manners, after all!). After I married my wife, my mother, Glynneth, became a wonderful mother-in-law who shared many recipes with my new wife. Those recipes were written on scraps of paper, covered in children's crayon scribbles, with notes about how to make the recipe perfect. I never turn down a meal cooked by my mother, but now I won't turn down a meal my wife makes, either! I love it when they make Lemon Artichoke Chicken.

Manhattan Rolls

Frozen bread dough (or fresh homemade
  bread dough)
2 lb. ground beef
1 10.75-oz. can cream of mushroom soup

1 10.75-oz. can cream of celery (or cream of
  chicken soup)
Homemade cheese sauce or Cheez Whiz,
  melted and thinned

Thaw bread dough per instructions. Brown ground beef; drain. Stir in undiluted soups. Roll out bread dough in a thin layer; spread mixture over top of dough. Roll bread up into a roll and cut into slices. Arrange on baking sheet. Bake at 350 until golden brown. Top with cheese sauce and serve. Makes 8 servings.

Arlene Russell
Lander Wyoming Ward
Lander Wyoming Stake
Hudson, Wyoming

I used to eat these in grade school and just loved them. I wanted to share them with my kids, so I made my best guess and came up with this recipe. My kids ask for these for their birthday dinners or other special occasions. My son, who has a family of his own, now makes them for his kids—a recipe handed down, and worth it!

Chicken Penne with Tomato Cream Sauce

1 lb. penne pasta
2 Tbsp. butter
1 onion, chopped
½ tsp. red pepper flakes
2 garlic cloves, minced
2 lb. Roma tomatoes, chopped

2 C. cream
1 C. frozen peas
½ tsp. salt
Fresh ground pepper
Whole roasted chicken, boned and chopped

Cook pasta according to package directions. In a large pan, melt butter; stir in onion and red pepper flakes and cook until soft. Stir in garlic; sauté for a few minutes. Stir in tomatoes and cream. Increase heat to high. Cook until reduced and thick. Stir in peas, salt, pepper, cooked chicken, and cooked pasta. Stir to coat and enjoy! Makes 4–6 servings.

Shondra Ceci
Peachtree City Ward
Jonesboro Georgia Stake
Peachtree City, Georgia

I love to cook, and one day I created this dish. Now it is a regular on the menu. This recipe is so versatile that you can add broccoli instead of the peas, or just leave out the chicken.

Sausage Pasta Sauce

3 Tbsp. olive oil

6 good-quality Italian sausages

2 14-oz. cans diced tomatoes (can be puréed to make a finer texture)

1 6-oz. can tomato paste

2 cans water (tomato paste can)

1 can cooking sherry (tomato paste can)

2 Tbsp. garlic powder or whole cloves of fresh garlic (use more if using fresh garlic)

1 celery rib (with leaves is better)

1–2 carrots, peeled

1½ tsp. Italian seasoning or to taste

¾ tsp. nutmeg (I grate mine)

¼ tsp. pepper (can add cayenne sparingly instead, or in addition to, for a creole-tasting sauce)

Salt to taste

In a large skillet, heat oil to medium or medium-low. Slice sausages lengthwise, remove from the casing (if needed), and brown in the oil. Stir in tomatoes, tomato paste, water, and cooking sherry. Cook until bubbly. Add garlic or garlic powder, celery, carrots, Italian seasoning, nutmeg, and pepper. After it cooks a little while, taste to see if you need more of any of the spices; add salt to taste. (I don't use very much salt.) Let simmer at least an hour. Remove celery and carrots before serving. Makes 6 servings. *Note:* Depending on your taste, you can use ground chicken, fish, or clams instead of sausage. You can also use shredded or chopped chicken. This dish is also good with a chopped onion or chopped black olives. We love it served over Gnocchi (see p. 169).

Tiffany Wardle de Sousa
Cherry Glen Ward
San Jose California South Stake
San Jose, California

My appreciation for good food all began when I was very young, and it began with my mom and her pasta. We usually had pasta for Sunday dinner. This usually meant the smell of the sauce started to permeate the house sometime on Saturday night. This was especially cruel on those fast Sundays when I managed to make a good effort. I'd have to go out of my way to avoid the kitchen at all costs. But I digress. My mom loves our family, and she always went out of her way, no matter how tight the budget became, to create a wonderful dinner for us every night. She is a great example to me, and I hope to continue this tradition in my family. My mom isn't perfect, and she makes no such claim, but I could argue that her pasta is perfect—especially her Sausage Pasta Sauce.

Gnocchi

6 C. potatoes, boiled and pushed through a
    ricer
3 C. flour
½ tsp. salt

2 Tbsp. olive oil
4 eggs, slightly beaten
Extra flour for kneading

In a large bowl, combine potatoes, flour, salt, and oil. Use a light touch. Add eggs; stir until blended and a ball of dough forms. Put dough on floured board and knead gently 15 times. You want dough to be as light as possible. Shape into a fat, round loaf; put on a clean floured spot; cover and let rest 15 minutes. Slice dough, flouring knife as you go, and roll into ¾-inch thick ropes about 12 inches in length. Cut each rope into 1-inch pieces (diagonally sliced pieces look nice). Lay pieces on a floured cloth, making sure that they don't touch each other. Let them dry for half an hour. To cook Gnocchi, drop dough pieces into boiling water in batches and boil for 5 minutes after they float. Drain; cover each layer with homemade pasta sauce (we love Sausage Pasta Sauce; see p. 168) and freshly grated Parmesan or Pecorino-Romano cheese. Makes 6 servings. *Note:* This recipe sounds difficult, but it really isn't after you've made it once. It's easier if you make the sauce the day before you make the Gnocchi. You can also make the Gnocchi a day ahead and reheat it in the oven.

Becky Grant
Cherry Glen Ward
San Jose California South Stake
San Jose, California

I think I was about eleven when my mom told me that presentation is everything when it comes to food. She was carefully spooning perfectly formed Gnocchi over a layer of delicately spread steaming marinara sauce in a stoneware dish. She spooned a few more ladles of sauce on top and carried the dish to an immaculately set table in an immaculate room. She fit right in, all the way to the impeccable bow of her apron at the back of her dainty waist. This is my mother—always picture perfect, and so is her food. She taught us to set the table, garnish the salad, and even garnish a bowl of cottage cheese—not just because it tastes good, because all of her food always does, but because food that looks delicious is even more of a treat. She didn't need a big centerpiece, because her food was the centerpiece. We all admired the care she put into cooking and serving our meals—and when she sat down, her presence was enough to complete the perfect Italian meal.

Peanut Butter Chicken

2–3 chicken breasts
¼ C. flour
½ tsp. salt
¼ C. oil
1–1½ C. water

1 Tbsp. chicken soup powder
1 tsp. cinnamon (or 2–3 pieces cinnamon bark)
¼ tsp. cloves (or 2–4 whole cloves)
½ C. peanut butter
¼–½ C. peanuts (optional)

Cut the chicken into halves or quarters. In a shallow bowl, combine the salt and the flour. Dredge chicken in flour, then lightly brown in hot oil. Place the cooked chicken in a 9 x 13-inch pan. In the pan that was used to brown the chicken, add the remaining flour to the drippings and brown. Gradually add water, stirring to make a thick sauce. Add the soup powder and spices. (The cinnamon bark and whole cloves are much tastier.) Continue cooking and stirring until the sauce is thick. Stir in the peanut butter. Pour the sauce over the chicken. Add peanuts if you like. Cover and bake at 400 for about 25 minutes. Uncover and bake another 7–10 minutes until the top is brown and bubbly. Makes 2–3 servings.

Eliana Hansen
Galilee Branch
Israel District
Hatzor, HaGlilit
Israel

This is my favorite thing my mom makes. I live in Israel, and I serve in the air force. Military service is mandatory here. All men and women who do not live in the Arab sector are drafted soon after graduating high school. We serve for at least two or three years. I have recently earned my sergeant stripes. When I go home or when my mom comes to visit me here on base, I always ask her to make Peanut Butter Chicken.

{ COOKIES & CANDY }

In the eyes of its mother, every beetle is a gazelle.

{ Moroccan proverb }

Mom's Best Chocolate Chip Cookies

½ C. shortening

½ C. butter, softened

¾ C. sugar

¾ C. packed brown sugar

2 eggs

1 tsp. vanilla

2 C. flour

1 tsp. salt

½ tsp. baking soda

Chocolate chips (as many as you want!)

Preheat oven to 350. Cream shortening, butter, sugar, and brown sugar. Add eggs and vanilla; blend well. Add flour, salt, and baking soda. Mix well. Stir in chocolate chips. Bake at 350 for 8–10 minutes. Makes about 3 dozen. *Note:* You can also scoop these out onto a waxed paper-lined baking sheet and freeze. Once frozen individually, put the cookies into a resealable plastic freezer bag. Bake as many or as little as you'd like! Simply increase cooking time to 10–12 minutes.

AnnDee Jones Jensen
Lakeside 10th Ward
Lakeside Utah Stake
Provo, Utah

One of my earliest memories involves my mom and this recipe. She sat me and my siblings on the counter and made these cookies. While we watched her working, Mom gave us a few chocolate chips to munch on. We anxiously waited for her to finish, because we knew we would be able to lick the beaters. (This became a problem when there were more than two of us—fighting ensued!) We then licked the beaters, got spoons, and ate the dough. Cookie dough became a family tradition and obsession. I now bake cookies all the time, and my little boy sits on the counter to watch. He's only five months old, so he doesn't get any cookie dough, but I look forward to passing on the tradition of making cookies together.

No-Bake Cookies

2 C. sugar

½ C. milk or cream

½ C. baking cocoa

½ C. butter

½ C. peanut butter

1 tsp. vanilla

3 C. oatmeal

In a large saucepan, combine sugar, milk, cocoa, and butter; bring to a boil. Remove from burner and add peanut butter, vanilla, and oatmeal. Mix well and spoon onto waxed paper to cool. Makes about 2 dozen.

This was the first type of cookie my mother taught me to make that I didn't burn or ruin. It is easy to make and a favorite of chocolate lovers. My children love it and make it themselves.

Jackie Loyd
Oakville Ward
St. Louis Missouri South Stake
St. Louis, Missouri

Applesauce Drop Cookies

1 C. raisins

1 C. thick applesauce

1 C. packed brown sugar

½ C. shortening

1 egg

2 C. flour

½ tsp. salt

1 tsp. baking soda

1 tsp. cinnamon

½ tsp. nutmeg

¼ tsp. cloves

1 C. nuts, chopped (optional)

Mix raisins and applesauce; set aside. In mixing bowl, combine brown sugar, shortening, and egg; beat until fluffy. Stir in applesauce and raisins. Combine dry ingredients; add and mix well. Stir in nuts. Drop by rounded teaspoonfuls about 2 inches apart on greased baking sheets. Bake at 375 for 13–15 minutes. Makes 4 dozen.

My grandmother made these cookies, and I always crave them in the fall. It must be the applesauce. In Pittsburgh, the winters are very long and dark. These cookies are very much a comfort food. My grandmother's theory in making these cookies was, "Why dirty up the dishes for just one batch? You should double the recipe!"

Evan McCall
Pittsburgh 4th Ward
Pittsburgh Pennsylvania North Stake
Pittsburgh, Pennsylvania

Mom's Rich Cookies

1¼ C. flour
1 tsp. baking powder
2½ C. quick oats
1 C. shortening
2 C. brown sugar

2 tsp. vanilla
4 eggs
½ C. milk (2%)
6 oz. semi-sweet chocolate chips
6 oz. butterscotch chips

In a large bowl, combine flour, baking powder, and oats. In a separate bowl, combine shortening, brown sugar, vanilla, eggs, and milk. Stir into dry ingredients. Stir in chocolate and butterscotch chips. Press cookie dough into a 9 x 13-inch glass dish; bake at 350 for 30 minutes. (Half a recipe fits into a 9 x 9-inch square dish.) Makes 18–20 brownie-size bars.

Toni Mann
Bountiful 10th Ward
Bountiful Utah North Stake
Bountiful, Utah

Even though Mom endured daily the pain of arthritis, she often surprised us kids with this recipe. She filled the house with warmth and holiday feelings even when it wasn't a holiday. It was difficult for her to stand up, but she volunteered this sweet dish made with love and care. It brought us together on many occasions, even when we were teenagers. She carried a sweetness and warmth of her own with her, and showed love through her cooking—especially with this recipe.

Magical Chocolate Chip Cookies

2¾ C. all-purpose flour
1 tsp. baking soda
1 tsp. salt
1 C. butter
½ C. sugar

1½ C. packed brown sugar
1 Tbsp. vanilla
2 eggs
2 C. semi-sweet chocolate chips

Preheat oven to 375. Mix flour, baking soda, and salt. In a separate bowl, beat butter, sugar, brown sugar, and vanilla until creamy. Add eggs and beat well. Gradually add flour mixture to the sugar mixture, beating well. Stir in chocolate chips. Drop by rounded teaspoonfuls onto an ungreased cookie sheet. Bake at 375 for 8–10 minutes, until lightly brown. Perfect. Magical. Makes about 5 dozen cookies.

Norberto Betancourt
Union City Ward
Caldwell New Jersey Stake
Union City, New Jersey

Peanut Butter Bars

1½ C. sugar
1½ C. packed brown sugar
1½ C. margarine
1½ C. peanut butter
3 eggs
1 tsp. vanilla
3 C. flour
1¼ tsp. salt

1½ tsp. baking soda
3 C. quick oats
3 Tbsp. cocoa
½ C. butter
3 C. powdered sugar
1 tsp. vanilla
6 Tbsp. milk

(recipe continued on next page)

(Peanut Butter Bars, continued)

Cream sugar, brown sugar, margarine, and peanut butter. Add eggs and vanilla. Mix well. Add flour, salt, baking soda, and oats. Mix well and press into a large ungreased cookie sheet. Bake at 325 for 10 minutes; raise heat to 375 and bake for 10–15 minutes longer. In a saucepan, melt cocoa and butter; add powdered sugar, vanilla, and milk. Stir until smooth and creamy; frost bars. Makes 20 servings.

Lynsie Mills
Middleton 7th Ward
Middleton Idaho Stake
Middleton, Idaho

Being a mom is one of life's greatest joys! My husband, Trevor, and I adopted a baby girl in July 2008, and we have loved every minute. I have always wanted to be a mom, and we were so happy when we had the opportunity to adopt. My mom did a great job raising us three kids. Thanks to her, I know how to raise my daughter. Moms are very special! Not living by my mom is very hard; I miss her all the time. I love you, Mom; thanks for all your advice. This is a Crandall family recipe that came from a school lunchroom. We had to resize the recipe down so we could make it at home!

World-Famous Cookies

2 C. butter

2 C. sugar

2 C. packed brown sugar

4 eggs

2 tsp. vanilla

4 C. flour

3–5 C. oatmeal, made into flour in blender

1 tsp. salt

2 tsp. baking powder

2 tsp. baking soda

24 oz. chocolate chips

1 8 oz. chocolate bar, grated

3 C. nuts, chopped (we prefer pecans)

Cream butter, sugar, and brown sugar. Add eggs and vanilla. Add flour, oatmeal, salt, baking powder, and baking soda to creamed mixture. Stir in chocolate chips, chocolate bar, and nuts. Roll into balls and place 2 inches apart on cookie sheet. Bake at 375 for 6–10 minutes. Recipe may be halved. Makes 112 cookies.

Louise Phelps
Groton Ward
Providence Rhode Island Stake
Ledyard, Connecticut

Granny's Butterscotch Cookies

4 C. flour

½ tsp. salt

1 Tbsp. baking powder

1 tsp. baking soda

2 C. packed brown sugar

1 C. butter

2 eggs

1 tsp. vanilla

1 C. walnuts, chopped

In a small bowl, mix the flour, salt, baking powder, and baking soda. In a large bowl, cream the brown sugar, butter, and eggs. Add vanilla; stir in flour mixture. Mix well and add walnuts. Divide into 2–3 sections, and form each into a 1 x 2-inch rectangle. Wrap in waxed paper and refrigerate overnight. Slice just thinner than ¼ inch and bake at 350 for 5–6 minutes. Makes 5–6 dozen.

Lena Laraux Gregory
Fairbanks 3rd Ward
Fairbanks Alaska Stake
Fairbanks, Alaska

My children know my mother—Lena Venes Laraux—as "Granny." She was born around 1902 or 1904 outside Bethel, Alaska, which is far out in the Alaskan tundra. My father is French Canadian, and I am one of their eight children. My mother was witty and funny, and had an excellent sense of humor. Standing her tallest, my mother came in at 4'6" and weighed about 80 pounds in her prime. She was tiny, but she worked hard; not only was she the hunter of the family, but she was a wonderful cook. My mother never learned to read, but was famous for this simple, delicious cookie that she produced liberally every Christmas.

Mom's Monster Cookies

1 C. butter
2 C. sugar
2 C. packed brown sugar
6 eggs
1 pt. jam
1½ lb. peanut butter

9 C. oatmeal
4 C. flour
4 tsp. baking soda
1 tsp. baking powder
1 bag M&Ms or chocolate chips

In a large bowl, mix butter, sugar, and brown sugar. Add eggs; mix well. Stir in jam and peanut butter. In a separate bowl, mix the remaining ingredients. Combine wet and dry ingredients; mix well. Bake at 350 for about 10 minutes. Makes 10 dozen.

Heather Munz
BYU 139th Ward
BYU 18th Stake
Provo, Utah

I have a wonderful mother. I wouldn't trade a single thing about her for any other traits. She did an amazing job raising us five children. I don't think she could have done anything better than she did, and I am eternally grateful for her. I am a fairly new mother. I have a twenty-two-month-old daughter, Keely, and a two-month-old son, Carter. I'm trying my best to be as good to them as my mother was to me. I am so blessed to have both of them in my life. Keely loved her new brother right away. She loves to hold him and give him kisses; it is the cutest thing in the world. She also likes to help me take care of him. The love little children have for everyone they meet is incredible. They never judge; instead, they are honest, loving, and forgiving. I find it interesting that I've always wanted to be like my mother—and now that I'm a mother, I find myself wanting to be like my daughter. They are both so amazing.

Hurry-Up Chocolate Chip Drops

3 C. graham cracker crumbs

1 6-oz. pkg. chocolate chips

1 14-oz. can sweetened condensed milk

1 C. shredded coconut

Preheat oven to 350. Mix cracker crumbs, chocolate chips, and milk in a bowl; form in small balls. Roll in coconut. Place 2 inches apart on a lightly greased baking sheet. Bake at 350 for 15 minutes. Makes 3–4 dozen cookies.

Michelle Mann Redfearn
Southglen 1st Ward
Littleton Colorado Stake
Centennial, Colorado

This is my favorite cookie recipe from my mother-in-law, Karen Owen Redfearn. When my husband, Ryan, and I were dating, I asked him what his favorite cookie was. He told me it was a recipe his mom always made. Having a sweet tooth myself and being a connoisseur of cookies, I said, "Just tell me what's in them; I bet I have a recipe." I was wrong! I hadn't even heard of these cookies. I have been married to Ryan for twelve years, and I have never had this cookie anywhere except at my mother-in-law's home—and now at mine! My mother-in-law is a fabulous mother. I lost my mother, and while no one could replace her, marrying into a strong LDS family was so important to me. After losing my mother, my father, and one sister, I wanted to marry into a large family to share the moments of life with. I wanted my children to have grandparents, aunts, uncles, and cousins! Ryan is the second of seven children—six boys and a girl—and all of us but his sister live in Colorado. This is the large family I dreamed of! Family get-togethers are big—thirteen adults and eleven children, with more coming as the months pass. Ryan's mother is the matriarch of this fabulous group. I can go to her with any child-rearing problems, questions, or concerns I have, and I know she has experienced firsthand every situation I lay before her. I trust her counsel and never feel judged. She is a shining example to me that motherhood does not have to be endured, but can be enjoyed. She has taught me to enjoy every moment. I love watching her watch my little boys and their cousins play. I see the joy in her face and realize that her "little" boys—my husband and his brothers—are running in the yard next door, creating even more wonderful memories.

Applesauce Chocolate Chip Cookies

4½ C. flour

1 tsp. salt

2 tsp. soda

1 tsp. cloves

2 tsp. cinnamon

1 tsp. allspice

2 C. sugar

1 C. shortening

2 eggs

1 16-oz. can applesauce

1 tsp. vanilla

1 C. nuts

1 12-oz. pkg. chocolate chips

Sift together flour, salt, soda, and spices. In a separate bowl, cream sugar and shortening. Add eggs, beating well after each one. Add applesauce and mix well. Add vanilla and beat. Add flour mixture and beat well. Stir in nuts and chocolate chips. Drop by teaspoonfuls onto cookie sheet. Bake at 350 for 9–11 minutes. Makes 6 dozen cookies.

Louise Phelps
Groton Ward
Providence Rhode Island Stake
Ledyard, Connecticut

As soon as I read the request for "Mom's Best Recipe," I instantly knew which recipe reminded me of my mom. I raced to my recipe box to see if I had the recipe I was looking for. My mom passed away four years ago, and I didn't know where to turn if I didn't have the recipe for her Applesauce Chocolate Chip Cookies. My mom was a real cookie maker, but these are the ones I remember most. I have not made these cookies since I moved away from home almost twenty years ago, so I made them this week. It's funny how the smell of the spices and dough brought memories flooding back. I can honestly say that taste buds have a memory! As soon as I tasted the batter (I know, I know, don't eat the uncooked batter—but we always did when Mom made cookies), I knew I had the right cookies. Funny how many more cookies this batch makes when you aren't busy eating dough! My kids have thoroughly enjoyed the cookies, and we have spent time talking about "Grandma Bev." My kids were just eight and six when she passed away, and baking these cookies has given me the opportunity to share some of my fondest memories of her with them.

Pineapple Bars

Bars:

2 C. flour

1 C. sugar

2 tsp. baking soda

1 20-oz. can crushed pineapple in heavy syrup;
   don't drain

1 tsp. vanilla

2 eggs, beaten

Frosting:

8 oz. cream cheese, softened

¼ C. butter

1¾ C. powdered sugar

1 tsp. vanilla

½ C. nuts, crushed

Preheat oven to 350. In a large bowl, stir flour, sugar, and baking soda. Add pineapple with syrup, vanilla, and eggs; mix well. Pour into a greased 11 x 17-inch cookie sheet (jellyroll pan) and bake at 350 for 25 minutes. While bars bake, prepare frosting by mixing all frosting ingredients. Spread over HOT cake and cut into bars when cool. Makes 20 servings.

Joni Hilton
Rocklin 5th Ward
Rocklin California Stake
Rocklin, California

My mother, Beulah Coralee Lemacks Pennock, was raised in Charleston, South Carolina, in an era when home skills were one of the marks of a truly refined Southern lady. I watched her make flawless pie crusts, perfect loaves of bread, killer dinner rolls, and, of course, treats like this one. These Pineapple Bars are the perfect potluck offering, a festive dessert for a ladies' luncheon, or simply a family favorite. You'll love how moist they are and how easy they are to make!

Six-Dollar Cookies

1 devil's food cake mix

1 small pkg. instant chocolate pudding

2 eggs

¼ C. water

½ C. oil

½ bag mini M&Ms

In large bowl, mix dry ingredients. Add eggs, water, and oil; mix until blended. Stir in M&Ms. Bake at 350 for 13 minutes. Remove from oven and allow to rest for 2 minutes; remove from cookie sheet and cool on a paper towel. DO NOT cool on a cookie rack; they will fall through. Makes 2 dozen cookies. *Note:* You can substitute chocolate chips and/or nuts for the M&Ms.

Summer Corbit
Richfield 7th Ward
Richfield Utah Stake
Richfield, Utah

I come from a very large family—my parents had ten children—and I remember for every holiday, even the small ones, my mom made cookies and let us help her. Even though she worked two jobs, she still spent quality time with her children. I just loved baking cookies with my mom and trying out fun new recipes with her. I think that's why I'm such a good baker: my mom took a little extra time to show me how. I am now expecting my first child, and I want to do the same thing with him. My mother showed me that by doing just the little things, you can show your children how much you love them.

Waffle Cookies

½ C. shortening

1 C. sugar

2 eggs

½ C. milk

1 tsp. vanilla

½ C. cocoa

2 C. flour

Frosting:

3 Tbsp. butter

3 Tbsp. cocoa

½ tsp. vanilla

1 Tbsp. corn syrup

1–2 C. powdered sugar

2–3 Tbsp. milk

(recipe continued on next page)

(Waffle Cookies, continued)

Cream shortening and sugar; stir in eggs. Stir in ½ C. milk and 1 tsp. vanilla. Add ½ C. cocoa. Add flour, 1 C. at a time. Mix well. While preparing cookie dough, heat up waffle iron. To bake, drop small teaspoonfuls of dough onto waffle iron and bake for 1–2 minutes. To make frosting, combine butter, 3 Tbsp. cocoa, ½ tsp. vanilla, corn syrup, and powdered sugar. Stir in enough milk to make smooth frosting. Frost cooled cookies. Makes 2–3 dozen.

This cookie is a classic. When I was little, my mom made these Waffle Cookies for me, and I loved them. Now I make them for my two children. The waffle texture is so fun for kids, and they love the yummy frosting on top.

Kristy Sinks
Glines 5th Ward
Glines Utah Stake
Vernal, Utah

Sour Cream Sugar Cookies

1 C. butter or margarine

2 C. sugar

2 eggs

1 C. sour cream

1 tsp. vanilla

½ tsp. baking soda

4 tsp. baking powder

4½ C. flour

½ tsp. salt

Cream butter, sugar, and eggs. Add sour cream and vanilla. Sift dry ingredients together and add to creamed mixture. Refrigerate. Line cookie sheet with parchment paper. Roll out dough, cut into desired shapes, and bake at 350 for 10 minutes. Makes 24 cookies.

I wanted to share this cookie recipe in honor of my mother-in-law. This is her recipe, and it is the best sugar cookie recipe I have ever tasted. They are so addicting and are perfect for cutting into shapes. The sour cream in these cookies gives them a little something extra and adds a creaminess that makes them perfect. We love you, Chickrae! Happy Mother's Day! Thanks for the best sugar cookies in the world.

Anna Wixom
Champions Ward
Klein Texas Stake
Houston, Texas

Applesauce Cookies

½ C. shortening
1 C. sugar
1 egg
½ Tbsp. baking soda
1 C. applesauce
½ Tbsp. nutmeg

½ Tbsp. cinnamon
½ Tbsp. cloves
½ Tbsp. salt
2 C. flour
Chocolate chips

In a mixing bowl, cream shortening, sugar, and egg on medium speed. In a separate bowl, combine baking soda and applesauce. Add the applesauce mixture to the sugar mixture on low speed. Beat in nutmeg, cinnamon, cloves, and salt on low speed. Mix in flour, 1 C. at a time, on low speed. Add as many chocolate chips as you'd like. (I prefer at least 1 C.) Bake at 350 for 10–12 minutes, or until edges are golden. Makes 3–4 dozen.

Skipper Coates
Pleasant Grove 2nd Ward
Pleasant Grove Utah Stake
Pleasant Grove, Utah

In our family, Applesauce Cookies were the only cookies we knew. My mom made them as a surprise after-school snack or as a reward for "being so good" at the store or at church. I didn't appreciate my mom making Applesauce Cookies for us until I became a mom myself. The first time I made them for my little boy, he helped me measure ingredients and pour them in. He helped eat the extra dough off the bowl and beaters—the same thing I did with my mom. When I called to ask her the origin of the recipe, she simply told me Grandma always made them for her—and that Great-grandma always made them for Grandma. I am so happy to be able to share this tradition with my own children. Thanks, Mom, for passing this recipe on!

Mom's Famous Chocolate Coconut No-Bake Cookies

½ C. butter
½ C. milk
2 C. sugar
¾ C. peanut butter

3 C. instant oatmeal
¼ C. cocoa
½ C. coconut

(recipe continued on next page)

(Mom's Famous Chocolate Coconut No-Bake Cookies, continued)

Boil butter, milk, and sugar for exactly 2 minutes (no more, no less!). Remove from heat and add remaining ingredients; stir until completely mixed. Spoon onto waxed paper, let cool for 5 minutes, and enjoy! Makes about 3 dozen.

Shawnnee Miranda
Weston 1st Ward
Boston Massachusetts Stake
Natick, Massachusetts

I grew up all over in a military family; no matter where we were, we could always count on our mom making great treats during the holidays. My favorites to sneak before they were done cooling were these no-bake cookies. These cookies always bring a homey feeling to me now that I am three thousand miles from home. Whenever I need a boost of home, I make my Mom's Famous Chocolate Coconut No-Bake Cookies.

Grandma Wilson's Raisin-Filled Oatmeal Cookies

1½ C. raisins
¾ C. water
½ C. sugar
1 C. packed brown sugar
1 C. butter, melted
1 egg

1 tsp. vanilla
2 C. oatmeal
2 C. flour
1 tsp. salt
1 tsp. soda

In a saucepan, boil the raisins, sugar, and water for 1 minute. Remove from heat and set aside. Combine brown sugar, butter, egg, vanilla, oatmeal, flour, salt, and soda into a dough. Divide into 2 parts. Cover bottom of 9 x 13-inch baking pan with thin layer of dough; press flat. Spread raisin filling over dough. Crumble remaining dough over the top. Bake at 350 until golden, about 20 minutes. Remove from oven and cool for 15 minutes before cutting into squares. You will love the nutty richness of these easy-to-make bar cookies! Makes 12–20 servings.

Steven D. Wilson
Gilbert 3rd Ward
Gilbert Arizona Highland Park Stake
Gilbert, Arizona

I count myself fortunate to have been raised at a time when Mom's home cooking was not an event, but a way of life. Oh, what a wonderful feeling it was to come home from school and catch the smell of homemade bread, scones, fruit being bottled, or best of all, raisin-filled cookies. My mom is the best.

Rocky Road Cookie Bars

1 C. butter or margarine

⅓ C. cocoa

2 C. sugar

4 eggs

1½ C. flour

Pinch salt

2 tsp. vanilla

1½ C. nuts, chopped

Miniature marshmallows

¼ C. butter, softened

⅓ C. cocoa

⅓ C. cream or milk

3–4 C. powdered sugar

1 tsp. vanilla

Pinch salt

Melt 1 C. butter; add ⅓ C. cocoa and sugar. Add eggs, one at a time, beating after each addition. Add flour, salt, 2 tsp. vanilla, and nuts. Spread into a 12 x 17-inch baking sheet. Bake at 350 for 25 minutes. Remove from oven and immediately cover top with miniature marshmallows. Return to oven for about 5 minutes. Remove and let cool. Combine ¼ C. butter, ⅓ C. cocoa, cream, powdered sugar, 1 tsp. vanilla, and salt. Mix well. Spread over top. Makes 20–24 servings.

Kathleen McClellan
Cedar Hills 3rd Ward
Cedar Hills Utah Stake
Cedar Hills, Utah

My mother was a wonderful example of service to others. It seems to me that she was always taking food to someone, including neighbors who were not members of the Church. I have a fond memory of being with her as we delivered baskets of goodies to several people at Christmastime. I took the basket to the door, rang the doorbell, and ran back to the car; we sped away and hoped people didn't recognize us or our car. She frequently made Rocky Road Cookie Bars for others and for special events. Everyone loved them except me, but now I make them for my grandchildren, who enjoy them.

Chocolate Chip Pudding Cookies

2¼ C. flour

1 tsp. baking soda

1 C. butter, softened

¼ C. sugar

¾ C. packed brown sugar

1 pkg. 4-serving vanilla instant pudding (Jell-O)

1 tsp. vanilla

2 eggs

12 oz. chocolate chips

Mix flour and baking soda; set aside. In a large mixing bowl, combine butter, sugar, brown sugar, pudding mix, and vanilla; beat until smooth and creamy. Beat in eggs. Gradually add flour mixture; mix well. Stir in chips. Drop by rounded teaspoonfuls onto cookie sheet about 2 inches apart. Bake at 375 for 8–10 minutes. Makes 3 dozen.

One of my mom's traditions I have tried to continue is after-school treats. When I came home from school, I could expect something special from my mom waiting for me. Now when we go to visit Grandma, she likes to have the cookie jar full of something sweet for her grandkids. Thanks, Mom!

Angela Harris
Foothills Ward
Golden Colorado Stake
Golden, Colorado

Great Grandma's Caramel

2 C. sugar

1¾ C. corn syrup

2 C. cream

1 C. butter

1 tsp. vanilla

Nuts, chopped (optional)

In a large saucepan combine sugar, corn syrup, cream, and butter. Boil over medium heat, stirring constantly, until the mixture reaches 255 on a candy thermometer. Stir in vanilla and nuts. Pour into 2 greased pie tins. Cool before cutting into pieces. Makes about 50 pieces.

I am fourteen and I never knew my grandmother, but I love to hear stories about her. I was practicing my signature and was frustrated by trying to make a pretty E. My mother remembered that my grandmother had a beautiful signature—Eula Lunt Romney—and she pulled out some notes that my grandmother had written before she died. I was so excited to copy the E. I love sharing this pretty E with my grandmother. I think it makes my mother happy, too.

Elise Frank
Battle Creek 10th Ward
Pleasant Grove Utah East Stake
Lindon, Utah

Grandma Mamie's Homemade Chocolate Peanut Butter Fudge

4 C. sugar

2 heaping Tbsp. cocoa

1 C. cream

1 C. milk

3 Tbsp. corn syrup

3 heaping Tbsp. peanut butter

In a saucepan, combine sugar and cocoa; add cream, milk, and corn syrup. Bring to a boil, stirring constantly! Boil for 15 minutes or until hard ball stage. To test, dip a spoonful into a cup of cold water; if it comes out in a hard ball, it's done! Dump the fudge out onto a marble slab and let cool for 1 hour. When it sets up, add peanut butter and whip until smooth by hand or in a mixer. Put the fudge onto a piece of waxed paper and form into a roll. Refrigerate and then enjoy! Makes 25–30 small pieces.

Teresa Kabonic
Kanab 7th Ward
Kanab Utah Stake
Kanab, Utah

I remember as a child cooking with my grandma. She made the BEST cookies, candy, pies, and, best of all, FUDGE. My grandmother was an inspiration to me. She cooked complete meals every day for any one of us that wanted to come over for lunch. Every Sunday she had all of the Hatches over for dinner. Her daughter (my Aunt Collette) also made this fudge, and although they were both taken away from us way too soon, I know that they are both smiling down from above, knowing that their recipe is being put in a Worldwide Ward Cookbook. I miss you both, and want you to know that I hope to keep your legacy alive by teaching my girls to cook and make GREAT fudge!

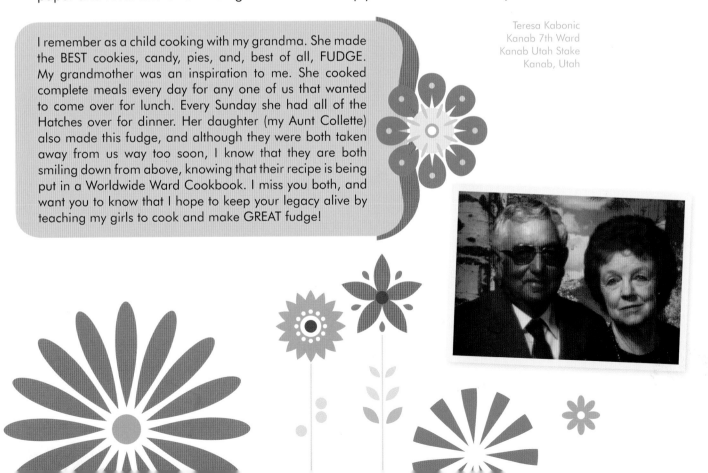

Microwave Caramel Popcorn

1 C. brown sugar
½ C. butter
½ C. corn syrup
½ tsp. vanilla

½ tsp. baking soda
4 qts. popped popcorn (2 bags microwave popcorn)

In a large glass bowl, combine brown sugar, butter, and corn syrup. Cook in the microwave for 5 minutes; you don't need to stir. Remove from microwave. Stir in vanilla and baking soda. The mixture will foam up. Pour over popped corn and stir. Shape into balls or just eat from the bowl. Makes 20 popcorn balls.

Shelly McDermott
Enterprise Ward
Morgan Utah North Stake
Morgan, Utah

I love being a mother of a large family. I have seven children; four are married, and I have five grandchildren. Life wasn't always this happy. My mother abandoned me and my siblings when I was sixteen, and my father took his own life soon after. I went to live with my grandmother, who died three months later. My brothers and sister have led tragic lives as a result of neglect, substance abuse, and depression. I wanted something more; I clung to the gospel and married a wonderful man. Together we have forged a life of happiness in spite of the tragedy all around me. Sometimes in our childhood we can lose our families through death, divorce, and separation, but when we have our own families we can heal and start over. We can start a new generation of love and support. Sometimes people frown on big families, but words cannot describe how much we love and support each other. Whether you have one child or ten children, you are signed up for life. You will invest every day in loving and being loved. You will be forever changed, and for the rest of your life, you get to be called "Mom." It will be your turn to make a difference, and you will make all the difference. It has been my lifelong quest to be the mother to my children that I have never had. I will forever be grateful to the Church and its influence in my life. My husband is as good as they come. The Lord has been very mindful of me. I have lived a full life. I look forward to sitting on my porch, laughing at my chickens as they chase the grasshoppers. Life was meant to be lived simply. There is so much joy in the silly moments. It's also where we find the salve for the pains of yesterday.

Peanut Butter Popcorn

2–3 bags microwave popcorn

1 C. sugar

½ C. corn syrup

½ C. honey

½ C. peanut butter

Pop corn and remove any unpopped kernels. Place popcorn in a big bowl. In a medium saucepan, combine sugar, corn syrup, and honey. Bring to a rolling boil. Boil for 1 minute. Remove from heat and stir in peanut butter. Pour over popcorn and stir. Makes 8 servings.

Tina Howard
Valdez Branch
Wasilla Alaska Stake
Valdez, Alaska

When I was young, all I can ever remember wanting to be was a wife and mother. I was the seventh child; my mother was forty-two and my dad fifty-two when I was born. I never really had a desire to cook. Of course, I knew how to make simple meals to provide for my own family, but I never felt a great love for cooking. I was raised in northern California, where I married and had four beautiful girls. We then moved to Utah, where we lived for about seven years. When I went through my divorce, some of the most wonderful people helped me through it. I was introduced to my good friend's brother-in-law, and we married three months after my divorce. I then moved to Alaska and had three more children—two sons and another daughter. Like my mother, I had seven children. My older daughters were a great strength and a wonderful help with the last three children. Thankfully my husband enjoys cooking, and so do a few of my daughters. I have lived in Alaska for the past thirteen years. What a beautiful place to be! This recipe was given to us by a wonderful friend here in Alaska. We enjoy making it when we are all together or have a bunch of friends over. It's very simple and very tasty!

Chocolate Rum Balls

2 C. powdered sugar

1 14-oz. can sweetened condensed milk

1 C. butter

½ tsp. vanilla

½ tsp. butter rum candy flavoring

12 oz. dipping chocolate

1 C. almonds, chopped

Combine all ingredients and beat until stiff. Drop onto a cookie sheet lined with waxed paper and put in freezer until set up. Roll into balls with hands and put back in freezer. In an electric frying pan turned to warm, melt dipping chocolate. Dip balls in chocolate and then roll in almonds. Freeze again until served. Makes about 49 balls.

This candy is definitely one of my mom's most famous and sought-after recipes! My dad is a professor at Weber State University, and one year he signed up to bring a dessert for the annual Christmas party. My mom decided to make Chocolate Rum Balls for him, and they were such a hit that every year since she is automatically signed up to make this now-famous treat. In fact, it has become such a highly anticipated tradition among colleagues, family, and friends that she doesn't want to disappoint anyone, so she makes them every year. My mom is also the GREATEST MOM IN THE WORLD, because she made more than 500 of these for my wedding reception—by herself!—which meant the world to me! They are the most unique and delicious treats ever!

Amy Hoyal
Prairie 8th Ward
Prairie Utah Stake
West Jordan, Utah

Grandma Donna's Popcorn Balls

½ paper grocery bag full of popped popcorn

½ C. margarine

1 C. corn syrup

2 C. sugar

1 tsp. vanilla

Food coloring (optional)

Place popped popcorn in a large bowl. In a medium saucepan, melt margarine and corn syrup; add sugar. Bring to a boil; boil for 1 minute. Remove from heat; stir in vanilla. If desired, tint with food coloring. Pour hot syrup mixture over popcorn and mix well to coat. Butter hands and form popcorn into balls. Place on waxed paper to cool. Makes 12–16 popcorn balls.

Renee Ransom
Hermiston Ward
Hermiston Oregon Stake
Hermiston, Oregon

{ PIES }

You never get over being a child, as long as you have a mother to go to.

{ Sarah Orne Jewett }

Coconut Custard Pie

2½ C. flour

1 tsp. salt

2 Tbsp. sugar

¾ C. butter, cut into pieces

½ C. shortening, chilled

5 Tbsp. ice water

Dried beans to use as weights

4 eggs

Butter as big as a hen's egg (2 Tbsp.)

2 C. sugar

⅓ C. sweet milk (whole milk)

½ C. freshly grated coconut

In a large bowl, mix the flour, salt, and sugar. Using a pastry cutter, two knives, or a food processor, cut the butter into the flour mix until you can no longer see it. Add the shortening and cut it into the mixture until only small bits remain. Add ice water 1 Tbsp. at a time until the dough just starts to stick together. (This recipe is enough for 2 thin double-crust pies, so you will have extra dough.) Chill the dough for at least 30 minutes. Divide in half, roll it out, and place in 2 9-inch pie pans. Refrigerate for 1 hour. Cover the dough by gently pressing aluminum foil over it; prick both the dough and the foil with a fork. Fill with beans to cover the foil. Bake at 400 for 15 minutes or until dough sets. Discard the beans and remove the foil. In a large bowl, combine eggs, butter, sugar, milk, and coconut. Mix well and pour into 1 baked pie shell. Bake at 400 for about 25 minutes, until knife comes out clean from center. Recipe makes 2 pie crusts and 1 Coconut Custard Pie—6–8 servings.

Jay and Obie Clark
Turlock 1st Ward
Turlock California Stake
Turlock, California

My family didn't say "I love you" a lot with words—instead, we said it with food. Lillie Lular (Miles) Lee taught me about love as I learned to cook at her knee. During the summer, the farmland of Louisiana was filled with so many beautiful and rich smells, but nothing beat the smells of love coming from our kitchen. It has been a long time since I have been in her kitchen, but there are still some aromas that take me back to that wonderful time.

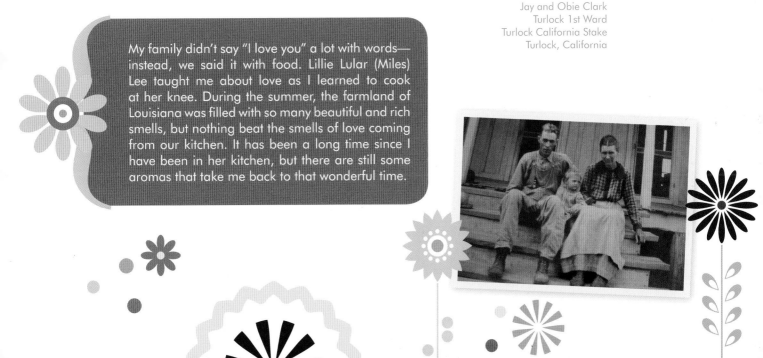

Grasshopper Pie

24 chocolate sandwich cookies (Oreos), crushed

¼ C. butter, melted

¼ C. milk

Drop of peppermint extract

1 7-oz. jar marshmallow cream

2 C. frozen whipped topping (Cool Whip)

2–3 drops green food coloring

Reserve ¼ C. crushed cookies. In a medium bowl, combine crushed cookies and melted butter; press into a 9 x 13-inch pan. Mix remaining ingredients and pour over the top. Sprinkle with reserved cookie crumbs. Freeze overnight. Makes 10 servings.

My mother always made us wonderful home-cooked meals. Her dinners fit the occasion: warm chili or stew on Halloween night before we headed out to trick-or-treat; delicious, comforting waffles with butter and syrup melting over them on a Sunday evening; and everybody's favorite—tacos! But when I think about which of her recipes is my favorite, there is no hesitation. Grasshopper Pie is my favorite thing my mother ever made, and I always knew it was a special occasion if she was preparing it. I would peek into the freezer at the enticing green dessert, smell the peppermint aroma, and just imagine how wonderful it would taste when it was ready to serve! Now I make this recipe and serve it to my own children, who love it just as much as I do. You often think of comfort food as being something warm—but my happy, comforting memories are laced with frosty peppermint and Oreo cookies.

Camille Whiting
Lander 1st Ward
Riverton Wyoming Stake
Lander, Wyoming

Peach Pie

½ C. butter, softened

2 Tbsp. sugar

1 C. flour

4 C. peaches, sliced (really ripe are best)

½ C. boiling water

3 Tbsp. cornstarch

1 C. sugar

1 Tbsp. butter

(recipe continued on next page)

(Peach Pie, continued)

Combine ½ C. butter, 2 Tbsp. sugar, and flour just until dough forms. Press into a 9-inch pie pan. Bake at 375 for 12–15 minutes. Crush enough peaches to make 1 C. Arrange the remaining peach slices in pie crust. Combine crushed fruit with water, cornstarch, and 1 C. sugar. Bring to boil. Cook over low heat until clear, about 2–3 minutes, stirring occasionally. Add 1 Tbsp. butter. Pour over peaches. Chill at least 2 hours. Makes 8 slices. *Note:* You can use bottled peaches in this recipe; if you do, use the juice instead of water.

Every peach season, we beg our mother, Susan, to bake this sweet pastry. The crust is so crumbly, and the peaches are so juicy. When these two powerhouse elements combine, it's like a punch of flavor to the face.

Jade and Haley Madison
Battle Creek 5th Ward
Pleasant Grove Utah East Stake
Pleasant Grove, Utah

German Chocolate Pie

2 envs. instant whipped topping mix (Dream Whip)

2 ¾ C. milk, divided

1 tsp. vanilla

2 small boxes chocolate instant pudding mix (Jell-O)

¼–½ C. mini chocolate chips

¼–½ C. coconut

¼–½ C. pecans or other nuts, chopped (optional)

1 baked pie crust

Whipped cream

In a large bowl, combine whipped topping mixes, 1 C. milk, and vanilla; beat with an electric mixer on high for about 6 minutes or until topping starts to form peaks. Add remaining 1¾ C. milk and pudding mixes; beat on low until mixed, then on high for 2 minutes, scraping the bowl occasionally. Stir in desired amount of chocolate chips, coconut, and nuts. Spoon into pie crust. Refrigerate at least 4 hours. Garnish the top with whipped cream and additional chocolate chips, coconut, and nuts, if desired. Makes 8 servings.

Kara Doty
Sheep River Ward
Foothills Stake
Okotoks, Alberta
Canada

Millionaire Pie

1 12-oz. container frozen whipped topping, thawed (Cool Whip)

1 14-oz. can sweetened condensed milk

¼ C. bottled lemon juice

1 20-oz. can crushed pineapple, well drained

½–1 C. walnuts, chopped

1 graham cracker crust

Mix whipped topping and sweetened condensed milk until thoroughly blended. Add lemon juice, then crushed pineapple. Mix well. Add chopped walnuts. (Amount varies according to your family's love of walnuts.) Pour into graham cracker crust. Refrigerate for at least 4 hours. Serve cold. Makes 8 servings. *Note:* This pie is also good if you use low-fat frozen whipped topping and pineapple that has no sugar added.

Debby Brissette
Taylorsville 39th Ward
Taylorsville Utah South Stake
Taylorsville, Utah

We love children. We are parents to seven, ranging in age from forty to sixteen. Four are biological and three are adopted from the foster care system—and we highly recommend it! The decision to become foster parents was an easy one. We knew that we could provide guidance, direction, but most of all love to a child in need. Little did we know that it would be the hardest job we would ever love doing. Two of our three boys came to us through the foster care system in 1995 with a multitude of problems and issues. But they came with a bigger need for understanding, guidance, direction, and unconditional love. These boys had been in situations where lack of food was a huge issue. Mikey, the oldest of these two biological brothers, spent many hours rummaging through dumpsters behind restaurants for food to feed himself and his brother, Tommy. When he came to live with us, he ate an entire box of cereal every morning; as time passed, he realized he could eat all he wanted and that there would always be plenty. In 1998, Jamie came along; he was only five, and was the cutest thing I had ever seen. Our first meal with him was pizza, and to this day, he reminds us of that meal whenever we have pizza. Mikey has now graduated from the University of Tampa and is in the process of starting a nonprofit organization for those who have aged out of the foster care system. Tommy is currently attending the University of Rhode Island, where he is studying business and Chinese. Jamie is attending the Academy of Math, Engineering, and Science at Cottonwood High School in Salt Lake City. They are all bright, wonderful, funny young men who have brought so much joy to us. Our biological children are amazing as well; they were willing to share their parents with these boys, and although the going was not always easy, we all got through it with humor, understanding, kindness—and, most of all, love.

Coconut-Pecan Chess Pie

3 large eggs, lightly beaten
1 C. sugar
1/3 C. buttermilk
2 Tbsp. butter, melted
1 Tbsp. cornmeal

1/2 tsp. coconut flavoring
3/4 C. flaked coconut
1/4–1/2 C. pecans, chopped
1 unbaked 9-inch pastry shell

Combine eggs, sugar, buttermilk, melted butter, cornmeal, and coconut flavoring. Mix well. Stir in coconut and pecans. Pour filling into pastry shell. Bake at 400 for 10 minutes. Reduce heat to 350, and bake 30 more minutes. Cool on a wire rack. Serve with whipped cream if desired. Makes 8 servings.

My mom is a big pie maker, and this is one of my favorites. It is so easy and quick to make; it's perfect for a busy holiday season!

Cassie Blake
Madison 3rd Ward
Huntsville Alabama Stake
Madison, Alabama

Grandma Millie's Pie Filling

1 C. sugar
1/4 C. cornstarch
1/2 tsp. salt
2 1/2 C. milk

3 eggs, separated
1/3 C. margarine
1 tsp. vanilla
1 baked pie shell

In a large saucepan, thoroughly mix sugar, cornstarch, and salt. Add milk; bring to a boil for 1 minute. Pour a little bit of the hot mixture into the egg yolks; stir, then pour egg yolk mixture into the saucepan and cook for 1 minute. Add margarine and continue cooking for 1 minute. Stir in vanilla. Let cool to room temperature. Add 2 bananas for Banana Cream Pie; add 3 Tbsp. baking cocoa for Chocolate Cream Pie; add 1/2–3/4 C. coconut for Coconut Cream Pie. Pour into pie shell. Refrigerate. Makes 8 servings.

Debbie Hatch
Panguitch 2nd Ward
Panguitch Utah Stake
Panguitch, Utah

Strawberry Rhubarb Pie

Pastry for a double-crust pie
4 C. rhubarb, chopped
2 C. strawberries, sliced
1¼ C. sugar
½ tsp. salt

½ tsp. orange rind
½ tsp. nutmeg
3 Tbsp. cornstarch or flour
Butter (optional)

Line pie plate with half the pastry to make bottom pie shell. Combine rhubarb and strawberries; pour into pie shell. In a medium bowl, mix sugar, salt, orange rind, nutmeg, and flour. Spread evenly on top of fruit. If desired, dot with butter. Place top crust over pie and crimp edges. Bake at 375 for about 1 hour, until crust is golden brown. Makes 8 servings. *Note:* For a particularly beautiful crust, roll pastry out larger than the pie plate. After placing top crust, trim both crusts about ¾ inch larger than pie plate. Fold under carefully and crimp evenly with fingers in a zigzag pattern all around the edge. Brush milk all over the top, not letting it pool too much at the edges, and sprinkle lightly with sugar before baking. Mom's family used black bear grease to make their pie crusts, and she says that it's especially delicious.

Zoanne Anderson
Bear Mountain Ward
Anchorage Alaska Chugach Stake
Chugiak, Alaska

My mother, Lena Laraux Gregory, was Yup'ik Eskimo from the Akiak/Bethel area of soutwestern Alaska. She left high school in Bethel to get married at the age of seventeen. She and my dad, Glenn, who was the proverbial bush pilot, moved to Koyukuk and later had seven daughters and one son. They ran a mercantile and flying service out of Tanana, Alaska, from 1964 to 1978. We kids grew up working hard and making our own entertainment. Our village of five hundred people had no televisions, little radio, and few phones. We played outdoors in the dirt, by the river, or in the woods. We grew up learning how to cook, sew, knit, crochet, embroider, and play musical instruments. We tried our hand at skin sewing and beadwork, but none of us became proficient at it. Our mother was an excellent example of the scriptural virtuous woman "whose price is far above rubies."

Cape Breton Pork Pies

Shells:
1 C. butter
2 C. flour
4 Tbsp. powdered sugar

Filling:
2 C. dates, chopped
1 C. water
1½ C. packed brown sugar
1 tsp. lemon juice
1 tsp. vanilla

Maple Icing:
3 Tbsp. butter, softened
½ tsp. maple flavoring
Dash salt
2 C. powdered sugar
2 Tbsp. warm cream

Shells: Cut butter into dry ingredients. Knead until well blended. Press in small muffin tins to form a tart. Bake at 425 for about 10 minutes. Set aside to cool.

Filling: Combine all ingredients in a large saucepan, and cook until dates are soft. Cool. Spoon filling into shells and top with maple icing.

Maple Icing: Cream butter, maple flavoring, and salt. Blend in powdered sugar alternating with cream. Add more sugar and cream if needed to get right consistency. Makes 12 servings.

Anne Donovan
North Sydney Branch
New Glasgow Nova Scotia District
North Sydney, Cape Breton Island
Nova Scotia, Canada

It is somewhat of a mystery how these delicious sweets got their name. Some suggest that originally pork fat may have been used instead of butter, or the name might simply reflect how funny Cape Bretoners are. Still others suggest that the recipe may have originated as a meat pie, similar to mincemeat pie, then evolved into more of a dessert pie using dates and other fruits like those used in Christmas mincemeat pies today. This pork pie recipe is one of my favorites, and it's hard to eat just one. I always make these at Christmas time, and now each Christmas my daughter makes them for family and guests. They are always a big hit. Nova Scotia is a small province on Canada's east coast that is famous for its seafood and great hospitality, and Cape Breton is an island that is part of the province. Cape Breton—which has repeatedly been voted one of the top islands in the world to visit—is famous for the Cabot Trail, which winds through its beautifully scenic mountains.

Mother's Meringue-Topped Cream Pie

2 C. milk
1 C. sugar
4 Tbsp. cornstarch
1 tsp. salt
6 eggs, separated
2 Tbsp. vanilla

2 Tbsp. butter
1 baked pie shell
½ tsp. cream of tartar
¼ C. sugar
1 baked pie shell

Put milk on to boil in a large saucepan over medium heat. In a medium bowl, mix 1 C. sugar, cornstarch, and salt; when milk is hot, gently blend sugar mixture into milk. Continue cooking until mixture starts to boil. (If too soupy, mix 3 Tbsp. cornstarch with ½ C. water until dissolved, and add a little at a time to the milk mixture until it begins to thicken.) In a separate bowl, beat egg yolks. Add a little of the hot mixture to the egg yolks, beat, and pour eggs into the saucepan. Cook until thick and bubbly. Remove from heat. Stir in vanilla and butter. For Vanilla Cream Pie, pour mixture into baked pie shell. You can also make a variety of pies with this filling:

Chocolate Cream Pie—Stir ¾ C. chocolate chips into milk mixture while cooking.

Coconut Cream Pie—Add ¾ C. coconut, reserving 2 Tbsp. to sprinkle on top of meringue.

Banana Cream Pie—Stir 1–2 sliced bananas into filling after it has been cooked.

To make meringue, stir cream of tartar into egg whites. Beat until stiff; gradually add ¼ C. sugar to sweeten. Spoon onto top of pie, using back of spoon to lift peaks. Bake at 350 for about 10 minutes or until lightly browned. Makes 8 servings.

Julie Renfrow
Clinton Ward
Jackson Mississippi Stake
Clinton, Mississippi

Fresh Peach Pie

1½ C. sugar

3 C. water

2 Tbsp. cornstarch

1 small cook-and-serve lemon pie filling
   (Jell-O)

Fresh ripe peaches

1 baked pie crust

Whipped cream

In a saucepan, combine sugar, water, cornstarch, and lemon pudding mix. Cook and stir until thick and bubbly. Remove from heat and allow to cool. Peel and slice peaches. Arrange a layer of peaches in pie crust. Cover with filling; continue to layer sliced peaches and filling to fill pie crust. Cool pie before serving; serve with real whipped cream. Makes 8 servings.

Donna Schulze
Granite Ward
Sandy Utah Granite View Stake
Sandy, Utah

I grew up in Holladay, Utah, on a one-acre farm. We grew everything we ate, including beef, chickens, fruit, and vegetables. I was taught to be thrifty and to not waste anything. My parents grew up during the Depression and prepared for the future by canning, preserving, and growing anything we needed. My father never borrowed money for anything in his life, including their house. What was not preserved for our family was either given away or sold on the sidewalk in front of our house. They did this to stretch the food budget.

We enjoyed the benefits of having fresh cream, eggs, fruit, and vegetables, and we learned to eat them all. My mother loved to cook, and she created many recipes, working until she had each one perfected. This Peach Pie is her own recipe; she made it with the fresh, sweet peaches they grew and served it with real whipped cream, fresh from the cow. My children share these recipes and remember having them at Grandma and Grandpa's house.

Caramel Pecan Pumpkin Pie

Pie:

1 30-oz. can pumpkin
1 C. sugar
1 5-oz. can evaporated milk
3 eggs
2 tsp. cinnamon

½ tsp. salt
1 yellow cake mix
1 C. butter or margarine,
   melted
1½ C. pecans, chopped

Caramel Sauce:

1 C. butter
2 C. packed brown sugar
1 C. cream
Whipped cream

Pie: Line 2 9-inch pie pans with waxed paper and coat with cooking spray. In a large bowl, mix pumpkin, sugar, and milk; beat in eggs, cinnamon, and salt. Pour into prepared pie pans. Sprinkle cake mix on top, drizzle with butter, and sprinkle with pecans. Press down. Bake at 350 for 50–60 minutes or until golden brown. Remove from oven; flip over onto plate and let cool for 2 hours.

Caramel Sauce: In a saucepan, combine butter, brown sugar, and cream; heat and stir over low heat until sugar is dissolved. Keep warm until ready to serve. Pour over slices of pie just before serving; top with whipped cream. Makes 2 9-inch pies.

Shauna Pearson
Rapid City 3rd Ward
Rapid City South Dakota Stake
Rapid City, South Dakota

My mom is quite a character. She is the mother of eleven children, and it has definitely made her a little crazy. My siblings and I often laugh about our Mom stories. One of my favorites is the day that she and my brother were trying to light the pilot light on the furnace, getting instructions over the phone from my dad, who was out of town. I was sitting in my bedroom when I heard a loud BOOM and a scream. I thought our house was being blown up! I jumped up and started running, along with the rest of my siblings. When we reached the furnace room, my mom was standing there with a look of shock on her face; her dark hair was standing straight up, and her face was black except for two white circles around her eyes. My brother was still talking to my dad and trying to light the furnace; after a second BOOM my mom went upstairs. I looked up the stairs and that little black face was peeking around the corner, crying. She hollered, "Tell him to forget it! He's going to blow us all up to heck!" My siblings and I just laughed. We all like to tease my mom, but I wouldn't trade her for any other mom on earth. She is a spiritual giant and I am truly blessed to call her Mom.

Dutch Apple Pie

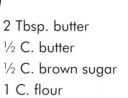

6–7 tart apples
⅔ C. sugar
1 tsp. cinnamon
2 Tbsp. flour
1 9-inch pie crust

2 Tbsp. butter
½ C. butter
½ C. brown sugar
1 C. flour

Peel, core, and slice apples. In a large bowl, combine sugar, cinnamon, and flour; stir in the apples. Pour into prepared crust. Dot with 2 Tbsp. butter. In a medium bowl, combine ½ C. butter, brown sugar, and flour until crumbly. Spoon on top of pie. Bake at 375 for 50–60 minutes. Makes 8 servings.

Chuck Melick
Grove Creek 10th Ward
Pleasant Grove Utah Grove Creek Stake
Pleasant Grove, Utah

My mom, Billie Melick, loved to cook and especially enjoyed baking. While some moms baked cookies or cakes, my mom's specialty was baking pies. In fact, her pies were always a favorite at the fund-raising bazaars that were held in my home ward in Mansfield, Ohio; people waited for Billie's pies to arrive so the bake sales could begin. Her pie crust was always marvelous, and she meticulously rolled out the dough, cut off the excess, and crimped the crust in her own unique way. I have tried for more than twenty years to recreate her crimping style, but have never learned to do it quite like she did. I remember one time she was making a fresh strawberry pie when the baked crust slid off of the counter and broke into pieces. She tasted a quick bite of the crust and found that it was flaky and beautiful—so, in an uncharacteristic move, she simply grabbed handfuls of the crust, placed them in bowls, spooned the strawberry topping on top of each, and served the pie just like that! She made lots of different pies—German chocolate, pecan, coconut cream, strawberry, and everyone's favorite, Dutch apple. It was always the first pie eaten at Christmas, Thanksgiving, or any other special family event. Today not a holiday goes by that my two sisters and I don't make a Dutch Apple Pie or two to serve to our families and think of mother's amazing pie-baking skills.

{ CAKES }

Heaven is at the feet of mothers.

{ Roebuck }

Can't Put Your Fork Down Carrot Cake

Cake:

1 Tbsp. baking soda

1 Tbsp. salt

2 C. flour

2 C. sugar

2 Tbsp. cinnamon

4 eggs

1 Tbsp. vanilla

1½ C. vegetable oil

4 C. carrots, shredded by hand

Icing:

2 8-oz. pkgs. cream cheese

1 C. butter

2 lb. powdered sugar

1 C. coconut (optional)

1 C. pecans, chopped (optional)

Sift dry ingredients together. In a separate bowl, beat eggs; add vanilla and oil. Mix with dry ingredients. Stir in carrots. Bake in three 9-inch greased and floured cake pans at 350 for 30–35 minutes. To make icing, combine cream cheese and butter. Stir in powdered sugar until thick and fluffy. Add coconut and pecans if desired; we love them, but you can leave them out if your family does not like them. Spread on each layer of the cooled cake. Makes 10 servings. *Note:* To decorate this cake for a wedding, wedding shower, or other special occasion, cut the stems of a dozen roses to about 2 inches in length; stick the flowers all over the top of the cake. Beautiful!

Reagan Leadbetter
"Good Things Utah"
ABC Channel 4
Salt Lake City, Utah

This is the very best carrot cake I have ever had. It is SO moist! My dad loves carrot cake, so this is what I make him every time he comes to visit his grandchildren. The great thing about this cake is that it is so easy, yet it tastes like it is from the best bakery in the world. And it is—it's from your kitchen! I am the mother of two boys, ages four and six. They are juicy delicious, and love to put their fingers in whatever I am making in the kitchen!

Strawberry Cake from Scratch

1 C. butter, softened

2 C. sugar

1 small box strawberry-flavored gelatin

4 eggs, room temperature and separated

2¾ C. cake flour, sifted before measuring

2½ tsp. baking powder

1 C. whole milk, room temperature

1 Tbsp. vanilla

½ C. strawberry puree made from frozen sweetened strawberries (use a blender to blend semi-thawed berries)

1½ C. cream

1 8-oz. pkg. cream cheese

1 C. sugar

⅛ tsp. salt

1 tsp. vanilla

Preheat oven to 350. Grease and flour 2 9-inch round cake pans. In a large bowl, cream butter, 2 C. sugar, and strawberry gelatin mix until light and fluffy. Beat in egg yolks one at a time, mixing well after each addition. In a separate bowl, combine the flour and baking powder; stir into the batter alternately with the milk. Blend in 1 Tbsp. vanilla and strawberry puree. Whip egg whites until fluffy; fold into batter. Divide the batter evenly between the prepared pans. Bake at 350 for 25–30 minutes, or until a small knife inserted into the center of the cake comes out clean. Allow cakes to cool in their pans over a wire rack for at least 10 minutes before tapping out to cool completely. In a small bowl, beat cream until stiff peaks form; set aside. In a large bowl, combine cream cheese, 1 C. sugar, salt, and 1 tsp. vanilla. Beat until smooth; fold in whipped cream. Frost cake. Makes 16 servings.

Elizabeth Mortonsen
Charleston 1st Ward
Charleston South Carolina Stake
Folly Beach, South Carolina

My mom made this cake for me every single birthday when I was a child. Making it today brings back so many great memories of her. She always sacrifices so much for her kids, and I love her more than words could ever say. I hope that I can be as great a mother as she was to me and my siblings. Even at thirty, I sometimes want to curl up in my mom's bed and talk forever. She's the kind of person that makes you laugh until you cry. I admire her in every way. She is beautiful inside and out; I definitely won the mom lottery!

Peanut Butter and Fudge Cake

1 yellow cake mix

½ C. smooth peanut butter

½ C. butter or margarine

½ C. cocoa

¼ tsp. salt

6 Tbsp. milk

1 tsp. vanilla

1 lb. powdered sugar

Mix cake according to package instructions. Stir in peanut butter. Bake according to package instructions. In a saucepan, melt butter; remove from heat and stir in cocoa until smooth. Add salt, milk, and vanilla. Add powdered sugar and stir until fairly smooth. Return saucepan to heat, stirring constantly until the mixture is a smooth spreading consistency. Frost the cake immediately, or the frosting will quickly become too hard to work with. Makes 20 servings. *Note:* Baking the cake as a single-layer sheet cake is the easiest way to make this recipe, because the frosting can simply be poured over the cake while still in the pan.

Charlotte Cantwell
Cobblestone Ward
Providence Utah Stake
Providence, Utah

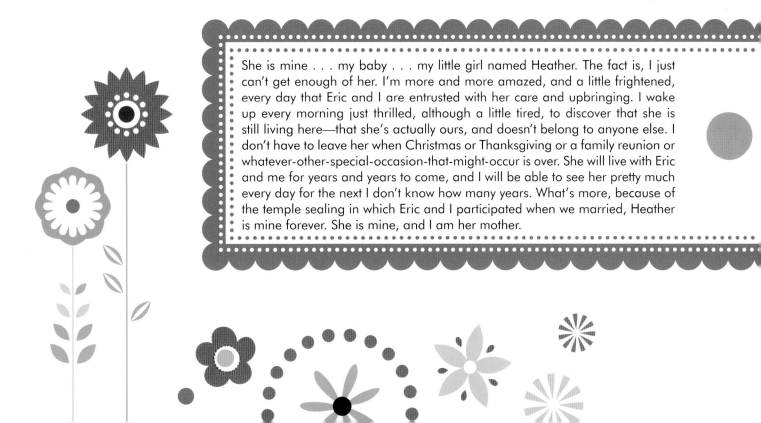

She is mine . . . my baby . . . my little girl named Heather. The fact is, I just can't get enough of her. I'm more and more amazed, and a little frightened, every day that Eric and I are entrusted with her care and upbringing. I wake up every morning just thrilled, although a little tired, to discover that she is still living here—that she's actually ours, and doesn't belong to anyone else. I don't have to leave her when Christmas or Thanksgiving or a family reunion or whatever-other-special-occasion-that-might-occur is over. She will live with Eric and me for years and years to come, and I will be able to see her pretty much every day for the next I don't know how many years. What's more, because of the temple sealing in which Eric and I participated when we married, Heather is mine forever. She is mine, and I am her mother.

Chocolate Crock Pot Cake

1 chocolate cake mix

1 small box instant chocolate pudding mix

1 C. sour cream

4 eggs

1 C. water

¾ C. vegetable oil

1 C. chocolate chips

Combine chocolate cake mix, pudding mix, sour cream, eggs, water, and oil. Beat for 2 minutes. Stir in chocolate chips. Pour into greased crock pot. Cook on low for 5–6 hours or on high for 3–4 hours. Cooking on low is preferred, because the cake tends to burn on the bottom if it is cooked too fast. Be sure to watch, though, because every crock pot is different. Makes 8–12 servings.

Heather Leishman
Paradise 2nd Ward
Paradise Utah Stake
Paradise, Utah

My mother has nine children: one boy, Jason, and eight girls—Laura, Mary, Amy, Emily, Tara, Kristy, Heidi, and me. My mother is the most amazing person. She can teach herself to do anything. She is very talented at sewing, cooking, and quilting, and is the best grandma in the whole world. My sisters and I get together at least once a month for "girls' night out." My family also gets together for birthdays and holidays. All of my sisters love chocolate, and we all love this Chocolate Crock Pot Cake. Even my brother's wife, Debbie, loves the chocolate cake. Jason prefers the vanilla cake, though, so sometimes I make that one for him. All eight of us girls are married, so maybe we can convince our husbands to prefer the vanilla so we can even things up a bit for Jason!

Celestial Cake

1 8-oz. pkg. ladies fingers (cookies)

Milk for dipping cookies

1 C. milk

1 Tbsp. cornstarch

3 egg yolks

1 ½ C. chocolate chips
   (milk, semisweet, or a combination)

⅔ C. butter

Use a spring-cake tin (spring-form pan). Line bottom with baking (parchment) paper. Cover bottom of tin with ladies fingers, dipping every one of the cookies in milk before putting it in the pan. In a saucepan, mix 1 C. milk, cornstarch, and egg yolks; heat over low, stirring constantly, until the mixture thickens like pudding. Remove from heat. Stir chocolate chips into the pudding until chips are melted. Stir butter into the pudding until butter is melted. Spoon ⅓ of the pudding over the layer of ladies fingers. Top with another layer of ladies fingers that have been dipped in milk. Spoon another ⅓ of pudding on top. Cover with a final layer of ladies fingers that have been dipped in milk. Spoon the last ⅓ of the pudding on top. Refrigerate, overnight if possible. Makes 10–12 servings. *Note:* You can decorate the top of the cake if desired. It is easy to increase the recipe by simply adding a little bit more of each ingredient.

Steven Heinrichs
Apeldoorn Ward
Apeldoorn Stake
Apeldoorn, The Netherlands

This cake is chocolate heaven! We eat it at birthdays and holidays. Its real name is Ladies Fingers Cake, but since everybody loves it so much we change the name to Celestial Cake. My mother always makes this cake on my birthday. I took this recipe with me on my mission, and since Mom wasn't there to make it for me, I decided to make it for myself on both birthdays away from home! On my mother's last birthday before I left on my mission, I wanted to treat her, so I made and decorated the cake for her. She was turning forty-one, but to tease her, I put a big forty-two on top of the cake. I guess my mom doesn't think about her age that often, because she didn't even question the forty-two! No one said anything to her about it being a joke, and she went on to believe she was forty-two for an entire year. The next year my dad kept telling her, "Well, you finally turned forty-two." So I guess I stole a year from her life, because in her mind she was never forty-one! I love my beautiful mother.

Graham Cracker Cake

5 eggs

3 C. graham cracker crumbs

1 C. butter or margarine, melted

1 C. pecans, chopped

2 C. sugar

1 20-oz. can crushed pineapple

¾ C. sugar

2 Tbsp. flour

1 8-oz. tub whipped topping (Cool Whip)

Additional pecans, chopped

Maraschino cherries

Beat eggs. In a separate bowl, combine graham cracker crumbs, melted butter, pecans, and sugar. Add to eggs. Mix well and pour into greased and floured 9 x 13-inch pan. Bake at 350 for 30–40 minutes. In a saucepan, combine pineapple, sugar, and flour. Cook and stir until thickened. When cake is cool, spread pineapple topping over cake. Top with whipped cream, chopped pecans, and cherries. Makes 24 servings.

Pam Harris
English Indian Ward
New Albany Indiana Stake
French Lick, Indiana

Mom's Boiled Raisin Cake

2 C. raisins

2 C. packed brown sugar

2 C. water

2 tsp. cinnamon

1 tsp. cloves

1 tsp. nutmeg

1 tsp. allspice

1 tsp. ginger

½ C. shortening

2 tsp. baking soda

2 tsp. salt

2 tsp. baking powder

2 C. flour

1 C. fruit or nuts

2 eggs

(recipe continued on next page)

(Mom's Boiled Raisin Cake, continued)

In a saucepan, combine raisins, brown sugar, water, cinnamon, cloves, nutmeg, allspice, ginger, and shortening. Bring to a boil and then allow to cool completely. In a separate bowl, mix the dry ingredients with fruit or nuts. Beat the eggs and add to the cooled raisin mixture. Add the liquid mixture to the dry mixture and stir well. Bake in a well-greased 9 x 13-inch pan at 350 for 50–60 minutes. Makes 12 servings.

Candy McKerchar
Lloydminster Branch
Edmonton Bonnie Doon Stake
Lloydminster, Saskatchewan
Canada

My mom often made this cake when she was expecting company; I remember coming home from school to the wonderful aroma of its spices. My mom taught me how to make this cake when I was about twelve in preparation for Thanksgiving guests. My mom passed away when I was fourteen; I love to make this cake, because the wonderful smell of it baking in the oven reminds me of when my mom made it. Now I love to make it for guests as well, especially during Thanksgiving!

Peanut Butter Cake with Peanut Butter Frosting

½ C. creamy peanut butter
½ C. butter, softened
4 eggs
1 18.25-oz. pkg. butter cake mix
⅔ C. water

½ C. butter, softened
1 C. creamy peanut butter
2 C. powdered sugar
3 Tbsp. milk, or as needed

Preheat oven to 325. Grease and flour 2 9-inch round cake pans. Combine ½ C. peanut butter and ½ C. butter or margarine; cream until light and fluffy. Add eggs one at time, mixing well after each one. Add cake mix alternately with water. Stir until just combined. Pour batter into prepared pans. Bake at 325 for 25 minutes or until cake tests done. Allow cakes to cool in pan for 10 minutes and then turn out onto a cooling rack to cool completely. In a medium bowl, combine ½ C. butter and 1 C. peanut butter; beat with an electric mixer. Gradually mix in powdered sugar; when the frosting starts to get thick, incorporate milk 1 Tbsp. at a time until all of the sugar is mixed in and the frosting is thick and spreadable. Beat for at least 3 minutes until fluffy. Assemble and frost cooled cake. Makes 16 servings.

Kadence Suiter
Stone Oak 1st Ward
San Antonio Texas North Stake
San Antonio, Texas

German Chocolate Icing or Coconut Pecan Icing

5 egg yolks
1½ C. sugar
½ C. butter
1½ C. evaporated milk

1 small can coconut or ½ bag shredded
  coconut
1 tsp. vanilla
1 C. pecans, chopped (optional)

In a saucepan, mix egg yolks, sugar, butter, and milk; cook over medium heat until thick, usually about 12 minutes. Stir constantly and be careful not to burn. When thickened, stir in coconut, vanilla, and pecans (if desired). Pour over warm cake. I poke holes in my cake with a butter knife so that the icing sinks down into the cake. This icing goes great over chocolate, devil's food, or German chocolate cake. Makes 8–10 servings.

Karan Burns
Senatobia Mississippi Ward
Memphis Tennessee Stake
Senatobia, Mississippi

This is a family recipe that came from a late aunt, and it is my all-time favorite cake icing. Recently we had a benefit garage sale for my son-in-law, who had suffered a brain injury in a car accident; part of the sale was a bake sale. My mom made this icing, put it on a devil's food cake, and sold slices at the bake sale; they quickly sold. Later that day, one of the customers called and asked who had made the cake; she raved about how wonderful it was, and asked if I thought my mom would make her a whole cake. I told her I was sure Mom would give her the recipe, but the customer said she wanted Mom to make her the cake. She has since made numerous cakes for this customer. Anyone who tries this icing recipe loves it! My husband likes to tease me that when we got married the only thing I could cook was German chocolate cake and no-bake cookies. I hate to admit it, but he is almost right. My brother says he doesn't eat many sweets today because I burned him out on sweets while we were growing up.

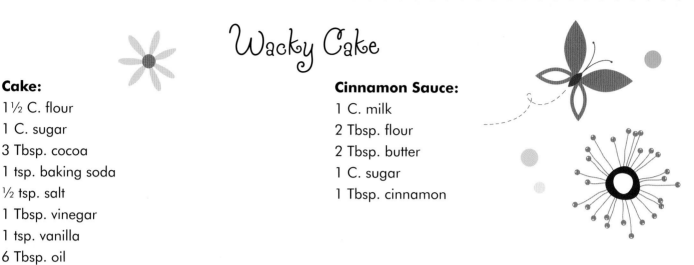

Wacky Cake

Cake:

1½ C. flour

1 C. sugar

3 Tbsp. cocoa

1 tsp. baking soda

½ tsp. salt

1 Tbsp. vinegar

1 tsp. vanilla

6 Tbsp. oil

1 C. lukewarm water

Cinnamon Sauce:

1 C. milk

2 Tbsp. flour

2 Tbsp. butter

1 C. sugar

1 Tbsp. cinnamon

Combine 1½ C. flour, 1 C. sugar, cocoa, baking soda, and salt in a greased 8-inch cake pan. Make three holes. Put vinegar in one hole, vanilla in one hole, and oil in the third hole. Pour water over all and mix well. Bake at 350 for 35–40 minutes. In a saucepan, whisk together milk and 1 Tbsp. flour. Whisk in butter and heat to a boil. Simmer for 1 minute. Stir in 1 C. sugar and cinnamon. Pour over cake. Makes 6–8 servings.

The Brockholt Cousins
Heatheridge 9th Ward
Orem Utah Heatheridge Stake
Orem, Utah

For birthdays, we all gather on a Sunday afternoon for dinner and cake. Wacky Cake has become really popular because it brings back memories for our dads and uncles of helping their mother make it. Now we all get to make it with our grandma. Jay, Wes, Kyla, Katryn, Lacy, and Bryce all crowd around the counter helping poke the holes in the cake mix and pour ingredients so we can all claim, "I made this cake for you! Happy birthday!"

Carrot Cake

Cake:

4 eggs

1 C. packed brown sugar

1 C. sugar

1½ C. vegetable oil

1 tsp. vanilla

2 C. flour

2 tsp. soda

½ tsp. salt

¼ tsp. allspice

1 tsp. cinnamon

3 C. carrots, finely grated

Cream Cheese Frosting:

½ C. butter, softened

3 oz. cream cheese, softened

2 C. powdered sugar

1 tsp. vanilla

Beat eggs, brown sugar, sugar, oil, and vanilla. Set aside. Combine flour, soda, salt, allspice, and cinnamon. Mix into wet ingredients. Add carrots. Bake at 350 for 40 minutes; check with toothpick to make sure the cake is done. Cool. For frosting, combine butter and cream cheese. Beat in powdered sugar and vanilla. Frost cooled cake. Makes 15 servings.

Charity Flanagan
Prairie 8th Ward
Prairie Utah Stake
West Jordan, Utah

My mom has made this cake since I was very little. I didn't even care that there were carrots in it—I just knew it tasted GOOD! Most kids ask for a chocolate cake for their birthday, but I wanted my mom's Carrot Cake. Cakes purchased at the store were good, but none compared to the one my mom made. I'm thirty-three now, and still request this carrot cake for my birthday; my husband and children love it, too!

Dump Cake

1 20-oz. can crushed pineapple

1 21-oz. can cherry pie filling

1 yellow cake mix

1 C. butter

Pour undrained pineapple into a 9 x 13-inch baking dish. Spread evenly across bottom of pan. Spoon cherry pie filling over the pineapple. Sprinkle dry cake mix evenly over top of fruit. Cut butter in slices and arrange over top of cake mix. Do not stir. Bake at 350 for about 1 hour. Serve warm with ice cream. Makes 12 servings.

Melanie Gilbert
Stockbridge Ward
Jonesboro Georgia Stake
Stockbridge, Georgia

White Chocolate Raspberry Cake

White Chocolate Cake:

1 white cake mix (without pudding)

1 small box instant white chocolate pudding mix

½ C. sugar

¾ C. applesauce

¾ C. water

4 egg whites

1 C. sour cream

¾ tsp. vanilla

White Chocolate Frosting:

6 oz. white chocolate, coarsely chopped

8-oz. pkg. cream cheese, at room temperature

4 Tbsp. butter, at room temperature

1 tsp. vanilla

2½ C. powdered sugar

White Chocolate Cream Topping:

1 small box instant white chocolate pudding mix

1 C. milk

8-oz. tub whipped topping, thawed

White Chocolate Curls and Fresh Raspberries:

White chocolate shavings and curls, or white chocolate chips, chopped

2 pts. fresh raspberries

(recipe continued on next page)

(White Chocolate Raspberry Cake, continued)

White Chocolate Cake: In a large bowl, combine cake mix, pudding mix, and sugar. Beat until blended. Add applesauce, water, and egg whites; mix for 2 minutes. Add sour cream and vanilla; blend for 30 seconds. Divide batter among 3 9-inch greased and floured round pans. Bake at 350 for approximately 15 minutes. Don't overbake. While cake is baking and cooling, prepare frosting, cream topping, and garnishes.

White Chocolate Frosting: In a small pan over low heat, melt chopped chocolate, stirring constantly. Remove from heat and let cool. In a large bowl, combine cream cheese and butter; beat for 30 seconds. Add melted chocolate and blend on low for 30 seconds. Add vanilla and powdered sugar and blend on low for 30 more seconds. Increase mixer speed to medium and beat 1 minute until fluffy. Keep refrigerated. Makes 3 cups frosting, enough to frost a 2- to 3-layer cake.

White Chocolate Cream Topping: Place pudding mix in medium bowl; gradually stir in milk. Beat with wire whisk for 2 minutes. Fold in whipped topping. Makes 4 cups.

Assembling the cake: Trim cake if needed so layers fit nicely together. Place bottom layer on cake plate. Frost bottom layer with White Chocolate Frosting and arrange up to ½ pt. raspberries on top, keeping ½ inch away from the sides. Place middle layer on top and frost, arranging up to ½ pt. raspberries on top. Place final layer on top and frost top and sides of cake with remaining frosting. Frost entire cake, including top and sides, with White Chocolate Cream Topping. Arrange white chocolate curls or chopped chips on top and garnish with raspberries as you see fit. Keep refrigerated; remove from refrigerator an hour before serving. Makes 8–12 servings.

Stephanie Valdez
Palo Verde Ward
Las Vegas Nevada Redrock Stake
Las Vegas, Nevada

My mom, Kathy Terry, got this recipe from a friend, and it is now a family favorite! While serving as stake Relief Society president for the BYU 13th Stake, my mom and her presidency—first counselor Sharon Call, second counselor Weezie Flagg, and secretary Linda Ellertson—had the privilege of serving dinner to President H. David Burton. Weezie brought this White Chocolate Raspberry Cake and, in the end, there wasn't a crumb left! Now we enjoy this decadent dessert in our own family whenever an occasion arises. My mom has always made parties and gatherings extra special with her fabulous desserts. Even though this cake takes a lot of work, it's completely worth it.

Pecan Carrot Cake

4 eggs
1 C. vegetable oil
¼ C. unsweetened applesauce
1 C. sugar
1 C. packed brown sugar
2 tsp. vanilla
1 8-oz. can crushed pineapple, drained
2 C. flour
2 tsp. baking soda
2 tsp. baking powder
½ tsp. salt

2 tsp. cinnamon
¼ tsp. nutmeg
3 C. carrots, grated (use coarse side of grater, or they become mush)
1 C. pecans, chopped
½ C. butter, softened
1 8-oz. cream cheese, softened
4 C. powdered sugar
1 tsp. vanilla
1 C. pecans, chopped

Preheat oven to 350. Grease and flour a 9 x 13-inch pan. In a large bowl, beat eggs, oil, applesauce, sugar, brown sugar, vanilla, and crushed pineapple. Mix in flour, baking soda, baking powder, salt, cinnamon, and nutmeg. Stir in carrots. Fold in 1 C. pecans. Pour into prepared pan. Bake at 350 for 40–50 minutes, or until a toothpick inserted into the center of the cake comes out clean. Let cool in pan for 10 minutes, then turn out onto a wire rack and cool completely. In a medium bowl, combine butter, cream cheese, powdered sugar, and vanilla. Beat until the mixture is smooth and creamy. Stir in 1 C. pecans. Frost the cooled cake. Makes 18 servings.

Karoline Bradley
Washington DC 3rd Ward
Washington DC Stake
Washington, DC

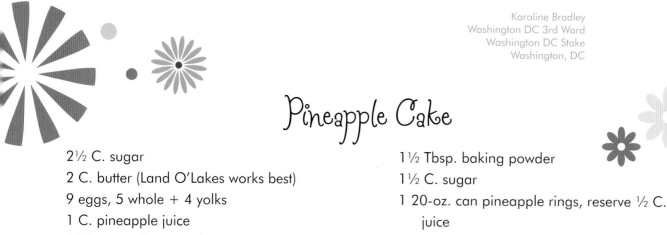

Pineapple Cake

2½ C. sugar
2 C. butter (Land O'Lakes works best)
9 eggs, 5 whole + 4 yolks
1 C. pineapple juice
1 Tbsp. vanilla
2¼ C. flour

1½ Tbsp. baking powder
1½ C. sugar
1 20-oz. can pineapple rings, reserve ½ C. juice
Berries

(recipe continued on next page)

(Pineapple Cake, continued)

In a large bowl, blend sugar and butter. Add eggs and yolks, one at a time, mixing after each one. Stir in pineapple juice and vanilla. In a separate bowl, mix flour and baking powder. Stir into the butter mixture one spoonful at a time. This takes awhile, but makes the cake spongy. In a saucepan, melt sugar until it's a deep caramel color. Spread sugar over the bottom of a well-greased bundt pan; lay pineapple rings on top of the sugar. Pour the cake batter over the pineapple. Bake at 325 for 1½ hours, or until a toothpick comes out clean. Turn cake out of pan. Prick the cake all over with a toothpick; pour ½ C. reserved pineapple juice over the top to keep the cake moist. Decorate with berries. Makes 12 servings.

Maria Baptista
Central Falls Ward
Providence Rhode Island Stake
Pawtucket, Rhode Island

Russian Apple Pie Cake

5 eggs
1 C. sugar
1 C. flour
2 tsp. baking powder

⅛ tsp. cinnamon
1 tsp. vanilla
3 apples, peeled and diced

In a large bowl, combine eggs and sugar; beat for 2 minutes. Add flour, baking powder, cinnamon, and vanilla. Lightly grease an 8 x 8-inch pan. Pour ⅓ of the batter into the pan. Spread ½ of the apples on the batter. Cover with ⅓ of the batter. Spread the rest of the apples on the batter. Pour the rest of the batter on top. Cook at 325 for 35–40 minutes. Makes 10–12 servings.

Sandi Henderson
Nakhodka Branch
Vladivostok Mission
Nakhodka, Russia

Wild Blueberry Cake

4 eggs, separated
1 C. shortening or butter
2 C. sugar
2 tsp. vanilla
3 C. flour

2½ tsp. baking powder
½ tsp. salt
⅔ C. canned evaporated milk (undiluted)
1½ C. blueberries
Extra sugar for sprinkling

Preheat oven to 350. Beat egg whites in mixer bowl until stiff. Remove and set aside. In same mixer bowl, cream shortening and sugar. Blend in yolks and vanilla. In a separate bowl, mix dry ingredients. Add dry ingredients and milk, alternately, 3 times each, to creamed mixture. Fold in beaten whites. Spread half of the batter in greased and floured 9 x 13-inch baking pan. Sprinkle half of the blueberries over the batter. Sprinkle sugar over top of blueberries. Repeat layers, sprinkling sugar over top of blueberries again. Bake at 350 for 25 minutes if using fresh berries, 65 minutes if using frozen berries. Test with toothpick. Makes 12 servings.

Lena Laraux Gregory
Fairbanks 3rd Ward
Faribanks Alaska Stake
Faribanks, Alaska

The only native fresh fruit we have in Alaska are wild berries—including blueberries, lowbush cranberries (lingonberries), highbush cranberries, crowberries, salmonberries, and, in some areas, wild currants. Though our berries are small and very tart, they are highly prized and sought after. I am Yup'ik Eskimo from the Akiak/Bethel area of southwestern Alaska; my husband, Glenn, grew up around Dolores, Colorado. We have seven girls and one boy. Glenn is a bush pilot, and together we ran a flying service out of Tanana, Alaska. We first learned about the gospel of Jesus Christ after an airplane accident Glenn had during a snowstorm outside Koyukuk in early 1952. He was nearly killed; the air traffic controller who took the accident report, Frank Coil, had recently been converted by reading the Book of Mormon, but had not yet been baptized. The Coils showed particular kindness to us. Within a couple of years, both our families moved to Fairbanks, and our friendship continued. By that time Frank was a member of the Church and was a stake missionary; he taught us, and we were baptized in 1954. On Halloween in 1956, we were in the Idaho Falls Idaho Temple after driving down the Alcan Highway with five little girls in minus-sixty-degree weather. Frank believes I am the first Eskimo to have been endowed in the temple.

Strawberry Heaven

4 egg whites
1 C. sugar
2 C. shredded coconut
1 C. shredded chocolate, divided

2 C. cream
1 10-oz. pkg. frozen sliced, sweetened
   strawberries, crushed

Whip egg whites and sugar until stiff peaks form. Carefully stir in coconut and all but 2 Tbsp. shredded chocolate. Grease and flour 2 spring-form cake pans. Bake at 350 on the bottom rack of the oven for 30 minutes. Remove outside rings from pans. Whip the cream; carefully fold crushed strawberries into the whipped cream. Spread half the strawberries and cream on one layer of cake; top with the second layer of cake, and spread with the remaining strawberries and cream. Sprinkle with remaining shredded chocolate. Makes 8–10 servings. *Note:* You can also increase the recipe by half.

Rebekka Ran Gudmundsdottir
Selfoss Branch
Reykjavik District
Selfoss, Iceland

My mother loves to cook, and she has taught me how. I prefer cooking simple things. There are seven in my family—my parents, two sons, and three daughters—and we all love it when my mother makes this wonderful strawberry cake.

Vanilla Crock Pot Cake

1 vanilla cake mix

1 small box instant vanilla pudding mix

1 C. sour cream

4 eggs

1 C. water

¾ C. vegetable oil

1 C. vanilla chips

Combine vanilla cake mix, pudding mix, sour cream, eggs, water, and oil. Beat for 2 minutes. Stir in vanilla chips. Pour into greased crock pot. Cook on low for 5–6 hours or on high for 3–4 hours. Cooking on low is preferred, because the cake tends to burn on the bottom if it is cooked too fast. Be sure to watch, though, because every crock pot is different. Makes 8–12 servings.

Jason Mathison
Forest Hills Ward
Valley View Utah Stake
Layton, Utah

My mother has nine children: eight girls—Laura, Mary, Amy, Emily, Tara, Heather, Kristy, and Heidi—and I'm her only son. I have never known a more loving and caring person than my mother. She is so willing to serve and help those that come into her life. My sisters get together at least once a month for "girls' night out." I'm not invited to these nights when they do whatever it is girls do when they get together, but I am invited to other family gatherings. All eight of my sisters love chocolate. I suspect they prefer the Chocolate Crock Pot Cake since they make it more often than they make the Vanilla Crock Pot Cake, but I prefer the vanilla. Again, I am outnumbered—but they're nice enough to bring the vanilla cake once in awhile!

Peach Cake with Caramel Sauce

Peach Cake:

1½ C. sugar

2 eggs

¾ C. oil

1⅓ C. mashed peaches

2 C. flour

1 tsp. baking soda

1 tsp. cinnamon

¼ tsp. salt

Caramel Sauce:

1 C. sugar

½ C. butter

⅔ C. evaporated milk

2 egg yolks

1 tsp. flour

1 tsp. vanilla

Peach Cake: In a large bowl, cream sugar, eggs, oil, and peaches. Add dry ingredients; mix well. Bake at 350 for 35 minutes or until golden brown and firm to the touch.

Caramel Sauce: Melt butter and sugar over medium heat. Whisk milk into mixture; add egg yolks and mix well. Add flour and vanilla. Stir until thickened and remove from heat. Pour caramel sauce over cake and serve with a dollop of whipped cream. Makes 12 servings.

Kristie Christensen
Mount Mahogany 1st Ward
Mount Mahogany Utah Stake
Pleasant Grove, Utah

When I was twenty-five, my mother was in a fatal motorcycle accident. I was married and had just started my family. I was one of six children. One sibling was on a mission, one was getting ready to leave on a mission, one was attending college, and two were still at home with my father. It was devastating to us all. Our mother was truly the heart of our home; she made each of us feel like we were the favorite, and she was constantly serving others, especially her children. She gave us the love of music and a love for life. It seemed that every occasion with her was a party, and she always had something good to eat! Everyone who knew her felt welcome in our home. I now have six children of my own, and I truly appreciate all my mother did for me and taught me. There have been many times I have needed my mother's advice and guidance while raising my family, and I have missed her desperately. But I know that she has been with me, silently helping me along. Most of all, she taught me what was important. I also know that when Heavenly Father closes a door, he opens a window, and I have felt His love through the love and support of my husband, children, siblings, father, loving step-mother, and everyone around me. We are all better people because my mother was part of our lives. One of my favorite recipes I learned from my mom is her Peach Cake with Caramel Sauce. I love this recipe because it is so simple to make and is so delicious! I think of her every time I make it.

Brown Sugar Pound Cake

¾ C. margarine

¾ C. shortening

1 lb. brown sugar

1 C. sugar

5 eggs

1 C. milk

2 tsp. vanilla

3 C. flour

Cream margarine, shortening, and sugars. Add eggs, milk, and vanilla. Stir in flour. Pour into a greased and floured tube pan. Bake at 350 for 1½ hours. Makes 8 servings.

Leslie Stanley
Desert Mountain Ward
Scottsdale Arizona North Stake
Scottsdale, Arizona

Lisa Stanley, standing only 4'10", is the tiniest, sweetest mom ever—a wonderful mother to me and my siblings, and the grandmother of my nieces and nephews. She is a wonderful cook and even better baker, creating cookies, breads, and this amazing Brown Sugar Pound Cake, which is to die for. She invests every ounce of love and concentration into this cake, making sure it's perfect every time. At sixteen, I love my mom more than anything in the world—sorry, Dad! She is a loving mother and valiant member of the Church who goes to church every Sunday, prepares Primary lessons for her students, then comes home and spends a wonderful Sabbath with her family. My mom not only makes a killer pound cake, but she is the best mother and daughter of God. I love her dearly with all my heart.

Rainbow Citrus Cake

Cake:

3½ C. flour

5 tsp. baking powder

1 tsp. salt

¾ C. shortening

2¼ C. sugar

4 eggs

2 tsp. vanilla

1½ C. milk

2 tsp. lemon zest, grated

2 drops yellow food coloring

2 tsp. orange zest, grated

2 drops orange food coloring

2 tsp. lime zest, grated

2 drops green food coloring

Lemon Curd Filling:

3 eggs

1 C. sugar

½ C. fresh lemon juice

¼ C. butter or margarine, melted

1 Tbsp. lemon peel, grated

Orange Cream Frosting:

⅔ C. butter, softened

3 Tbsp. orange zest

2 tsp. lemon zest

½ tsp. salt

2 egg yolks

8 C. powdered sugar

2 Tbsp. orange juice

4 tsp. lemon juice

 In honor of my mother, Rita Burke, I wanted to share her favorite cake. We make this every year around her birthday. She just loves it, and I must say it is delicious. It is time-consuming because of all the different layers, fillings and frosting, but it really is worth it. Thanks, Mom, for always being the most loving, organized, selfless mother in the world! Happy Mother's Day—we love you!

Cake: Preheat oven to 350. Grease and flour 3 9-inch round pans. Sift the flour, baking powder, and salt. Set aside. In a large bowl, cream the shortening and sugar until light and fluffy. Beat in the eggs one at a time, then stir in the vanilla. Beat in the flour mixture alternately with the milk. Divide equal amounts of batter into 3 bowls. In first bowl, stir in lemon zest and yellow food coloring; pour into prepared pan. In second bowl, stir in orange zest and orange food coloring; pour into second prepared pan. In third bowl, stir in lime zest and green food coloring; pour into third prepared pan. Bake at 350 for 30 minutes, or until a toothpick inserted into the center of the cake comes out clean. Let cool in pan for 5 minutes, then turn out onto a wire rack and cool completely. To assemble the cake, put layers together with Lemon Curd Filling. Frost sides and top with Orange Cream Frosting. Refrigerate until served. Makes 14 servings.

Lemon Curd Filling: In the top of a double boiler, beat eggs and sugar. Stir in lemon juice, butter, and lemon peel. Cook over simmering water for 15 minutes or until thickened. Let cool before spreading.

Orange Cream Frosting: Cream butter, orange zest, lemon zest, and salt. Add egg yolks and mix well. Add powdered sugar alternately with orange juice and lemon juice, beating well after each addition. Makes 4 cups frosting.

Lauren Langston
Lake Shawnee Ward
Topeka Kansas Stake
Shawnee, Kansas

{ DESSERTS }

Mighty is the force of motherhood!

{ George Eliot }

Mom's Homemade Ice Cream

Blender full of fruit (great with raspberries)
10 eggs
3 Tbsp. vanilla
½ tsp. salt

3 C. sugar
2 pints cream
1 12-oz. can evaporated milk
Milk

Blend fruit until blender is full. Beat eggs. Combine fruit, eggs, and all remaining ingredients; pour into ice cream freezer. Add milk to fill; freeze according to manufacturer's directions. Makes about 1 gallon.

Trudy Evans
Syracuse 1st Ward
Syracuse Utah Bluff Stake
Syracuse, Utah

Nothing brings back great summer memories as well as my mom's homemade ice cream! It was a great tradition to pick fresh raspberries and make this ice cream together as a family. It's also fun to see this tradition continue with my own children at Grandma's house. This ice cream was served every 4th of July as well as at countless barbecues with family and friends. I have yet to find any recipe that beats this one. It reminds me of very happy and carefree summers at my mom and dad's house. It's a simple recipe, but so delicious!

Banana Loaf

½ C. butter
1 C. sugar
1 tsp. vanilla
2 eggs

2 C. flour
2 tsp. baking powder
4–6 bananas
½ tsp. salt

Beat butter and sugar until creamy. Add vanilla. Add the eggs one at a time, beating well after each addition. Sift dry ingredients together and add to butter mixture. Mash bananas thoroughly with a fork and add to batter. Blend well and divide between 2 small greased loaf pans. Bake at 350 for 1 hour. Makes 2 loaves.

Janine Vorster
Roodepoort South Africa Ward
Roodepoort Stake
Wilropark, Roodepoort
South Africa

This recipe was passed down to me as soon as I was able to start baking; my mother taught me how to make it. It is a quick, easy, simple dessert—the perfect little sweet after a meal.

Louisiana Cornbread

1 lemon cake mix
1 small box lemon gelatin (Jell-O)
4 eggs
¾ C. oil
¾ C. water

1 tsp. lemon extract
¼ C. melted butter
½ C. lemon juice
2 C. powdered sugar

Combine lemon cake mix, gelatin mix, eggs, oil, water, and lemon extract. Mix by hand, stirring 50 strokes. Bake in a well-greased and floured bundt or tube pan at 325 for 55–60 minutes. Combine melted butter, lemon juice, and powdered sugar; mix well. After the cake has been out of the oven 5 minutes, poke holes in top and pour glaze over top. Makes 10 servings.

Kathy Vanbeck
Clayton North Carolina Ward
Goldsboro North Carolina Stake
Angier, North Carolina

English Trifle

1 6-oz. pkg. raspberry gelatin (Jell-O)
1 12-oz. pkg. frozen raspberries
1 angel food cake

1 large box cook-and-serve vanilla pudding
1 8-oz. container whipped topping (Cool Whip)

Mix gelatin as directed, decreasing water to 1⅔ C. Stir in raspberries. Cut angel food cake into small pieces and add to gelatin/fruit mixture; mix well and refrigerate to set up. Cook pudding according to package directions. Set aside and cool. Pour cooled pudding over set gelatin. Top with whipped topping. Makes 10–12 servings.

Shantaila Lamb
Cedar 2nd Ward
Central Idaho Stake
Pocatello, Idaho

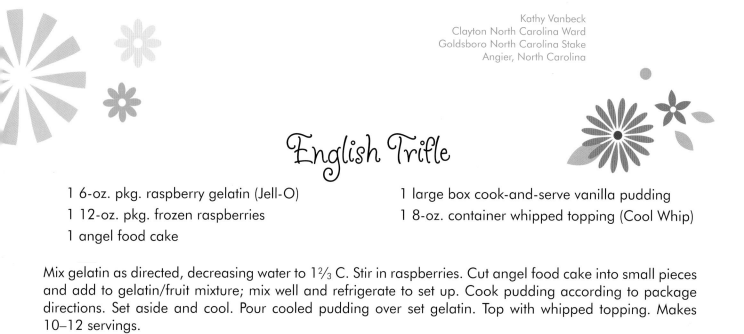

This is my Grandma Carol's recipe, and it was a must at every family event. Now that I am grown, Grandma knows that she has to bring the trifle—whether it's for a baby blessing or just a picnic. Grandma married at a very young age, and through trial and error, she became the best cook in the entire world!

Baked Devil's Float

1 C. sugar, divided
1½ C. water
2 C. miniature marshmallows
2 Tbsp. shortening
1 C. flour
½ tsp. salt

1 tsp. soda
3 Tbsp. cocoa
½ C. milk
1 tsp. vanilla
½ C. nuts (optional)

In a saucepan, combine ½ C. sugar and water; boil for 5 minutes. Pour over miniature marshmallows in a 4-quart casserole dish. Combine shortening, flour, salt, soda, cocoa, milk, vanilla, and nuts. Drop by dollops into marshmallow mixture. Bake at 350 for 45 minutes. Serve hot with vanilla ice cream on top. Makes 6 servings.

This recipe passed down from my grandmother has become a favorite with my family. While my three sons were on their missions, each wrote to ask for this recipe. When I told my youngest son to take the recipe with him because he would want it on his mission, he reminded me that he probably couldn't find the ingredients in the Baltics. He never could find any marshmallows, and his first request when he came home was for Baked Devil's Float.

Julene McConkie
Pleasant Valley 3rd Ward
Pleasant Valley Utah Stake
South Odgen, Utah

Dominican Flan

1 12-oz. can evaporated milk
1 14-oz. can sweetened condensed milk
5 large eggs

Flavoring of choice (vanilla is good)
½ C. sugar (optional)

Pour all ingredients into a blender; mix, but don't beat too long—it toughens the eggs. Cook either in the oven in a pan placed in another pan of water, covered with foil, at 350 for 1 hour 20 minutes; remove foil halfway through. Or cook in the top of a double boiler for about 30 minutes, until a knife comes out clean. Makes 8 servings. Note: If you like extra sweetness, caramelize ½ C. sugar in the pan before you pour in the liquid; you'll get a dark brown sweet sauce. You can also caramelize the sugar separately and pour it over the cold flan; it will harden like candy.

Arden Hansen
Bonao 1st Ward
La Vega Stake
Las Cuevas, Dominican Republic

Blackberry Cobbler

¼ C. butter, softened
½ C. sugar
1 C. flour
2 Tbsp. baking powder
¼ Tbsp. salt

½ C. milk
1–1½ C. blackberries
¼–½ C. sugar
1 C. fruit juice or water

Beat butter and sugar until well mixed. Sift flour, baking powder, and salt; stir into shortening/sugar mixture. Add milk and beat until smooth. Pour into a greased 8 x 8-inch pan or dish. Spoon blackberries over the batter. Sprinkle sugar over the fruit. Pour fruit juice or water over the sugar. Bake at 375 until golden brown, 35–45 minutes. Serve with ice cream. Makes 4–6 servings.

Dorry Lou Wharton
Spanish Fork 17th Ward
Canyon Ridge Utah Stake
Spanish Fork, Utah

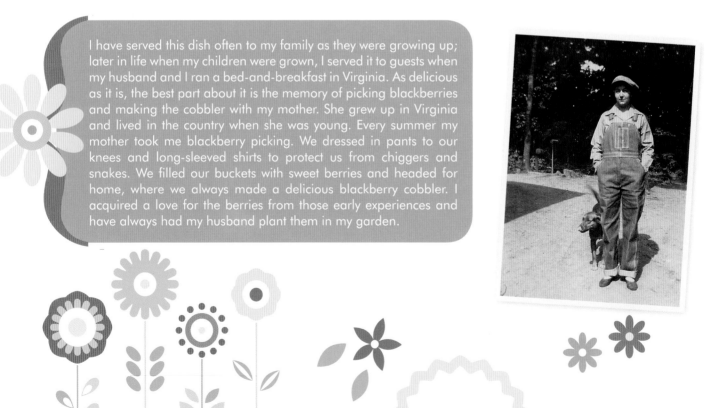

I have served this dish often to my family as they were growing up; later in life when my children were grown, I served it to guests when my husband and I ran a bed-and-breakfast in Virginia. As delicious as it is, the best part about it is the memory of picking blackberries and making the cobbler with my mother. She grew up in Virginia and lived in the country when she was young. Every summer my mother took me blackberry picking. We dressed in pants to our knees and long-sleeved shirts to protect us from chiggers and snakes. We filled our buckets with sweet berries and headed for home, where we always made a delicious blackberry cobbler. I acquired a love for the berries from those early experiences and have always had my husband plant them in my garden.

Fried Creamy Pastry

1 box frozen puff pastry dough, thawed

2 Tbsp. sour cream

1 8-oz. pkg. cream cheese

1 Tbsp. lemon juice

1 C. chocolate hazelnut spread (Nutella)

Oil for frying

Cut dough into 3 x 3-inch pieces. Combine sour cream, cream cheese, and lemon juice. Put Nutella in a pastry bag or in a resealable plastic bag with the corner cut off. Spoon about 1 tablespoon of the cream cheese mixture onto each square. Squeeze Nutella on top of the cream cheese mixture; don't put so much that you can't close the squares. Wet the edges with a little water, fold the edges together, and seal the edges. Just before serving, deep fry until golden, about 1 minute on each side. Sprinkle with powdered sugar and serve. Makes about 20 servings.

Marisol Rivera
Ocoee Ward
Orlando Florida South Stake
Orlando, Florida

I'm twenty years old and a graduate of West Side Tech for Commercial Foods; I have lived in Orlando, Florida, my whole life. My mother and I are very close and have a lot of things in common—we both make friends in an instant, we both love the gospel and all of its teachings, and we both love to cook. I learned my love for cooking from her when I was a little girl. Whenever we got to feed the missionaries, she let me help in the kitchen, and I was always in charge of making the dessert. I was always trying something new and different, and the missionaries were my test subjects! I loved to turn the kitchen into my experiment lab. I love to look at a recipe and make changes to it so the recipe is my own. I love making something new out of something old. I love making a difference in everything that I do. I would love to do more studying in pastry arts and food, but my greatest desire is to become a mom like my own and to teach others the things I've been able to learn.

Nanner Puddin'

2 large pkgs. instant vanilla pudding mix

Milk per pudding package directions

2 8-oz. pkgs. cream cheese, softened

1 large contaner frozen whipped topping, thawed (Cool Whip)

Vanilla wafer cookies (Nilla Wafers)

Bananas, sliced

Make pudding as directed on the package. Beat in cream cheese. Fold in Cool Whip. Refrigerate. Line a large bowl with cookies; cover cookies with sliced bananas. Pour in half the pudding mixture. Cover pudding with another layer of cookies; cover cookies with another layer of sliced bananas. Pour in remaining pudding mixture. Crumble a handful of cookies on top. Refrigerate until ready to eat. Makes about 20 servings.

Teresa Mansker
Abilene 3rd Ward
Abilene Texas Stake
Abilene, Texas

Well, my MOMMY is the very best cook on the face of the planet! She knows just about everything about food; if I ever have a question, I can call her, and she knows the answer. She's been making this Nanner Puddin' for as long as I can remember. My brothers and I didn't like it warm, so Mom figured out a way to make it cold. We LOVE it. My four brothers don't like bananas, so Mom always made them a special bowl with no "nanners" in it. My four brothers and I have all left home and married, and all of us make this all-time favorite recipe for our own families, for extended family get-togethers, and for ward activities. Mom is the Maw-Maw of twelve beautiful grandchildren, and they all love Nanner Puddin' too! I hope y'all will love this as much as we do! I love you, Momma! You're the best.

Grandma Jo's Magic Marshmallow Treats

2 8-oz. cans refrigerated crescent roll dough

½ C. sugar

½ tsp. cinnamon

16 jumbo marshmallows

½ C. butter, melted

Preheat oven to 375. Separate crescent rolls into individual pieces; set aside. Combine cinnamon and sugar; set aside. Roll one marshmallow in butter, then in cinnamon/sugar mixture. Place marshmallow inside crescent roll and pinch dough closed around marshmallow. Roll crescent roll in butter, then cinnamon/sugar mixture. Place crescent in greased muffin tin. Repeat for all marshmallows and rolls. Bake for 10–12 minutes. Makes 16 delicious rolls.

Lisa Coombs
Battlecreek 10th Ward
Pleasant Grove Utah East Stake
Pleasant Grove, Utah

I remember the first time my mother made these for us kids! It was such a surprising treat! We were all a little skeptical at first, because we were used to crescent rolls being used for dinner, and now all of a sudden Mom was putting a marshmallow inside each one. They were absolutely delicious! The best part is that the marshmallows dissolve inside the crescent roll, so when you bite into the roll, it is hollow. One of my favorite things about taking my husband and kids home to visit my family is begging my mom to make these for my kids, because I can always see the wonder in their eyes when they bite into Grandma Jo's "Magic Marshmallow Rolls"! Thanks, Mom, for creating such a great memory!

Della's Fruit Cobbler

¼ C. butter or margarine

1 C. flour

2 C. sugar, divided

¼ C. water

½ tsp. baking soda

1 tsp. salt

1 tsp. baking powder

1 egg

Milk or buttermilk

3–4 C. fruit

Preheat oven to 375. Melt butter or margarine in an 8 x 8-inch pan. In a small bowl, mix flour and 1 C. sugar. In a 1-cup measuring cup, mix water, baking soda, salt, and baking powder. Stir to mix well; add egg. Stir; fill to 1-cup mark with milk or buttermilk. Stir to mix well. Pour into flour/sugar mixture. Mix well; and pour into pan over melted butter. Mix fruit with remaining 1 C. sugar or to taste; spread over batter, but do not stir fruit into the batter. Bake at 375 for 45 minutes to 1 hour, until top of cake is brown. Time varies depending on amount of fruit used. Makes 6–8 servings. *Note:* Blackberries, blueberries, and firm fruits are good. Strawberries and raspberries are also good, but are best when mixed with rhubarb or other firm fruit. For a 9 x 13-inch pan, double the batter and use 5–6 cups fruit.

Blain Nelson
Ferndale Washington 1st Ward
Bellingham Washington Stake
Ferndale, Washington

This recipe is named for my mother, Della Carnefix Nelson, who adapted it from a recipe given to her by her sister. Mom almost always cooked from scratch, and usually by "touch," rather than from a recipe; she never felt comfortable preparing a meal out of a box with instructions to "add water and stir." She liked this recipe because it's so easy and because the batter starts out underneath the fruit and cooks through it, picking up flavor from the fruit on its way through. It was one of two recipes we had her dictate while she was in hospice care, shortly before her death from cancer in July 2006.

Cruellers

4 C. flour
4 tsp. baking powder
½ tsp. salt
½ tsp. cinnamon
2 Tbsp. butter, melted
1 C. sugar

2 eggs
1 tsp. vanilla
1 C. milk
Oil for frying
Powdered sugar

Mix flour, baking powder, salt, and cinnamon. Stir in melted butter, sugar, eggs, vanilla, and milk, forming a soft dough. Do not knead. Roll out a little at a time, pinch off in pieces, and deep fry. Drain on paper towels and roll in powdered sugar. Makes 2 dozen.

Katia Tishnya
Cherkassy Tsentrainy Branch
Ukraine District
Cherkassy, Ukraine

The Closest Thing to Heaven on Earth

Cake:
2 dark chocolate cake mixes
2 small boxes instant chocolate pudding
8 eggs
⅔ C. vegetable oil
1 ½ C. sour cream
1 ½ C. water
2 12-oz. bags semi-sweet chocolate chips

Chocolate Chunks:
Chop 4 1.55-oz. milk chocolate bars into chunks. Set aside.

Chocolate Curls:
Using a swivel-blade vegetable peeler, shave small curls from the side of a large milk chocolate bar. Shave enough to cover the top of the cake completely. Set aside.

Simple Syrup:
1 C. sugar
1 C. corn syrup
1 C. water

Cream Cheese Frosting:
2 8-oz. pkgs. cream cheese, at room temperature
½ C. butter, at room temperature
4 C. powdered sugar
2 tsp. vanilla
1 6.7-oz. milk chocolate bar

Assembling the cake:
1 16-oz. bag mini chocolate chips

(recipe continued on next page)

(The Closest Thing to Heaven, continued)

Cake: Preheat oven to 350. Spray 3 round 10-inch pans with nonstick spray and dust lightly with flour. Blend all ingredients except chocolate chips for 2 minutes on low. Fold in both bags of chocolate chips. Bake at 350 for 30–35 minutes until the cake tests done. Remove the layers from the oven and cool.

Cream Cheese Frosting: Blend all ingredients except chocolate bar together until light and creamy. Scrape down the sides and bottom of the mixture bowl so no clumps of cheese remain. Melt chocolate bar in the microwave. Blend the melted chocolate bar into the frosting.

Simple Syrup: In a saucepan, combine all ingredients and bring to a full boil. Allow to cool before using. Brush a generous amount (about 2 Tbsp.) of simple syrup on each cake layer. Be sure to get the edges extra well.

Assembling the cake: Place little squares of waxed or parchment paper on the platter you are going to place your cake on; tuck them just under the edge of your first layer of cake so that you can pull them out easily when you are done decorating the cake. This will keep your platter clean as it collects all the chocolate that falls while you are decorating the cake. Place first layer of cake on platter. Frost the top with Cream Cheese Frosting and sprinkle with one of the chopped chocolate bars. Repeat with second layer. Place third layer on cake. Frost the remaining cake. While frosting is still moist from spreading on cake, push mini chocolate chips into the frosting on the sides of the cake. It works best if you pour some in your hand and lightly press them into the frosting starting from the top of the cake sides and moving to the bottom. Sprinkle chocolate shavings on the top of the cake. Carefully slide out the wax or parchment paper that is under the bottom cake layer. Makes 24 servings. Note: If desired, you can give your cake a more finished look by piping the top and bottom edge of the cake with chocolate frosting using a star-shaped frosting tip.

Christy Dye
Mount Mahogany 4th Ward
Pleasant Grove Utah Mount Mahogany Stake
Pleasant Grove, Utah

This chocolate cake didn't really have a name, so I called my sister and asked her what we should name it. I overheard her husband say, "It is so good, call it 'The Closest Thing to Heaven on Earth.'" With more than four pounds of chocolate, it truly is that! Our mom taught us that we can achieve anything we set our minds to. She always said, "If anyone can do it, it will be you." One year my sister, Andy Arko, and I wanted to do something special for her for on her birthday to thank her for all the wonderful things she has done for us in our lives. She loves chocolate, so we created this chocolate cake in her honor.

Glazed Potato Doughnuts

1 pkg. yeast (1 Tbsp.)

¼ C. warm water

¼ C. scalded milk

¼ C. shortening

¼ C. sugar

1 tsp. salt

¾ C. mashed potatoes (you can use instant)

2 eggs, beaten

5–6 C. sifted flour

Oil for frying

1 lb. powdered sugar

6 Tbsp. water or milk

Dissolve yeast in ¼ C. warm water. Combine milk, shortening, sugar, and salt. Cool to lukewarm. Stir in yeast, potatoes, and eggs. Gradually add enough flour to make a soft dough. Knead until smooth. Let rise in greased bowl until doubled, 1–1½ hours. Roll to ½ inch thick and cut with 3-inch cutter. Let rise until doubled. Fry in hot oil. Drain. Combine powdered sugar and water or milk. Glaze doughnuts while still hot. Makes 3½ dozen.

David Lee
Greenwood Ward
Fort Smith Arkansas Stake
Hartford, Arkansas

My mother, Verona Lee, is a great cook, and she loves to make treats for all her children and grandchildren. I enjoyed her doughnuts as I was growing up; whenever she came to visit me after I was married and had children, she made her doughnuts for us again. She always gathered the kids around and let them help make the doughnuts—a highlight of her visits. Doughnuts were cooling over every surface in the kitchen, and many fingers were reaching to grab one. During her most recent visit she made doughnuts with my granddaughters, Caroline and Holly. It was a special time to see a new generation helping Great-Grandma make her doughnuts. Grandma, love, and doughnuts just seem to go together.

Marle's American-English Trifle

1 yellow or white cake mix, cut into cubes (can use purchased angel food or pound cake)

1 pkg. raspberry or strawberry Danish Dessert (can use Jell-O)

1 packet custard mix (can use a large box of instant vanilla pudding)

1–2 C. frozen strawberries or raspberries, thawed

2 bananas, sliced

1 C. cream, whipped and sweetened

As long as a day before assembling the trifle, prepare the cake mix, Danish Dessert, and custard mix according to package directions; allow to cool properly. In a trifle dish or glass bowl, layer all ingredients in the following order: cake cubes, Danish dessert, custard, fruit, and bananas. Repeat layers if you can—a trifle dish will usually allow two layers, but a glass casserole dish will usually allow only one. Top with whipped cream and refrigerate until ready to serve. Don't assemble the trifle more than six hours before serving, or the cake will get soggy and the bananas may turn brown. Makes 12 servings.

Josi S. Kilpack
Willard 1st Ward
Willard Utah Stake
Willard, Utah

As a stay-at-home mother of nine kids, my mom—Marle Schofield—didn't have many opportunities to make "fancy food." But when she did, she did it in style. Throughout my life Mom made trifle for Christmas Eve dinner, and it was something we all anticipated. She usually made two of them to ensure there was plenty, and it was always a challenge to be the first to remember the leftovers Christmas morning. I grew up assuming trifle was a fairly common dessert, and it wasn't until I was a teenager that I realized that while most people had heard of trifle, not very many had ever eaten it. As adults, my siblings and I still equate Christmas Eve to Mom's version of English trifle—which, while different than traditional English trifle, is phenomenal and not as difficult as it might appear. When I began considering the second book in my Sadie Hoffmiller culinary mystery series, *English Trifle* was a perfect title and set the stage for a really fun book. It's equally fitting because in addition to teaching me how to cook, my mom was also a voracious reader, setting an example that has changed my life. I will ever be grateful for all the wonderful gifts my mother has given to me and can only hope I can give equally valuable gifts to my children as well. Thanks, Mom.

Italian Cream Cheese Cake

½ C. margarine or butter
½ C. vegetable shortening
2 C. sugar
6 egg yolks
2 C. flour
1 tsp. soda
1 tsp. baking powder
1 C. buttermilk
1 tsp. vanilla

1 C. pineapple tidbits
1 small can flaked coconut
½ C. pecans, chopped
6 egg whites, stiffly beaten
1 8-oz. pkg. cream cheese
1 lb. powdered sugar
¼ C. margarine or butter
1 tsp. vanilla
½ C. pecans, chopped

Cream ½ C. margarine, shortening, and sugar; mix until smooth. Add egg yolks and beat well. Combine flour, soda, and baking powder; add to creamed mixture, alternating with buttermilk. Stir in 1 tsp. vanilla, pineapple, coconut, and nuts. Fold in stiffly beaten egg whites. Bake in 3 8-inch cake pans or 1 pound cake pan at 350 for 25 minutes or until done. Mix cream cheese and ¼ C. margarine until smooth. Add powdered sugar and mix well. Add 1 tsp. vanilla and beat until smooth. Add ¼ C. pecans; spread between layers and on top of cake. If using pound cake pan, spread on top and sides. Makes 12 servings.

Ruth Haywood
Stockbridge Ward
Jonesboro Georgia Stake
Stockbridge, Georgia

Tapioca Pudding

4 C. milk
2 eggs, lightly beaten
⅔ C. sugar

½ C. small pearl tapioca
½ tsp. vanilla

In a blender or food processor, combine the milk and eggs; mix very well. Pour into a slow cooker; stir in the sugar and tapioca. Cover and cook on medium for 3 hours or on low for 6 hours, stirring every 40 minutes or so. Stir in vanilla halfway through cooking process. Serve warm. *Note:* You can find pearl tapioca in Asian markets or on the ethnic aisle of the grocery store.

Regina Tucker
Montpelier Ward
Montpelier Vermont Stake
Montpelier, Vermont

Momma's Forbidden Chocolate Dessert

2 C. flour

1 C. butter, melted

1 C. pecans, chopped

2 8-oz. pkgs. cream cheese

1 8-oz. tub whipped topping (Cool Whip)

2 C. powdered sugar

2 large pkgs. instant chocolate pudding mix

Preheat oven to 350. Mix flour, butter, and pecans; press into a cookie sheet or 4 pie pans, depending on desired thickness. Bake at 350 for 7–10 minutes, or until golden brown. In a mixing bowl, blend cream cheese, whipped topping, and powdered sugar; set aside. Once the crust is cool, evenly spread the cream layer over the crust. In a separate mixing bowl, prepare instant pudding according to directions. Pour pudding over the cream layer. Refrigerate overnight. Makes 12 servings. *Note:* We like to top this dessert with additional whipped topping and sprinkle with chopped nuts.

Kimberlie McBride
Westland Ward
Columbus Ohio West Stake
Galloway, Ohio

Mom was always cookin' up meals for families in the ward and neighborhood. She seemed to enjoy few things more than bringing meals to families in need. Her meals were always delicious and seemed to always include yummy chocolate brownies or her amazing chocolate dessert. When it was her brownies—made from scratch with lots of love—there always seemed to be extras for us at home to have and enjoy. But her chocolate dessert was usually made specifically for the family in need, and no one else! We came home from school or play and could only wish that the Forbidden Chocolate Dessert was for us. That's partly why I consider her chocolate dessert so valuable and amazing: it was so untouchable when it looked so available. Her creamy dessert was off-limits so often that I think we probably became conditioned to admire it more than we normally would! Either way, everyone agrees that it is amazing, creamy, and delicious!

(Regina Tucker) My mom is no longer with us, but this dessert always reminds me of her. She loved tapioca pudding, and she made the best pudding. She was an amazing woman. She lived with cancer for more than twenty years, and she never complained or let it get her down. She always said she was going to live to be a hundred, no matter what her health was like. She had a heart of gold and was a woman of strength and courage. I hope that during trials and tribulations I can be the type of mother and friend that she was to me.

Tarteletas Frutales (Fruit Tarts)

Pastry:
⅔ C. butter
2½ C. flour
¾ C. powdered sugar
3 egg yolks
1 tsp. vanilla

Crema Pastelera:
2 C. milk
6 egg yolks
½ C. sugar
⅓ C. cornstarch
1 tsp. vanilla
Bananas, kiwis, cherries, peaches, strawberries
(almost any fruit), cut in pieces

In a food processor, combine butter, flour, and powdered sugar; pulse a couple of times. Add egg yolks and vanilla; beat to form dough. Refrigerate for at least 30 minutes. On a lightly floured surface, roll dough into a circle about ⅛ inch thick (size depends on the size of the tart pan; you can make individual ones). Dust excess flour from both sides. Place dough in a lightly greased tart pan. Cook at 400 for 15–20 minutes, until dough gets slightly brown. Cool. To prepare Crema Pastelera, boil the milk. In a separate bowl, mix egg yolks, sugar, and cornstarch. Pour milk into egg mixture, stirring constantly; it's important to stir constantly, or the egg yolks will cook. (If that happens, put the mixture in the blender and blend until smooth.) Cook the mix, stirring constantly, until thick. Stir in vanilla. Cover and chill in the refrigerator. Fill the tartlets with the Crema Pastelera and decorate with pieces of fruit. Makes 12 servings.

Cecilia Haedo de Mazal
Chacarita Ward
Belgrano Stake
Capital Federal, Buenos Aires
Argentina

I love these tarteletas; they are my favorite, and I even choose this as my birthday "cake." When we were kids, my sisters and I used to go to my aunt's house, and she let us cook and decorate our own tarteletas! I love cooking and sharing with my family. I always wanted to have children, so when I got married, that was on the top of my mind. The moment finally came eighteen months ago, and I simply love it! All the love I receive from Santi and all the experiences we have with him are priceless. I also love cooking for my family; I think the best way to show my love for them is to bake something they enjoy. I'm so happy to have a wonderful family!

Aunt Betty's Ice Cream Dessert

1 C. packed brown sugar

½ C. butter or margarine

2½ C. cornflakes

½–1 C. nuts, chopped

8 oz. shredded coconut

½ gal. vanilla ice cream, softened

Chocolate syrup (optional)

In a medium saucepan, melt sugar and butter over low heat. Stir in cornflakes, nuts, and coconut. Put half the mixture on the bottom of an 8 x 12-inch or 10 x 10-inch pan. Carefully spread softened ice cream over crust. Spread remaining mixture over top. Freeze until firm. To serve, cut into squares and drizzle with chocolate syrup (optional). Makes 24 servings. *Note:* Any flavor of ice cream works well, and crispy rice cereal can also be used instead of cornflakes. If you like a thicker crust, use as much as 4 C. cornflakes.

Andrea Dickinson
Grandview 2nd Ward
Mesa Arizona Central Stake
Mesa, Arizona

When I was twelve, my mom and grandma took me on a road trip from Arizona to Pennsylvania and Michigan to visit Grandma's brothers. There were three generations of girls crammed into one small Camaro. While in Michigan, I met my lovely Great-Aunt Betty, who brought this delicious dessert to a big family gathering. The moment we tasted it, my mom and I wondered if anyone would notice if we took the pan and hid somewhere with a fork to eat as much as we could. Since we weren't able to escape with the dessert, we begged for the recipe and have been enjoying it ever since.

Canadian Butter Tarts

1¼ C. flour

½ tsp. salt

1 Tbsp. sugar

½ C. butter

⅛–¼ C. ice water

2 eggs

2 C. brown sugar

2 Tbsp. vinegar

1 tsp. vanilla

½ C. butter, melted

1⅓ C. currants or raisins

Pie crust dough

(recipe continued on next page)

(Canadian Butter Tarts, continued)

In a food processor, combine flour, salt, and sugar; pulse until mixed. Add butter and process until the mixture resembles coarse meal, about 15 seconds. Pour $1/8$ C. ice water in a slow stream, processing until dough forms. Add more water if necessary. Gather dough into a ball. Flatten into a disk and wrap with plastic. Refrigerate for about an hour. Divide dough into 12 balls. Roll each ball out into a 4-inch round. Line the 12 cups of a muffin tin. Cover and refrigerate for about 30 minutes. Beat eggs only until well blended. Beat in brown sugar. Add vinegar and vanilla. Stir in melted butter and currants. Fill each pastry-lined cup $1/3$ to ½ full of mixture. Bake at 450 for 7 minutes; lower temperature to 350 and continue baking for 10–15 minutes, or until firm. Be careful, as they have a tendency to spill over while baking. Makes 12 tarts.

Enjoy something truly Canadian! My mom's name is Judy Tiede, and she is extremely talented at making Butter Tarts. She is also extremely talented at poetry and calligraphy, and she is an extraordinary teacher. She always had a way of explaining things to her five children, and she raised all of us wonderfully.

Spencer David Tiede
Sunridge Ward
Calgary Alberta East Stake
Calgary, Alberta
Canada

Stewed Rhubarb

1 lb. rhubarb (about 3 C.)
2 C. water
¼ vanilla bean
$1/3$ C. sugar

2½ Tbsp. cornstarch
¼ C. water
1 Tbsp. sugar
1 Tbsp. almonds, chopped

Cut rhubarb in 1-inch pieces and boil for 10 minutes in 2 C. water with split vanilla bean. Pour through a strainer; remove vanilla pod and beans. Stir sugar into the rhubarb and bring to a boil. Take the pot off the heat. In a small bowl, combine cornstarch and ¼ C. water; stir into rhubarb. Put back on heat; cook and stir until thickened. Pour into a bowl. Sprinkle with sugar and let cool for 2–3 hours. Sprinkle with almonds just before serving. Makes 4 servings.

Mille Norgaard
Randers Branch
Aarhus Denmark Stake
Randers, Denmark

Jelly Whip (Jell-O Whip)

1 12-oz. can evaporated milk, chilled

2 Tbsp. sugar

2 small pkgs. jelly (Jell-O)

1 C. boiling water

1 C. cold water

Using electric beater, whip evaporated milk; add sugar. In separate bowl, mix Jell-O mixes with 1 C. boiling water until fully dissolved. Stir in the cold water. Slowly add the Jell-O to the whipped evaporated milk, 1 spoonful at a time. Refrigerate until set. Makes 8 servings. *Note:* For variety, add canned fruit—for example, add pineapple chunks to lemon Jell-O or peach slices to peach Jell-O. Don't try it with fresh fruit—the Jell-O won't set. You can also pour this dessert into various molds for variety.

Beverly Ledward
Pioneer Ward
Herriman Utah Stake
Herriman, Utah

This is a very easy and inexpensive dessert to make. We grew up calling it *spookasem,* which is the Afrikaans word for cotton candy; the direct translation would mean "ghost's breath." It melts in your mouth. You can make whatever flavor your children love. Sundays in our family of twelve usually meant roast chicken, lamb, or beef with roast potatoes, pumpkin or hubbard squash, and peas, followed by this light dessert! The kitchen used to get pretty crowded with everyone doing something to get lunch ready after church. It's only now as I actually think of recipes that I remember the wonderful times our family had doing things together. The best thing my mom did was to teach us to cook from an early age. I guess my dad should get credit, too; I remember standing on a bar stool at the stove when I was five so he could teach me how to make a big pot of porridge for breakfast. I am originally from Roodepoort Ward in South Africa; I immigrated to the United States in 2001.

Banana Caramel Tart

½ C. butter, room temperature

¼ C. sugar

1 large egg yolk

1 tsp. vanilla

¼ tsp. salt

1 C. flour

3 large bananas, thinly sliced

1 Tbsp. butter, melted

1 Tbsp. sugar

1 C. cream

1 C. sugar

1 Tbsp. freshly squeezed lemon juice

¼ C. butter

In a large bowl, beat butter and sugar with an electric mixer until blended. Beat in egg yolk, vanilla, and salt. Add flour and beat until moist clumps form. Press dough into bottom of 9-inch tart pan with removable bottom. Pierce with fork and refrigerate for 1 hour. Bake crust at 450 for about 15 minutes or until golden. Cool. Reduce oven temperature to 375. Overlap banana slices on crust, covering completely. Brush melted butter over banana slices and sprinkle with 1 Tbsp. sugar. Bake until just warmed through, about 3 minutes. In a heavy saucepan, heat the cream over medium low heat until bubbles form along the edges of the pan. Keep warm. In a heavy saucepan, combine 1 C. sugar and lemon juice until well mixed. Cover the pot and place it over medium-high heat until the sugar melts and bubbles, about 4 minutes. Remove the cover and occasionally swirl the pan or stir the mixture until the syrup is a golden amber color, 5–8 minutes. While cooking, brush the sides of the pan with a wet brush just above the bubbling sugar to keep crystals from forming. Stirring constantly, slowly pour in the warm cream. Bring to a boil, continuing to stir constantly. Cook until slightly thickened, about 3 minutes. Remove the sauce from the heat, add the butter, and stir until the butter melts and the sauce is smooth. Serve immediately or cool to room temperature. Drizzle the banana tart with some caramel sauce. Sprinkle with macadamia nuts. Serve with ice cream (vanilla or coconut) and pass extra caramel sauce around. Cover any leftover caramel sauce tightly and refrigerate for up to two weeks; reheat in a pan of simmering water or a microwave. Makes 6 servings.

Dhadha Zulueta
University Ward
Manila Stake
Manila, Philippines

Chocolate Banana Gag

1½ C. graham cracker crumbs

¼ C. sugar

⅓ C. butter, melted

1 8-oz. pkg. cream cheese

2 Tbsp. milk

¼ C. sugar

1 8-oz. tub frozen whipped topping (Cool Whip), thawed and divided

2 bananas

1 large instant chocolate pudding mix

2½ C. milk

Combine graham cracker crumbs, sugar, and melted butter. Press onto bottom of 9 x 13-inch dish. Chill 15 minutes. In a bowl, beat together cream cheese, milk, and sugar. Fold in 1¾ C. whipped topping. Spread over crust. Slice bananas and arrange in a single layer over cream cheese layer. In a large bowl, beat pudding mix and milk. Pour over bananas. Chill several hours. Top with remaining whipped topping and serve. Makes 12 servings.

Erin Miner
Springcreek 21st Ward
Springville Utah West Stake
Springville, Utah

This is my favorite dessert. Every year for my birthday my mom made this dessert for me because I would rather have this than birthday cake. Even now that I am married, my mom still makes it for my birthday. I still request it even though the combination of pudding and bananas makes me gag by the end of my piece. My mom renamed the dessert "Chocolate Banana Gag" just for me. Now that I am soon going to be a mom, I am looking forward to figuring out my kids' favorite food and making it for them, even if it makes them gag.

Creamy Caramel Flan

¾ C. sugar

1 8-oz. pkg. cream cheese, softened to room temperature

5 eggs, room temperature

1 14-oz. can sweetened condensed milk

1 12-oz. can evaporated milk

1 tsp. vanilla

Preheat oven to 350. In a small, heavy saucepan, cook sugar over medium-low heat, stirring constantly until golden. The sugar will melt; just keep stirring. Pour into a 10-inch round baking dish that has been warmed in the oven for a few minutes. Tilt to coat bottom and sides. Set aside. In a large bowl, beat cream cheese until smooth. Beat in eggs, one at a time, until well incorporated. Beat in sweetened condensed milk, evaporated milk, and vanilla until smooth. Pour into caramel-coated pan. Line a roasting pan with a damp kitchen towel. Place baking dish on towel inside roasting pan, and place roasting pan on oven rack. Fill roasting pan with boiling water to reach halfway up the sides of the baking dish. Bake at 350 for 50–60 minutes, until center is just set. Cool one hour on wire rack, then chill in refrigerator 8 hours or overnight. To unmold, run a knife around edges of pan and invert on a rimmed serving platter. Makes 6 servings.

Danielle Martinez
Covington Ward
New Orleans Louisiana Stake
Abita Springs, Louisiana

When my firstborn was a week old, I decided to take him to the store. I was really nervous because it was my first time taking him out by myself. After spending about an hour getting ready, we left the house. I locked the front door of my house and put my key chain in my pocket. Minutes later, I buckled my son into his car seat and closed the car door. I went around to the driver's side door, and the door was locked. I went back around to the passenger side, and it was locked too. I sat on the hood of my car crying for about an hour (while my baby slept in his car seat), thinking about what a terrible mother I would be. Then I remembered that the keys were in my pocket! I unlocked the car door and took the baby back into the house. When my husband came home and I told him about it—still crying—he laughed so hard. To this day I still get teased about it. Sometimes being a mom isn't about doing everything perfect; sometimes you just have to laugh at your mistakes and say, "They'll survive."

Ice Cream Roll

Ice Cream Roll:

¾ C. flour

¼ C. cocoa

1 tsp. baking powder

¼ tsp. salt

3 eggs

1 C. sugar

⅓ C. water

1½ tsp. vanilla

Powdered sugar

½ gal. vanilla ice cream

Hot Fudge Sauce

Hot Fudge Sauce:

½ C. granulated sugar

1 C. packed brown sugar

¼ C. flour

5 Tbsp. cocoa

4 Tbsp. butter

1 C. evaporated low-fat milk

Ice Cream Roll: In a small bowl, combine flour, cocoa, baking powder, and salt. In a larger bowl, beat eggs for 5 minutes. Gradually add sugar. Add water and beat on low speed until mixed. Add vanilla. Stir flour mixture into eggs. Beat just until smooth. Line a cookie sheet (jelly roll pan) with waxed paper and grease well. Pour cake mixture onto cookie sheet. Bake at 375 for 15 minutes. Turn onto a dish towel sprinkled with powdered sugar. Carefully remove the waxed paper and roll up cake. Leave rolled until cool. Unroll cooled cake. Spread with softened vanilla ice cream. Roll back up and freeze. Serve with additional ice cream and Hot Fudge Sauce. Makes 8 servings.

Hot Fudge Sauce: Mix all ingredients until smooth. Pour into a saucepan or double boiler and cook over medium heat, stirring occasionally, until boiling. Let boil, stirring continuously, for 3 minutes or until thickened. Remove from heat. Makes 8 servings.

Tiffeny Pickett
Bountiful 41st Ward
Bountiful Heights Utah Stake
Bountiful, Utah

For as long as I can remember, this has been my absolute favorite dessert. Growing up, I requested it every single birthday, and my mom happily obliged. Even now that I am married and on my own, Mom still makes it for me anytime I visit home close to my birthday, and now I make it for my own girls. The Hot Fudge Sauce is a must and should be applied liberally!

Bread and Butter Pudding with Butter Sauce

4 slices bread (about ½ inch thick)
Butter
2 large·eggs
¼–½ C. sugar
¼ tsp. salt
3 C. milk

Butter Sauce:
1 C. sugar
½ C. butter
1 Tbsp. water
1 C. cream

Butter bread and arrange slices, buttered side down, in a greased ovenproof dish; the depth of the dish needs to be at least twice the height of the bread. Beat eggs, sugar, salt, and milk. Pour over the bread and allow to soak for about 30 minutes. Cover and bake at 350 for half an hour. Remove cover and allow to brown for an additional 10 minutes. Serve warm with butter sauce. To make sauce, melt sugar, butter, and water in a saucepan. Be careful not to burn mixture. When slightly brown (caramelizing), add the cream and allow to come to a boil. Serve warm. Makes 4–6 servings.

Debra James
Roodepoort Ward
Roodepoort Stake
Roodepoort, Gauteng
South Africa

I learned this recipe from my mother, Lesley Nell, when I was about twelve. It was a staple Sunday dessert because it was so quick and easy to make and was a great way to use bread that was beginning to go stale; in fact, this recipe tastes better with stale bread. As the oldest child I had many opportunities to practice and perfect the recipe, and today I can still make it without having to look at the recipe. I learned so many lessons from my mother. Being mother to six girls and four boys spread over eighteen years cannot have been easy, but she made it seem that way. I think the most important lesson I learned from her was to be happy in whatever situation I find myself. Even when things were really tough for my parents, Mom just kept on being herself and doing the best she could. Even when she faced a physical battle against cancer during the last years of her life, she tried to find some humor in the situation for us. My mom is the person I'd most like to be like; even though I fall far short of the mark now, I keep on striving, because she taught to never to give up . . . ever!

Cinnamon Ice Cream

1 C. sugar
1½ C. half-and-half cream
2 eggs, beaten
1 C. cream

1 tsp. vanilla
2 tsp. ground cinnamon
Waffle cones, crushed

In a saucepan over medium-low heat, stir the sugar and half-and-half. When the mixture begins to simmer, remove from heat; whisk half of the mixture into the eggs, whisking quickly so the eggs don't scramble. Pour the egg mixture back into the saucepan with the rest of the half-and-half mixture; stir in the cream. Continue cooking over medium-low heat, stirring constantly, until the mixture is thick enough to coat the back of a metal spoon. Remove from heat; whisk in vanilla and cinnamon. Set aside to cool. Pour cooled mixture into an ice cream maker and freeze according to the manufacturer's instructions. Serve with crushed waffle cones. Makes 6 servings.

Danielle Martinez
Covington Ward
New Orleans Louisiana Stake
Abita Springs, Louisiana

As someone once said, you never realize how much your mother loves you until you explore the attic—and find every letter you ever sent her, every finger painting, clay pot, bead necklace, Easter chicken, cardboard Santa Claus, paper lace Mother's Day card, and school report since day one. Now that I am a mother, I feel I am rediscovering my own mom in a sense. Things my mom did that drove me crazy as a kid now seem not so crazy. When my mom cried the day I got my driver's license, I realize now they were probably tears of pure fear—even though she said she was just sad I was growing up. When my mom stayed up through the night sewing a Garfield Halloween costume, even though she had to be at work the next day, I now know it was because she just wanted to bring a smile to her child's face. I now know why she always bragged about what a genius I was, even though I was only a B student, because I remember rocking my own six-month-old child and feeling sure he was the next Einstein. I now understand why she always said that being a mother of a toddler means never being able to go to the bathroom in privacy. In motherhood, there are so many unexpected emotions that take you by surprise—but one thing is certain: being a mother is a lifetime journey filled with fears, tears, laughs, and dreams. It's a journey that never ends, and I am so blessed to be able to know what true sacrifice and love really feel like.

Blueberry Cheesecake

1 C. graham cracker crumbs

¼ C. packed brown sugar

¼ C. butter, melted

1 env. whipped topping mix (Dream Whip)

1 8-oz. pkg. cream cheese

½ C. powdered sugar

1 21-oz. can blueberry or cherry pie filling

In a medium bowl, combine graham cracker crumbs, brown sugar, and melted butter. Press into a pie pan. Prepare whipped topping as directed on package. Add cream cheese and powdered sugar. Beat well. Pour into crust. Chill. Top with blueberry or cherry pie filling. Chill a few hours before serving. Makes 8 servings.

Bradley Val Buxton
Providence Ward
Nashville Tennessee Stake
Nashville, Tennessee

Mom made sure all eight of us—Mom, Dad, five sons, and a daughter—attended our church activities, and at home we always had family home evening and celebrated the holidays together. She also made sure that everything was done with good food and happy spirits. As a child, I took these things for granted. I looked forward to these events because I knew I would have fun. As an adult, I appreciate the preparation and work that was necessary to pull off those activities. Mom—now Grandma—is still the star of our family get-togethers. She always asks us what special dish or dessert she can make for us. Her cheesecake recipe is a pretty regular choice. You can make it with any canned fruit topping, or use a topping of your own. I have made it myself a few times, and it is really good, but not as good as when Mom makes it. But isn't that true with all of Mom's recipes? Mom just adds that extra little delicious bit of love.

Birthday Peach Cobbler

1 C. sugar

1 C. water

12 fresh peaches, pitted and sliced OR 2 32-oz. cans sliced peaches with juice

Blackberries or raspberries (optional)

1 white or yellow cake mix

½ C. butter

1 8-oz. pkg. cream cheese (not in a tub)

¼ C. sugar

½ tsp. cinnamon

Dash of nutmeg (optional)

Preheat the oven to 350. Butter a 9 x 13-inch baking dish. If using fresh peaches, combine 1 C. sugar and water; stir until sugar is fully dissolved; set aside. If using canned peaches, drain the peaches and save ½ C. syrup; set aside. Spread the peaches evenly along the bottom of the buttered baking dish. If you are using the oh-so-incredible but oh-so-optional blackberries or raspberries, scatter them over the peaches. Sprinkle the dry cake mix over the peaches. You may not have to use the whole mix; just make sure all the peaches are covered. Cut the butter into thin pats and dot evenly across the peaches. Do the same with the cream cheese. Pour the sugar/water mixture or the canned syrup evenly over top. Combine ¼ C. sugar and cinnamon; sprinkle over the top. (You can use as much of this as you like; I use the entire thing, and then some.) If desired, sprinkle with a dash of nutmeg. Bake at 350 for about 45 minutes. I like to put it under the broiler for about 5 minutes just before I think it's done to brown the top just a bit and make it extra crunchy! It should be golden brown and bubbly and not too juicy; the cake mix should soak up a lot of the juice and create a wonderfully crusty surface. We love to serve it with vanilla ice cream, but whipped cream is definitely acceptable as well! (Be prepared: this recipe is neither healthy nor easy to resist!) Makes 10–12 servings.

Krystal Webb
Sharon 8th Ward
Sharon Utah Stake
Orem, Utah

This recipe has very special meaning to me. My mom died of pancreatic cancer in April 2009. For her fiftieth birthday—the last birthday I spent with her—we had a celebration of her life with all of our family. My mom's family flew in from California, and my brother and sister-in-law brought their little boy—my mom's only grandchild—from North Carolina to surprise her. The entire day was filled with reunions and celebrations, and I was in charge of one of the most important parts: the birthday cake. My mom requested something different from my typical cake from a box, and told me to surprise her with whatever I wanted. Being a full-time college student, I ended up making this easy peach cobbler, which my family still adores to this day. Although my mom isn't with us anymore, we still love to gather and remember her and the most wonderful birthday we ever had together. I love you, Mom. Thanks for inspiring me to love to cook.

A Cookbook Representing Moms from Around the World!

Recipes in the *Worldwide Ward Cookbook: Mom's Best* were submitted by members of the Church living in all fifty of the United States and the District of Columbia.

Recipes were also submitted by Church members living in thirty countries outside the United States, including:

Argentina	Denmark	Mongolia	South Africa
Australia	Dominican Republic	Nicaragua	Taiwan
Belgium	Estonia	Peru	Thailand
Brazil	Germany	Philippines	The Netherlands
Canada	Guatemala	Portugal	Ukraine
Chile	Iceland	Puerto Rico	United Arab
China	Israel	Russia	Emirates
Colombia	Mexico	Singapore	

Italicized entries in the index will help you find recipes from a specific state or country.

Index

A

B